British History in Perspective
General Editor: Jeremy Black

PUBLISHED TITLES

Please see overleaf for forthcoming titles

FORTHCOMING TITLES

Peter Catterall *The Labour Party, 1918–1940*
Eveline Cruickshanks *The Glorious Revolution*
John Davis *British Politics, 1885–1931*
David Dean *Parliament and Politics in Elizabethan and
Jacobean England, 1558–1614*
Susan Doran *English Foreign Policy in the Sixteenth Century*
David Eastwood *England, 1750–1850: Government and Community
in the Provinces*
Colin Eldridge *The Victorians Overseas*
Brian Golding *The Normans in England 1066–1100:
Conquest and Colonisation*
Steven Gunn *Early Tudor Government, 1485–1558*
Richard Harding *The Navy, 1504–1815*
Angus Hawkins *British Party Politics, 1852–1886*
H. S. Jones *Political Thought in Nineteenth Century Britain*
Anthony Milton *Church and Religion in England, 1603–1642*
R. C. Nash *English Foreign Trade and the World Economy, 1600–1800*
W. M. Ormrod *Political Life in England, 1300–1450*
Richard Ovendale *Anglo-American Relations in the Twentieth Century*
David Powell *The Edwardian Crisis: Britain, 1901–1914*
Brian Quintrell *Government and Politics in Early Stuart England*
Alan Sykes *The Radical Right in Britain*
Ann Williams *Kingship and Government in Pre-Conquest England*
Michael Young *Charles I*

History of Ireland

Sean Duffy *Ireland in the Middle Ages*
Hiram Morgan *Ireland in the Early Modern Periphery, 1534–1690*
Toby Barnard *The Kingdom of Ireland, 1641–1740*
Alan Heesom *The Anglo-Irish Union, 1800–1922*

History of Scotland

Bruce Webster *Scotland in the Middle Ages*
Roger Mason *Kingship and Tyranny? Scotland 1513–1603*
John Shaw *The Political History of Eighteenth Century Scotland*
John McCaffrey *Scotland in the Nineteenth Century*
I. G. C. Hutchinson *Scottish Politics in the Twentieth Century*

History of Wales

A. D. Carr *Medieval Wales*
Gareth Jones *Wales, 1700–1980: Crisis of Identity*

Please also note that a sister series, *Social History in Perspective*, is now
available, covering the key topics in social, cultural and religious history.

CHURCH, STATE AND SOCIETY, 1760–1850

WILLIAM GIBSON

St. Martin's Press

First published in Great Britain 1994 by
THE MACMILLAN PRESS LTD
Houndmills, Basingstoke, Hampshire RG21 2XS
and London
Companies and representatives
throughout the world

A catalogue record for this book is available
from the British Library.

ISBN 0-333-58756-1 hardcover
ISBN 0-333-58757-X paperback

Printed in Hong Kong

First published in the United States of America 1994 by
Scholarly and Reference Division,
ST. MARTIN'S PRESS, INC.,
175 Fifth Avenue,
New York, N.Y. 10010

ISBN 0-312-10363-8

Library of Congress Cataloging-in-Publication Data
Gibson, William.
Church, state and society : 1760–1850 / William Gibson.
p.   cm. — (British history in perspective)
Includes bibliographical references
ISBN 0-312-10363-8
1. Church of England—History—18th century.   2. Church of
England—History—19th century.   3. Church and state—England-
-History—18th century.   4. Church and state—England—History—19th
century.   5. England—Church history—18th century.   6. England-
-Church history—19th century.   7. Great Britain—History—18th
century.   8. Great Britain—History—19th century.   I. Title.
II. Series.
BX5088.G53   1994
261.7—dc20
93–28945
CIP

For my family and friends

CONTENTS

Contents

PREFACE

The aim of this book is to provide the undergraduate with an accessible examination of the principal themes and issues in the history of religion and society in the period. The years covered by this book were perhaps the most turbulent in the development of religion in British history. It should be borne in mind that this was perhaps the last period in British history in which popular piety was a reality rather than a goal. The British State in the early nineteenth century was still a strongly Christian one; Victorian Britain relied on the churches as instruments of social control. These factors raise questions about the pattern of religious practice and activity which this book seeks to address.

Although this book examines issues and events that stretch from North America to continental Europe, it is predominantly a work of English history. Its principal subjects are the relationships between the Church of England and the State, society, Nonconformity and Dissent. It is not intended that this book duplicate the perspective or material already admirably covered by writers like Ward or Gilbert in their detailed examinations of Nonconformity. Rather, this book attempts to explore the common heritage, social context and political issues that the Established Church shared with Nonconformity.

I should like to record my thanks to the many people who have helped me with the research and production of this book. In particular I would like to thank Jeremy Black for inviting me to contribute this volume, and for his support and advice during the writing. Vanessa Graham, my publishing editor, has provided me with guidance and reassurance. I owe a particular debt to those people who read and commented on earlier drafts of this book:

William Price, my former tutor and supervisor, commented with characteristic thoroughness and generosity, as did Jeremy Black and Eileen Gibson. Their combined criticisms have preserved me from grosser errors than this book yet retains.

There are numerous other acknowledgements I should make, to librarians, archivists, scholars and colleagues. But my principal debt of gratitude is to those people, family and friends, whose sense of humour and forbearance has supported me.

WILLIAM GIBSON

INTRODUCTION

In 1788 the Archdeacon of Exeter, at a meeting to vote thanks to William Pitt on the resolution of the regency crisis, claimed that the strongly Tory city of Exeter now regarded the Revolution of 1688 as truly glorious.[1] This speech reflected a significant shift on the part of the clergy of Exeter, who had been tainted with Jacobitism for the first half of the century. It was a change that arose, in part, from the policy of cooperation that the Whig Church establishment had adopted with the Hanoverian regime. The policy was controversial: but the bishops who had supported the new regime were vindicated. There was no danger for the Church in the Hanoverian succession. From 1760 onwards the challenges that confronted the Church came from social and economic changes, rather than from political turbulence. For whilst there were political forces which threatened the Church: the French Revolution, Catholic emancipation and the Whig reforms of the 1830s, they were for the most part illusory. The most dramatic change which the Church of England had to accommodate was the transition from the role of the Established Church with a virtual monopoly, to being one of a number of denominational churches.

This dramatic transformation was in part a consequence of economic change. Industrialisation and urbanisation bewildered the clergy of all denominations. In Sheffield, which grew in population from 14,105 in 1736 to 45,758 by 1801, the clergy of the Church of England were joined in their inability to respond quickly and effectively by the Methodists and other Nonconformists. In 1779 and 1780, John Wesley preached in Sheffield to crowds which staggered him by their size. However quickly church building was undertaken and however tireless the clergy in visiting their new parishioners, they could not keep pace with the population growth. Moreover urbanisation was only one of a plethora of changes which confronted the Church. Enclosure and economic improvement of land effected changes in the life of men and women in the countryside which placed the Church in rural areas under as great a threat as it was in towns. For the majority of people in the country these changes meant that traditional patterns of life were abandoned. The men and women who worked in factories and mills became another commodity for industrialists, like raw materials and steam power. Yeoman farmers, who enjoyed the autonomy of modest owner occupation, became tenants of large landowners, paid to undertake the drudgery of farm labour. Child labour and unsanitary conditions, which had always been a feature of traditional patterns of production, became a part of the cold unemotional face of commerce. King Cotton brought with him King Cholera. Of most concern to the Church was that patterns of religious practice were broken by these changes. Whether turned from religion by exhaustion, bitterness or cynicism, many people broke away from the Church of England. Some turned to other churches, a few slid into apathy and neglect of religion. Virginia Woolf's *Orlando* described the turn of the eighteenth century as a period in which the misery of industrialisation created cold and uncaring attitudes which promoted scepticism and unbelief.

For the State the breach in the wall of religious observance was worrying. It eroded one of the instruments of social control and opened the way to the growth of class politics. In 1760 most men, whatever their politics, were adherents of the Church of England, by 1850 the differing sections of society could choose a religious denomination which suited their political complexion. The churches realised gradually that they had to respond to changes in society. The Church of England found this response more difficult to achieve since its role and status was a matter of State policy. Nevertheless, the Victorian view that there was no commitment to change before the 1830s is quite erroneous, the Church was prepared to undertake structural reform of itself from 1780 onwards. By 1850, the Church also reached an accommodation with a spectrum of theological opinions. Tolerance of Tractarianism, Christian Socialism and even of fringe sects indicated that the Church was no longer a single track with High Church and Latitudinarian furrows, but a broad avenue with many paths. The accommodation that the Nonconformist churches had to make tended to be easier since it was most frequently the management of expansion. Their problems were those which accompanied the creation of national structures and institutional growth.

In spite of these changes, widespread loss of faith was a feature of mid-Victorian Britain, rather than of the preceding century. Moreover, the Church of England in 1850 retained, in the words of one writer, 'an air of ineluctable legitimacy'. [2] Its institutional position in national life gave it a strong gravitational pull, even for those who had chosen to support Nonconformist churches. Church marriages and burials still retained a greater respectability than those of the chapel. It was a popular joke in the nineteenth century that the affluent dissenter's horse knew its way to the parish church as well as to the chapel. The Church in 1850 still exercised a preponderance of control over the universities and education and the clergy were accorded the deference due to gentlemen. Great national ceremonies were those of the Established Church as well as of the State. The momentum which the Victorians inherited from the Hanoverian Church carried them into missionary work to Britain's colonies and beyond. Whilst to many people Victorian Britain is synonymous with religious and moral strength, it is perhaps worth reminding ourselves that this strength was the harvest of the religious seedcorn sown in the years after 1760.

1

THE ESTABLISHED CHURCH IN 1760

The Established Church in 1760 was more secure than at any time in the preceding century and a half. It had survived the dangers of the Hanoverian succession and the risings of 1715 and 1745, and had understandably allied itself with the Whigs, the party which most strongly represented anti-Jacobite opposition to Catholicism. By 1760 the Church had secured its position, though it had done so at the cost of neglecting church reform. In 1760, *quieta non movere* remained the adage that best exemplifies the Church's cautious policy to any change. There were many reasons for following such a policy. Dissent and Methodism were growing in popularity, the challenges of American independence and the French Revolution destabilised politics, and economic forces were swiftly eroding the bedrock of rural Anglicanism. In an era of flux the Church clung to a structure, a system of patronage and an association with the State which it inherited from the seventeenth century. This does not, of course, mean that the Church did not also inherit the popular piety and clerical scruples of an earlier age also. It was easy for the Victorian historians to overlook these features. They denigrated the unreformed features of the Church without consideration of the Church's difficulties, or any understanding of the evolutionary changes that were effected after 1760. Between 1760 and 1830 attitudes to the Church's structures, finances, deployment of clergy and parish life underwent subtle changes, without which the reforms that followed could not have been achieved.

The Church's Involvement in Politics

One of the principal sticks used to beat the Church in the mid-eighteenth century was its involvement in politics. It was regarded as a feature of the State's control over the Church, known as Erastianism, which promoted corruption and abuse. At all levels the Church involved itself in politics. County elections, especially those in clerical centres like Oxfordshire, were frequently opportunities for clergy to preach and publish their support for the Whig and Tory factions.

The visible support of the Church was important for both sides. In Northamptonshire in 1806, for example, the incumbent of Bugbrooke promised that his tenants would make a strong display at the polls. Clergymen of this type often acted as agents for one interest or another. In the same election, the Revd Mr Bonney acted as the agent for the parishes of the 7th Earl of Westmorland, a major local landowner, and the Revd Isaac Knott did for those of his opponent Mr Cartwright. Some clergy were sufficiently committed to a political interest to seek office.

William Buller, later dean and bishop of Exeter, was elected Mayor of East Looe in 1760, 1767, 1774 and 1780. In each case he was able to influence the subsequent election of the borough's MP. In the Middlesex elections of 1768–9 Parson Horne, nicknamed 'the Brentford Parson', was a significant voice and was even depicted harbouring aspirations for a parliamentary seat, though he was ineligible by Common Law, and by statute after 1801. But for the most part clergy were content to support a political party with local intelligence. In 1760, for example, Dean Green of Lincoln warned Lord Hardwicke, the Lord Chancellor, that the gentlemen of the Lincoln Militia were banding together to insist on the right to determine the proper persons to represent the county. The Duke of Newcastle, the Whig minister with responsibility for church patronage, recognised the value of clerical supporters and agents. In 1761 he asked the Dean of Canterbury to act on his behalf to fix the Canterbury election so that the Whig interest was preserved. This was not merely a feature of the eighteenth century; in 1852, the theologian the

Revd Rowland Williams wrote from Lampeter that 'the election bids fair to stir people here, and my principal neighbour will, as usual, be more busy than reverend, in the turmoil of the affair'. Nor was it simply the latitudinarian clergy, whose religious and political outlook enabled them to tolerate a range of opinions, who took an active political role. Samuel Horsley, a High Churchman who had strong views on the standing of the Church and the sacraments, was particularly active in politics. As bishop of St David's in 1789 he canvassed the clergy for his candidate in the Carmarthen election, concluding his letter 'I hope I shall not have the mortification to find a single clergyman in my diocese who will . . . give his vote for any [other] man.'

At a national level, bishops were an integral element in the political structure. Throughout the early Hanoverian period the government distributed sees and church dignities through ecclesiastical agents like Bishop Edmund Gibson of London (1720–48) and Newcastle. Newcastle has been the object of considerable criticism for his partisan discharge of the crown's church patronage, although recent research suggests that 'compared with the period that had gone before, the stewardship of Newcastle appears as something of a golden age'.[1] Even contemporary opinion, like that of the statesman Edmund Burke (1729–97), accepted that while the system of ecclesiastical patronage in England was 'sometime unworthy', alternatives were infinitely worse.

In the House of Lords, bishops played a part in political debates. The historian Richard Pares regarded them as 'a laughing stock for their subservience'. However, the bishops' attendance at the Lords was by no means consistent or regular. Mather has pointed out that it was unusual for more than eight bishops to attend an ordinary debate. In the fifteen years after 1760 the bishops attended only half of the votes in numbers consistent with their proportional membership of the House. Equally bishops did not assiduously use their proxies. Nor did they venture into debate on overtly political topics very often. Moreover, as McCahill has shown, bishops were frequently prepared to vote against the government. In all, twenty one of the thirty-one bishops who sat in the Lords between 1760 and 1775 voted against the government in one division or other.

During the 1760s there were also significant numbers of episcopal protests registered in the Journals of the House of Lords. Such protests could solidify into more general opposition: for example, Lord Shelburne's government in the late eighteenth century had particular problems with the bishops. Some bishops were noted rebels: Richard Watson, bishop of Llandaff, saw his role in the Lords to withstand 'the corrupting influence of the Crown'. At least sixteen bishops can be identified as independent in politics or willing to oppose the government. In fact Lowe has concluded that 'the bishops fell far short of upholding their reputation as a ministerial voting bloc'.[2] Even a convinced Tory bishop, like Horsley, was prepared to oppose the government when his conscience dictated.

The level of involvement of the lesser clergy in politics has also been exaggerated. There were clergy who sought to avoid involvement in political contests. Parsons Hinds and Tutte of Northamptonshire decided that, since they held opposing views, they would both agree not to attend the county elections. Bishops also felt that political contests could damage the Church; Bishop Secker of Oxford tried to diminish the worst effects of electoral splits in his diocese.

The Church's involvement in politics was, in part, a function of its role as a property owner. In 1806 the nomination of Sir William Dolben as the parliamentary candidate for Northampton by the Revd William Shippen Willes reflected his status as the owner of the Astrop estate rather than his clerical calling. Moreover, clergy as landowners had to provide a lead for their tenants. In the Northampton election, the Revd H. B. Harrison and Bishop Pretyman Tomline of Lincoln were among the clergy who promised their candidates that they would persuade their tenants to vote for them. Parson Anderson of Northamptonshire was affronted that he had not been canvassed by one of the candidates as befitted his status as a freeholder. In the same year, Thomas Johnes of Hafod in Wales carefully canvassed the support of the Revd John Jenkins of Cilbronnau in the same way as many other candidates sought that of their parish clergy. Such views indicate that the Church in the eighteenth century was necessarily involved in politics because it existed in an age in which landownership *ipso facto* carried a political interest and thrust the clergy into the arena.

A further factor which encouraged clergy to become involved in politics was that in 1760 Church and State still felt threatened by the Jacobite factions which they feared would destroy the foundations upon which the Church was built. In 1745, the Church had been an important instrument for drawing support to the Hanoverian regime against the threats from Jacobite invasions. Archbishop Herring had raised the government's standard in the north and was tireless in organising the militia. The perception of a Jacobite threat – though in reality Jacobitism decayed as the century progressed – did not recede. The mid-eighteenth century saw as much terror of rumoured Jacobite plots and covert activities as 1714. Even churchmen were accused of treasonable views, and dignitaries like Dean Cowper of Durham, Bishop Johnson of Gloucester, and numerous Oxford clergy, had to fight hard to throw off allegations of Jacobitism. Prebendary Pyle of Winchester even questioned in 1757 whether the militias would desert to the Jacobites in the event of another rumoured invasion. In such an atmosphere, the Church saw a natural interest in promoting and supporting the Hanoverian order, and for preaching the doctrine of subservience to the established order.

Clerical involvement in politics also reflected the nature of ecclesiastical patronage in the eighteenth century. The clergy were rewarded for the part they played in politics: for example, in 1753 George Bubb Doddington applied to Newcastle for preferment for the two parsons who supported his election to parliament. In 1760, the Duke of Marlborough and Lords Harcourt, Macclesfield and Parker petitioned Newcastle for preferment for the Revd Thomas Bray, who had used his fortune to buy Oxford freeholders' franchises for the Whig interest. Bray in due course became a canon of Christ Church and dean of Raphoe. There is, however, no evidence that the normal standards required for such clergy were relaxed and the government rejected those unworthy clergy who were nominated for political reward. Nor is there evidence that this sort of use of patronage was unique. The Church was treated in this way in the seventeenth century and was undoubtedly used by successive prime ministers to reward political service in the nineteenth century.

What made the Church's involvement in political service distinctive in the eighteenth century was that it formed part of a systematic use of patronage by a governing faction to establish a network of obligations. Bubb Doddington described it well when he wrote 'service is obligation, obligation implies return'. The distribution of church livings formed part of this wider web of patronage in politics and society. Dean Cowper, for example, having been advanced to the deanery of Durham in 1744 was expected to bind himself to the government's interest and to use his own modest patronage as dean in its service. If he condescended to take up such clients he in turn received obligations from them as well as gratitude for continued service from the government. Often clientage and patronage were practically indistinguishable. In 1760, for example, the fusion of patronage and clientage was apparent when Newcastle was urged by a Mr Knight to prefer his brother-in-law, the Revd Henry Galley, to a Nottinghamshire living. Knight owned a fortune of £30,000 and had the potential to be troublesome to the government. Thus church livings became, like judgeships, excise offices, commissions, places at court, honours and peerages, part of what Curtis has called the 'pagoda of patronage'. It is easy however to exaggerate the monolithic nature of the government's control of patronage.

The Crown owned only 9.6 per cent of the advowsons in the country, compared with 26 per cent owned by bishops and 53.4 per cent by laymen. Furthermore, recent claims that ecclesiastical 'patronage empires' existed in the hands of aristocrats has been undermined by evidence that only 2.5 per cent of private patrons owned more than one advowson.[3] For the most part church patronage lay in the hands of local landowners and gentry, far beyond the reach of government influence.

What is often forgotten in discussions of patronage and the Church is that the world view of most people in the eighteenth century included the assumption expressed by George Lawson in the late seventeenth century that 'Politics are from God . . . politics, both civil and ecclesiastical belong unto theology, and are but a branch of the same.' As Jonathan Clark has shown the nature of the Church–State relationship in the eighteenth century was much closer than we are inclined to recognise. Most recently the research of Stephen Taylor has emphasised how unrepresentative William Warburton's *Alliance between Church and State . . .* was of eighteenth-century clerical thought. Most people accepted the necessity of an Established Church and viewed it as indistinguishable from the State. Warburton's view of two allied but separate institutions was rare. Equally the level of commitment to the Church was also much greater than historians allow, and the eighteenth century is perhaps the last period in which popular faith can be taken for granted. As a result, well into the nineteenth century it was religious rather than political allegiance which defined the nature of popular politics.

The Development of the Clerical Profession

The eighteenth century saw the development, initiated at the Reformation, of the Church as a profession. In particular three features of the Church as a profession emerged during the eighteenth century: the differentiation of a hierarchy within the clerical profession and the related rise in the social status of the clergy; the association of the profession with the establishment; and the creation of a professional community.

The emergence of a hierarchy within the Church and the elevation of the status of the clergy are inextricably linked. The eighteenth century saw the development of a ladder of preferment in the Church. The wealthy living, cathedral dignity, deanery, royal chaplaincy and bishopric were becoming discrete rungs on this career ladder. Even within the episcopate there was differentiation of rank indicated by the varying wealth and prestige accorded to sees. By 1761 this perception of a hierarchy found expression in Newcastle's answer to a request from the Earl of Albemarle for preferment for his clerical brother. Newcastle replied that he must 'rise by degrees, and not go all at once'. Each rung developed separate functions: William Paley pointed out to ordinands at Carlisle, in 1781, that their role on the lowest rung as deacons and curates was to remain close to their congregations and learn about the lives of the ordinary people.

As the hierarchical structure became evident, raising the status of those at the top, it inevitably attracted men of noble birth. Prime Minister George Grenville's comment in 1764 to Bishop Thomas Newton of Bristol (1761–82) that there were 'bishoprics for men of ability and learning, and bishoprics of ease for men of family and fashion' reflects the growth in numbers of noble sons entering the ministry. But it is easy to forget that Newton felt this trend was often a useful one for the Church. Commenting on Bishop Edmund Keene's elevation from Chester to Ely in 1771, Newton recorded his approval that a man of 'liberal fortune as well as a liberal mind' had spent his time at Chester building a new episcopal palace and his fortune on building Ely House in London and on parsonages within his diocese.

Whilst the rise in the incomes available from the Church may have attracted noblemen into Orders, there is some evidence that they were less likely than others to obtain the highest rewards. Daniel Hirschberg has indicated that noble prelates such as the Hon. Henry Egerton (Bishop of Hereford 1724–46) and his successor Lord James Beauclerk (1746–81) were more likely to 'toil til the ends of their days in middling sees for . . . lamentable profits'. Contemporary opinion recognised the value of noblemen in Orders for the Church as a whole. Newton wrote in 1760 that

> though the apostles for wise reasons were chosen from among men of low birth and parentage; yet times and circumstances are so changed that persons of noble extraction by coming into the Church, may add strength and ornament to it, especially as long as we can boast of some, who are honourable in themselves as well as in their families, and whose personal merits and virtues, if they had not been nobly descended, would have entitled them justly to the rank and pre-eminence that they enjoy. God forbid that the Church of England should ever be reduced to the state of the Gallican church, incumbered with the weight of prelates of quality without learning or merit.[4]

Norman Ravitch's comparison between the French and English churches confirms Newton's view. The Church of England and the English aristocracy rewarded the talents of the meritorious, and drew the brilliant and able into the Establishment. The noble bishops of the late eighteenth century were also men of learning and merit. The 2nd Viscount Barrington, a Whig minister, soliciting for his brother the Revd Shute Barrington in the 1780s, rested his claim on his brother's accomplishments and on the esteem he attracted from others. Bishop Barrington turned out to be one of the best diocesans of his generation. One writer in 1828 wrote of him that it was a pity that his reputation seemed to rest on his family connection rather than his own piety and character. In 1765, Newcastle recommended two noble bishops to the King for promotion, Bishops Frederick Cornwallis of Lichfield and Coventry (1750–68) and William Ashburnham of Chichester (1754–98), concluding that they were both meritorious.

As the clerical profession became crowded and the struggle to obtain preferment became more difficult there is no evidence that merit as a criteria for appointment declined. Qualifications of character, service and education all rated more highly than those of family connection. The Carlisle vacancy of 1787 illustrates the reaction of the government to attempts by grandees to prefer unworthy relatives. Carlisle diocese was often held by bishops with a connection with the area. In 1787, the local Carlisle magnate, Lord Lowther, attempted to force his kinsman, William Lowther, rector of Aikton, on to the see. Lowther was an entirely unacceptable candidate and immediately rejected in favour of the more modestly born John Douglas whose principal qualifications were his academic success and clerical experience. It is easy to exaggerate the numbers of noble bishops and clergy. In the thirty-eight years prior to 1760 26.4 per cent of bishops were from the families of nobles, the gentry and the armigerous, and 20 per cent of all clergy have been estimated to have had connections with a noble house. Whilst the noble clergy enjoyed disproportionate representation on the bench of bishops, the emergent middle classes dominated both the lesser clergy and episcopate.

One of the characteristics of a profession in the eighteenth century, before the emergence of the commercial professions, was its association and connection with the Establishment. This is certainly the case for the army and the Law, and in a more subtle way for medicine. In its crudest expression, the professions generated wealth and support for the regime which afforded them protection, legitimacy and monopoly. This applied to the Church also. Bishop Richard Watson of Llandaff wrote that the safety of the government relied on the hopes of another world entertained by the people it ruled. Watson propagated this view among the clergy. In 1769, he wrote that it was the role of clergy to cooperate in promoting peace, respect and good order in society.

The fields in which clerical adherence to the State were demonstrated were not confined to the spiritual. Clerical magistracy increased in the eighteenth century as the Church endowed its personnel with the rank of 'gentlemen by profession'. Appointment to the bench was still very much in the control of the local nobility and lords lieutenant. Certainly by waiving the usual property qualification for the clergy the Commission for the Peace recognised them as having gentry status. Before 1740 clerical magistrates were few, yet in 1761 alone their number was increased by 1038, and continued to rise, by 1836 3266 clergy were JPs. Levels of clerical magistracy varied across the country: in Lincolnshire it rose as high as 47 per cent of the total bench. Magistrates could also form the backbone of the bench: in Oxfordshire, in 1780, 82.6 per cent of convictions were signed by clerical magistrates. Lord Redesdale wrote in 1824 that, in Gloucestershire, the clerical magistracy made up a substantial bulk of the bench: 'in this county the business could not be done without them; indeed they do nearly the whole'.

The role of clerical magistrates was varied. The Revd Francis Witts, the diarist and rector of Upper Slaughter in Gloucestershire, recorded his activities as a magistrate. He regularly sat on the bench at the Quarter Sessions, hearing cases of vagrancy, poaching, theft, desertion, bastardy, assault, threats, drunkenness, and even riot. In addition he was actively involved in the administration of the poor laws and as Chairman of the Board of Guardians of the Poor for Stow district from 1836 he supervised the workhouse. Witts also acted as chairman of the justices' accounts committee and as a member of the local turnpike trust. He occasionally ministered to those he had condemned, as when in 1820 he visited Gloucester Gaol and exhorted a sheep stealer to confess his crime after he had been sentenced to execution. That Witts saw his principal role as maintaining the peace in the countryside is illustrated by his condemnation of riots among the factory operatives in Stroud and his determination to punish them so as to prevent further outbursts.

A further characteristic of the professions in the eighteenth century was the development of a professional community. This was achieved in two ways, first, through the development of opportunities for clergy to meet and associate, and second, in the development of a hereditary element in the profession. The emergence of professional associations, like the Gentlemen Practitioners in the Courts of Law and Equity, of the Honourable East India Company and in 1768 of the Society of Advocates of Doctors' Commons, are the most tangible examples of the formal ways in which professional groups generated a community within which to operate. In the clergy such a professional community operated less formally. The formal mechanism for clerical expressions of opinion, the Upper and Lower Houses of Convocation, had been suspended in 1717. Thus denied formal opportunities for debate, the Church developed informal means, involving far more clergy than Convocation. Perhaps the most common were the clerical societies set up across the country. From the multifarious activities of bodies like the Society for Promoting Christian Knowledge, the Society for the Propagation of the Gospel and the Society for the Reformation of Manners to the more narrow Society for the Suppression of Vice, set up in 1787, clergy were offered opportunities to take part in evangelism and the improvement of society. The Cornish evangelical revival was stimulated by the work of evangelical clergy, like Samuel Walker, meeting together for prayer, study and readings. Clerical societies were established in Huddersfield, later known as the Elland Clerical Society, by the Revd Henry Venn in 1767, by Mr Stillingfield at Hotham, and by the end of the century existed in York, Bristol, Creaton, and Islington. Bishop Thomas Burgess of St David's encouraged monthly meetings of clerical societies. At visitations also the clergy met together, often to hear a visitation sermon, to dine together and to exchange books and ideas. The publication and distribution of a visitation charge was also designed to generate a sense of a community of clergy. The charge of Bishop Thomas Sherlock of London (1748–61) to his clergy in 1759 emphasised that they had a special function and role that set them apart from the rest of society. It is significant that in the American colonies, devoid of episcopal oversight, clerical societies were equally widespread.

Another feature of the development of such a professional community was the emergence of a hereditary element in the profession. Indeed, one of the strong features of the Church in mid-eighteenth century England was the development of clerical families. At Wells, for example, the sons, and occasionally grandsons, of Bishops Creighton, Hooper, Willes and Moss (four of the eight bishops between 1670 and 1802) became members of the cathedral chapter and attracted the patronage of successive bishops. Such generosity to the offspring of predecessors suggests that a sense of responsibility to a wider professional community of clergy was alive in the episcopate. It was equally strong in the way episcopal chaplains were absorbed into the families of their patrons.

The work of the Corporation of the Sons of the Clergy, which developed fully in the eighteenth century, is further testimony to the way in which the clerical profession had developed a sense of a wider community of clerical families. But the highest form of a hereditary clerical community was the way in which livings became dominated by a single family. The Compton family, which passed the two livings of Minstead and Sopley in Hampshire from clerical member to clerical member from 1742 to 1930, was one of many. Livings like those of Cheddon Fitzpaine, Somerset, St Michael's on Wyre, Lancashire, and Munslow, Shropshire saw the monopoly of individual families for many generations. Eased by bonds of resignation, which allowed a clergyman to be presented to livings to fill a brief vacancy – usually to keep the living warm for a son at university – families enjoyed the material and moral security of representatives at both the manor and the rectory.

Higher up the ecclesiastical hierarchy this promotion of family interests allowed nepotism to operate. Nepotism has attracted considerable criticism, yet the evidence suggests that it possessed a validity in eighteenth century society which legitimised its use in the Church. Its operation, through mechanisms like the privilege of Founders' Kin, was widespread. In the Church nepotism had a particular function. The death of a bishop or clergyman lost for members of his family both their means of support and their home. Given the huge fees, and first fruits, payable on entry to a diocese it is unsurprising that some bishops were burdened with heavy debts for years. Bishops in the century up to 1760 rarely saw more than ten profitable years in their episcopates. It thus became an important need for bishops to provide for their families. Moreover, the State encouraged provision for family among the episcopate: it obviated the need for the unseemly petition of 1757 by Archbishop Secker of Canterbury and Bishop Hay Drummond of St Asaph on behalf of the penniless widow of Bishop John Conybeare of Bristol.

There was also a strong functional motive behind nepotism. Bishops, beset with a plethora of administrative and parliamentary duties, needed a corps of supporters who would give effect to their control of their dioceses. Members of the bishop's family inserted into a chapter or into administrative roles ensured not merely an income for a family member, but also that a bishop was well supported. This certainly stood Bishop Willes in good stead during a series of fraught cathedral disputes at Wells in the mid-eighteenth century. Those posts which provided an income from fees for members of a bishop's family also acted in the interests of the Church as a whole, since they earned income in direct relation to the activity of the post holder.

The Character of the Episcopate

The episcopate in eighteenth-century England has suffered from the pall of the reputations of Bishops Benjamin Hoadly and Richard Watson. Both bishops have been judged representative of the worst in the eighteenth-century Church. Hoadly, who died in 1761, was appointed to the bench largely as a reward for his Whig penmanship in the reign of Queen Anne. He did the government's bidding in defending the Hanoverian succession, and was rewarded by his elevation, successively, to Bangor, Hereford, Salisbury and Winchester. Hoadly was disabled and was unable to ride a horse or kneel to pray; his episcopal functions therefore were largely undertaken by brother bishops. Sykes wrote of Hoadly that 'the aptest illustration of the fulsome reward accorded to party services was seen in the rapid progress of Hoadly through a series of episcopal promotions'. But Hoadly was unique in the eighteenth century. Alone of all his brethren on the bench he was allowed three translations, the majority of bishops either remained in one see or were allowed one translation, respectively 51.4 per cent and 36.6 per cent of the bishops between 1660 and 1760. The myth that bishops were regularly translated through the ranks of poor sees to middling ones before final elevation to a rich one as a reward for political rectitude has unjustly damaged the reputation of the Hanoverian Church.

At the latter end of the eighteenth century the Church has been dogged by the reputation of Bishop Watson of Llandaff (1782–1816). Like Hoadly, Watson was a trenchant Whig, who attracted the patronage of the Dukes of Grafton and Rutland. His involvement in Cambridge University politics brought him the gratitude of the Whig government, which appointed him to Llandaff in 1782. Watson devoted his time to politics, speaking on the ministry's behalf on the 1789 Regency Bill and supporting repeal of the Test and Corporation Acts in 1787, 1789 and 1790. In 1798, he championed the legitimisation of the Catholic Church in Ireland and Catholic Emancipation in England. What made Watson comparable to Hoadly was his retreat to his estate at Calgarth Park in the Lake District and his apparent neglect of his diocese. He rarely visited Llandaff, though he undertook confirmations and ordinations in his diocese, and used diocesan patronage to promote the interest of his lakeland friends. Watson, rightly, railed against the structure of the Church which made him dependent on commendams and denied him sufficient income as bishop to build an episcopal residence in his diocese. But like Hoadly, Watson was unique. No other bishop held pluralities in such numbers – at one time they numbered as many as sixteen livings. No other bishop neglected his diocese on the scale that Watson did; certainly there is no evidence of other bishops who so signally failed to discharge the duties of their office. Indeed, episcopal biographies, as opposed to general histories, almost without exception praise the quality of the episcopate.

For the most part the bishops were industrious men, devoted to the Church, who strove to overcome the unique problems of their era with great credit. As Sykes wrote, 'in the face of the many obstacles of unwieldy dioceses, limited means of travel, pressure of other avocations, and the infirmities of the body incident to mortal flesh, the bishops of Hanoverian England and Wales strove with diligence and not without due measure of success to discharge the spiritual administration attached to their offices'.

The best evidence for the character of the episcopate in late eighteenth-century England is the manner in which its members discharged the function of visitation. The eighteenth-century Church saw the completion of the evolution of visitations. One by one the bishops adopted the system of distributing visitation articles to their clergy to discover the true state of the Church in their dioceses. It is an irony that the efficiency of episcopal administration in obtaining information about dioceses produced information which was used to charge the bishops with neglect of their duties.

Yet the bishops seem to have taken great care to visit their dioceses. The eighteenth century also saw the separation of visitations from confirmation tours. In this way, by the end of the century many bishops had effectively doubled their work by undertaking twice as many visits to their dioceses. Bishop Moss, for example, who was nominated to Bath and Wells in 1773, carried out his visitations and confirmations with such regularity that he must have been a frequent sight on the roads of the diocese. Indeed, Moss began the practice in Bath and Wells of dividing the diocese into three parts and visiting each third in successive years, rather than visiting the whole diocese triennially. Moss's final visitation in 1797 was begun when he was 86 years old, though it was completed by a surrogate. It has been calculated that from 1727 to 1745 visitations in Lincoln diocese were held every three years, and that between 1748 and 1781 the bishops adopted that practice already noted at Bath and Wells. They divided the diocese into two and visited the two halves in alternate years. Thus Bishops Thomas, Green and Thurlow, responding to the enormity of the task of visiting a huge diocese, exceeded the canonical requirements. Bishop Barrington's visitation of Salisbury diocese in 1783 affords further evidence of diligence in record keeping. The visitation records indicate that the registrar planned an itinerary in extraordinary detail, allowing accommodation in seventeen places for the bishop and his party. Among the information available to the bishop was that on the state of the roads and lists of clergy and benefices. A circular letter was sent to all innkeepers explaining the need for chambers for the entertainment of visiting clergy. Visitations of archdeaconries were equally well discharged, the publication of visitation records from Derby and Stafford in the first half of the nineteenth century indicate the determination of archdeacons to attend to the churches in their care.

Pluralism and Non-residence

The Church's work in the parishes of England and Wales has been a subject of great debate, principally because the level and quality of its services and its clergy provides one of the yardsticks against which the Church in the late eighteenth century has been judged. Anecdotal material can be used to suggest that there were parishes which suffered neglect and others which were served by diligent clergymen. Quantitative sources suggest that there is apparent evidence of systematic neglect, but they must be viewed with extreme caution. In Salisbury diocese, for example, the visitation returns in 1783 show that of 232 parishes only 90 were served by resident clergy. But a further 119 parishes were served by clergy who lived less than five miles distant. And no church was served by a cleric living beyond ten miles from it. In spite of this evidence a recent survey of six counties by Virgin, including Wiltshire, concluded that the technical residence level in the 1770s and 1780s varied widely: from 59 per cent to 22 per cent. The conclusion that in the case of Wiltshire only 39 per cent of clergy were resident was not tempered by a detailed analysis of visitation returns and must be reconsidered in view of the evidence that 'technical non-residence' is a worthless term. In neighbouring Somerset the levels of non-residence varied so widely from deanery to deanery that they make any generalisation for the diocese meaningless.

In 1791, Bishop Moss's visitation revealed that in Axbridge deanery non-residence was at the disturbing level of 84 per cent, yet in nearby Redcliffe and Bedminster deanery it was at 39.4 per cent. The diocese had an average non-residence rate of 38.1 per cent, suggesting that the strenuous condemnation of non-residence by the evangelical tract writer Hannah More, who lived in Axbridge, may apply to the deanery in which she lived, but not for the whole diocese.

Elsewhere the evidence of non-residence has been overstated. In Oxford diocese, where in 1788 100 clergy were non-resident, the existence of the university in the heart of the diocese meant that a significant number of incumbents studied and attended to their parishes as well. In Exeter diocese, in 1779, there were 231 resident clergy and 159 non-residents. But of the non-residents, only 24 resided outside the diocese, 34 had parishes adjacent to their parish of residence and 63 had a second parish within 30 miles radius, a further 17 were unable to reside due to lack of a parsonage. In Derby archdeaconry, visited by Archdeacon Butler in 1823, only one-sixth of those clergy who were technically non-resident were actually living so far from their parish as to make services impossible. For the remaining five-sixths their non-residence was purely technical and did not inhibit the performance of their duty.

There was also little evidence of pastoral neglect arising from non-residence. Nevertheless, Dean Percy of Carlisle held the view that the effects of non-residence were so serious that he could tell at a glance whether a parish had a resident cleric from 'the civil or savage manner of the people'. On the other hand, the Revd John Skinner recognised that a non-resident parson did not necessarily damage the worship of a parish. In 1801, he visited Linton parish church, served by a curate from nearby Ilfracombe, and commented that the church was 'so fully crowded there was scarcely room for my attendance'.

Some bishops went to considerable lengths to prevent non-residence. Bishop Moss of Bath and Wells incurred the wrath of Lord Bridport in 1796 by insisting that Bridport's newly appointed chaplain should vacate his living. Other bishops were also stern in their attitudes to non-residence: in 1809, Bishop Pretyman Tomline of Lincoln prosecuted curates who were non-resident. In contrast, some bishops were sympathetic to the unavoidable causes of non-residence. Richard Watson, the non-resident bishop of Llandaff, recognised that to enforce residence without giving clergy the income to build parsonages and to maintain their families was a nonsense. The clergy themselves often took great pride in their residence: the Revd William Jones of Broxbourne, Hertfordshire, confided to his diary his satisfaction that, in over twenty two years as curate and vicar, he had been absent from his parish for only three Sundays.

Episcopal failure to eradicate non-residence was in part the result of an inability to overcome the intractable problem of lack of parsonages. In the diocese of Llandaff, in 1763, absence of a parsonage was the largest single cause of non-residence and this was by no means a product of recent decay or neglect. In some parishes, typically where populations were very small, clergy had been non-resident for centuries. Elsewhere parsons rented houses to be near their parishes but did not have the funds to build or repair a parsonage. A further disincentive to bishops to act in cases of non-residence was the frequently technical nature of absenteeism.

Whilst in law non-resident, a clergyman often provided a curate to provide services or lived a short distance from the parish, or found the income of the parish too low to survive on and made his living by serving a cluster of livings near one another. Equally bishops could not legally deny exemptions from residence to certain clergy. Tenure of a fellowship at Oxford or Cambridge, of a cathedral dignity, of a chaplaincy to a nobleman or to a member of the royal family were all qualifications for a certificate allowing legitimate non-residence. Significantly, the legislation of the 1830s confirmed the exemptions for the first two categories of non-resident clergy. Legally, the sons of noblemen and MAs could apply for an exemption from residence too. Moreover ill health, teaching at a school – and in Wales the language barrier – prevented clergy from residing on their cures for acceptable reasons. Thus, as Geoffrey Best pointed out, there were circumstances by the end of the eighteenth century which 'made it impossible or cruel, in practice and theory alike, to expect each benefice to support a resident clergyman'.[5]

Non-residence frequently went hand in hand with pluralism, both in function and in the opprobrium it attracted. Like non-residence, the level and impact of pluralism may well have been exaggerated. In Salisbury diocese, of 262 beneficed clergy, 124 were technically pluralists. The detailed evidence suggests that pluralism did not necessarily entail pastoral neglect. Of the 124 pluralists, 68 held two livings and a further 25 acted as incumbent in one and curate in a second parish. All but 6 pluralists held their posts within the diocese or in adjoining counties and all but 15 resided on one or other of their livings. Had the 1838 Pluralities Act (which allowed and legalised pluralism inside a ten mile limit) applied in Salisbury diocese there would have been few clergymen who violated it. In Oxford diocese, pluralism seems to have grown in the nineteenth century rather than the eighteenth. Even so in 1834 Bishop Bagot conceded that, as in Exeter diocese, pluralities in his diocese of Oxford were caused by the poverty of some parish incomes. In 1793, the registered pluralist clergy of Oxford tended to be the wealthier rather than the poor clergy, the majority held livings with incomes between £100 and £200 in value. But these figures must be tempered by evidence that a further 29 pluralists, for whom there was no dispensation for plurality, held very poor livings: only two held livings which exceeded £100 in value, the majority held livings yielding less than £40 a year.

Bishops recognised that the reasons that lay behind much pluralism were valid. One of the qualifications for dispensation for pluralism was higher study at one of the universities. Pluralism in such a case was an incentive for a clergyman to advance his knowledge and thereby benefit the Church through study. But there are other explanations and justifications. One radical explanation by Peter Virgin is that pluralism in the mid-eighteenth century was due to a collapse in entrants to the Church, and that, rather than being an overcrowded profession in the eighteenth century, the Church was suffering from a prolonged famine of clergy which made for an increase in pluralism. This explanation flies in the face of accepted views of the Church as a crowded profession in the eighteenth century, however it may apply to some particular areas of the country.

It is also important to see pluralism from the perspective of the eighteenth century rather than from that of a later age. Ideas of merit and advancement were not yet connected with the world of competitive examinations or grades of employment within a hierarchy of incentives. Pluralism therefore supported the differentiation within the clerical profession. Before the equalisation of incomes from sees, dignities and parishes, many of the cathedral and diocesan dignities which were technically rewards for merit had inadequate incomes. Thus one way of establishing the middle rungs on the developing ladder of preferment was to allow pluralism for clergy marked out for advancement. Indeed this was the oblique intention of the 41st Canon of 1604, which allowed a dispensation for pluralism to one of 'learning, and very well able and sufficient to discharge his duty'. Masters of Arts, chaplains to the King, bishops and nobles, and a plethora of office holders – the church's 'middle management' – were rewarded by pluralism. It was an argument which contemporary opinion accepted. Edward Berens in 1828 argued that for the clergyman pluralism 'enlarged his own sphere of professional activity'. And it was argued that pluralism was the best way to make use of energetic and diligent clergy. By 1832 Archbishop William Howley of Canterbury conceded that pluralism allowed 'the remuneration of professional merit'. This resolves the apparent paradox that often the best clergy, the most diligent and painstaking, were also pluralists. An example of strong and effective clergy who were pluralists was the pocket of Somerset evangelical clergy in the eighteenth century. From the 1770s at least eight clerics were evangelical pluralists. Among them were Thomas Biddulph, John Richards, William Havergal, James Vaughan and William Farrish. Another evangelical, Richard Whalley, justified his pluralism by the opinion that had he not taken the additional living of Chelwood the parishioners would not have had regular services. Thus for many clergy pluralism improved the Church's effectiveness.

A further argument used to defend pluralism is that it was the lever which effected a rise in the social standing of all clergy. As we have seen, standing alongside the poorest curate the noble canon inevitably raised the former's status. In examining pluralism among wealthy clerics in Durham, W. B. Maynard suggests that it was the product of a system of clerical advancement. There were few rewards for parish clergy other than the acquisition of other benefices and livings of increasing value.[6] By 1783 the majority of the 262 clergy in Wiltshire were estimated to have come from the families of the gentry or professions. Pluralism was thus the ecclesiastical equivalent of granting privileges to noblemen, gentlemen and armigers at the universities and schools and had the same function: to attract men of status and connection and thereby raise the standing of the whole institution. By the mid-point of the eighteenth century there is evidence that sons of noblemen and gentry were entering Orders in greater numbers. Among contemporaries this argument was accepted as legitimate. Wharton and Stanhope believed that pluralism encouraged those who would become the 'ornaments of the Church'. They also held the view that pluralism enabled young clergy to be trained and inducted into Orders under the direction of experienced, well qualified and distinguished clergy. An example of a clergyman who saw pluralism as rewarding his abilities was Archdeacon William Paley of Carlisle. Paley resigned his Cambridge fellowship in 1775 to reside in Carlisle diocese. There he received a number of livings and cathedral dignities. Yet he was a conscientious cleric and author of the famous *Evidences of Christianity*, *The Clergyman's Companion in Visiting the Sick* and *The Young Christian Instructed in Reading*. Alternatives to pluralism were by no means either attractive or easily implemented. In 1786, it was calculated that a wholesale redistribution of church incomes (including those of the episcopate and dignitaries) would yield an average income of £60 a year for each clergyman. Redistribution would simply create a beggarly clergy too poor and low in esteem to do any good.

The impact of pluralism and non-residence should perhaps be judged by the way they affected the spiritual lives of the parishes. Certainly there is no correlation between non-residence and pluralism and lack of services. In 1783, the Salisbury visitation revealed that only five Wiltshire churches had less than one weekly service. Elsewhere figures for two Sunday services, or 'double duty', are respectable: in Chester diocese in 1778 it stood at 66 per cent; in Oxford diocese in 1783 it stood at 85 per cent; in Shropshire and Hereford archdeaconries 83 per cent and 63 per cent between 1716 and 1722. In the West Riding of Yorkshire, in 1764, 91 per cent of churches had two services and in south Lancashire the figure reached 95 per cent. Figures for celebration of Holy Communion are equally respectable. The canons of 1604 required at least three communion services annually. In Wiltshire, 73 per cent of churches held quarterly or more frequent celebrations. In Exeter diocese, by 1744 the vast majority had quarterly celebrations, and by 1799 41 churches had monthly celebrations and a further 71 had between 6 and 8 a year. In Llandaff diocese a majority of parishes exceeded the canonical minimum and some parishes were moving towards monthly celebrations. Infrequency of celebration should not, however, always be taken to mean that spirituality was ebbing. In the case of the Duke of Newcastle infrequent reception of Communion certainly reflected a piety unnoticed by the nineteenth century, indeed Newcastle was tormented by fears of his own unworthiness to receive the sacrament. The most thorough analysis of Georgian churchmanship has concluded that another factor in the frequency of celebration of Communion was the reluctance of the laity to receive it. There were prejudices that it was associated with the elderly and that it was reserved for the leisured classes and those of 'high attainment'.[7]

The Church and the People in 1760

Measurement of the level of churchmanship and spirituality among the people of late eighteenth century England and Wales is problematic. Contemporary opinions differed widely. Many observers held the view that the Methodist revival grew from the soil of the failure of the Church of England. Colonel John Byng held that if only the Church had been more active the people would have been receptive to the spiritual comfort which it offered. Similarly, one historian has recently concluded 'if there is an expectation of lethargy, this expectation is not disappointed'.[8] There is much evidence to support this view. The examination of visitation returns by Bishop John Butler of Hereford (1788–1802) in 1788 suggests that there had been a marked decline in church attendance, and in Lincolnshire in 1800 it was estimated that attendance had fallen to one-third of the population.

It is not difficult, however, to find examples of opposing views. A Frenchman in England in 1784, the Marquis de Rochefoucauld, commented that 'confirmation is regarded as much more necessary [than confession], in fact . . . it is practically indispensable'. The diary of the schoolmaster Samuel Teedon also suggests that there were men who inculcated a fear of God into the people, and in particular warned the people of the perils of Satan. The clerical diaries of the era suggest that, for the most part, the clergy were well motivated and conscientious. In 1799, for example Parson Jones of Broxbourne, indicated the expectations that he had of the clerical profession.

A clergymen's life should be chiefly spent among his books, and particularly in studying, upon his knees, that best & most useful of all books, the Bible. Whatever time he can spare should be laid out in exhorting, advising, comforting, & assisting his poor parishioners, especially those who are sick. In other respects, his life cannot be too recluse. If he mixes with the rich, he will be very apt, if of my volatile, naturally gay temper, to speak 'unadvisedly' & 'unguarded with his lips'. How must this damp, & daunt, his spirits, for some time afterwards, in his pulpit exertions! How destructive of his usefulness as a minister, must be every instance of misconduct![9]

Jones was convinced that his diary was an important means of self-inspection and used it as such. Equally suggestive of a high view of the clerical life was the anxiety of William Cole, the rector of Bletchley, Buckinghamshire, in 1766 that he was not worthy of the priesthood. In August of that year he recorded in his diary, 'I ought to examine my own conduct, & to live better than I do. God forgive me my greater failings, & enable me to live better for the future.' Cole in fact was an exemplary pastor, regularly visiting the houses of his flock. Visiting was also undertaken by clergy like the Revd Miles Atkinson, vicar of Kippax, who spent five or six hours a day in the homes of his congregation. The strength of the churchmanship in this period has led Jonathan Clark to invert traditional interpretations and conclude that the 'new branches' of Methodism and evangelicalism were evidence of the Church's vitality.

These two views, of neglect and spiritual strength, are not mutually exclusive. What historians and contemporary observers have failed to emphasise in the search for a single view is that the Church of England encompassed both strong and weak parsons, it had parishes in which clerical duties were well performed and the people benefited from them as well as parishes in which the clergy were negligent. A quantitative examination of this issue has yet to be devised and undertaken, but clearly needs to go beyond the superficial issues, like technical residence. The most recent qualitative examination of the state of Georgian churchmanship has concluded, however, that

> English Churchmanship of the Georgian epoch was 'higher' in the spiritual sense than is commonly supposed. It cannot simply be described as Latitudinarianism . . . Catholic inclinations weakened only gradually . . . they did not go out with the Nonjurors, or even with the Hanoverians . . . It was part of the outlook of moderate divines – Gibson, Wake, Warburton, Secker, Porteus and Moore – who, as bishops, sought to preserve what they could of the old, while laying their flocks open to the benefits of the new. These were more typical of the Georgian church than extreme latitudinarians like Hoadly or Richard Watson.[10]

The established view that the existence of the Non-jurors eliminated a High Church 'wing' of the Church has been challenged. High Church clergy and attitudes seem to have been diffused through the Church, but more prevalent than is often supposed. The works of High Church writers like Robert Nelson, William Law and Charles Leslie were very popular in the mid-eighteenth century. Bishop Wilson's work on the sacrament and Nelson's *Great Duty of Frequenting the Christian Sacrifice* went respectively into their twenty-fourth and thirteenth editions in 1796 and 1756.

Clerical Incomes

The tithe in eighteenth-century England and Wales was still the principal source of clerical incomes – together with farming the glebe, surplice fees and Easter offerings. Tithes, literally a tenth of a parishioner's income, were levied on all the produce of a parish. The rector, or the lay impropriator, was entitled to the great and small tithes; vicars were entitled only to the small tithes. (Great tithes being those of corn, hay and wood, small tithes being those of wool, livestock and garden produce.) By the eighteenth century custom had developed many local variations in the nature and collection of tithes. Tithes by 1700 were no longer payable on personal income, only on crops and increases in farm animals, and in many places a *modus decimandi*, or commutation to a fixed money payment, had taken place. The advantage of moduses was the ease with which they could be collected, but they could not keep pace with inflation and tended to be eroded in value. In 1803, the decision of the incumbent of Wisbech to reject the usual modus from his parishioners in preference for tithes in kind was met by a fierce legal battle taking five years. This was not surprising given that the court's decision was for the incumbent, whose income rose accordingly from £360 in 1775 to £2000. A great number of court cases arising from tithes were a product of the desire of a parson to break out of the straitjacket of a modus which had not kept pace with inflation.

Tithes were, moreover, notoriously difficult to collect. In part, as Eric Evans has demonstrated, tithe disputes were a reflection of new forms of cultivation and a rise in prices which meant, for the first time, that smaller farmers paid tithes – though in Bath and Wells diocese, where farmers were comparatively prosperous, there were protracted lawsuits for tithe payment. Between 1801 and 1805 there were forty tithe lawsuits entered in the Wells

Episcopal Court, and between 1826 and 1830 the figure had risen to fifty-seven. The cost of collecting tithes grew as resistance to payment stiffened. Where a clergyman turned collection of tithes over to an agent, or tithingman, it was common by the end of the eighteenth century for his charge to be a quarter of all monies collected. Clergy who could not afford an agent were often forced to come to an expensive bargain with farmers to avoid costly and protracted litigation. Often such bargains dragged down the income of a parish.

At the beginning of the eighteenth century 3826 livings of the total 9180 had incomes of less than £50 per annum. But the eighteenth century was one of growth of clerical income, largely as a result of the general growth in the income from land. Enclosures increased the yield of land and incumbents often supported their introduction at advantageous commutations agreed with the landowner. On occasion enclosures afforded the opportunity for tithes to be commuted into a land settlement. The enclosures at Wigston in Leicestershire allowed the incumbent a farm of 88 acres in exchange for the small tithes. Thus was the parson turned into a 'squarson'. In Oxfordshire, the enclosures created a gulf between the dispossessed yeoman class and the clerical land-owners. Occasionally, as in the case of the Vicar of Headington in 1819, a clergyman protested against the effects enclosures had on the poor. But clergy were understandably attracted to enclosures, particularly given the example of the richest living in the country, Doddington in Cambridgeshire, where fen drainage and enclo-sures caused the parish's income to rise to £7306.

The clergy were also affected by the increase in the price of corn resulting from the protectionist policies in operation from 1773 and from the Napoleonic Wars. By 1800 wheat stood at the inflated price of 127s a quarter, and the clergy, like all land-owners, profited from the rise. Where clerical incomes were known they had almost without exception risen. The profits of Glandford chapelry in Norfolk doubled between 1727 and 1780; those of Cockthorpe from £69 to £116 between 1744 and 1777. The living of Long Melford in Suffolk saw an increase from £303 in 1735 to £460 by 1790. In that year the rector renewed the financial arrangements of the living and increased the income to

£532. By 1800 it had increased to £732 and by the incumbent's death in 1819 it yielded £1219. Significantly, all these increases took place during a time of relatively low inflation. Further sources of increase in clerical incomes were surplice fees in large populous parishes. As the population grew, the fees payable on marriage and burial grew too. In 1833, St Pancras in London yielded £1147 in surplice fees.

This did not mean that all clergy benefited. Those with a large glebe did best. Those reliant on their parishioners for tithes were the most at risk. Jones of Broxbourne was bitterly upset by the difficulty of extracting tithes, and many clergy had to resort to law, if they could afford it. This was a particular problem of collecting tithes in kind, rather than of having them commuted to a modus. Moreover, there were problems with relying on the income from land. After the Napoleonic Wars the agricultural depressions of the periods 1813–15, 1819–23, and 1832–6 all saw major falls in the income from land. In Derbyshire between 1824 and 1832 the value of the average benefice declined by £15 a year. As a result, of course, there were destitute clergy. William Wilberforce in 1806 told the Commons of a clergyman who had been forced into weaving to supplement his income.

In many cases, of course, clerical income depended directly upon the effectiveness of estate management. Most bishops left the management of their estates to stewards and secretaries. Bishop Moss of St David's was an exception. On his elevation to St David's in 1766 he sent for the account books of episcopal estates and began a thorough overhaul of the diocesan income. By careful management of the lease renewals of the numerous and scattered lands of the bishopric he was able to restore their value. In one case he noticed that a lessee had forgotten to record that his lease included the rights to forestry and to operate a fair; he increased the lease fine accordingly. Even small rises, like that of the shilling increase imposed on Robert Brigstock's lease on land at Jordanston, were extracted. Additionally, Moss employed one of the canons of St David's as his financial agent in the diocese during his absence and retained a land umpire to resolve disputes over ownership. As a result of Moss's measures, in part at least, by the end of the eighteenth century St David's had caught up the income growth rate of the English dioceses. St David's was not alone, however. Between 1760 and 1835 the incomes of the six bishoprics of Canterbury, York, London, Oxford, Bristol and Llandaff rose from a total of £16,500 to £49,312; an increase of 199 per cent. In the same period cathedral chapters increased their incomes by a similar figure.

Recent research suggests some remarkable average rises in incomes between 1700 and 1835. A sample of 312 parishes appearing in records in both years suggests an average increase in rectories and vicarages of 462 per cent, and in perpetual curacies of 686 per cent. In part, this latter figure was a product of the growth in the augmentations available from Queen Anne's Bounty at the end of the eighteenth century because of the relaxation of the Bounty rules. But it has been confirmed by figures for the incomes of curates in Bath and Wells diocese where between 1814 and 1837 the average curate's income rose by over 100 per cent. Some bishops, like Horsley of St David's, were assiduous in increasing curates' incomes. Horsley in 1788 made his first priority an enquiry into levels of curates' income and refused to licence a curacy which offered less than £15 a year. In his first year the incomes of curates in a hundred livings were increased.

It is easy to exaggerate the level of clerical incomes; by 1835 there were only 76 incumbents with incomes in excess of £2000 a year and all but sixteen held some cathedral preferment as well as a parish. In Wales, where clerical incomes were lowest, 25.6 per cent of clergy received less than £100 a year, in England a comparable figure was 1081 or 15.6 per cent of the total. Regional differences were striking: Cumbria's clergy earned 60 per cent less than their brothers in the rest of England.

One further feature of tithes was the way in which they may have contributed to rural anticlericalism. Eric Evans suggests that, at times of economic distress, the Church was as unpopular in the countryside as it has been assumed that it was in some towns. The Select Committees on the state of agriculture in the 1820s and 1830s were littered with accounts of the oppressive impact of tithes. Evans emphasises that from the late eighteenth century onwards the clergy were increasingly determined to collect higher and higher tithes. Clergy even established their right to the potato tithes after lengthy court battles. The acrimonious disputes that high tithe demands generated promoted absenteeism from services and hostility to both incumbent and the Church as an institution. Clerical prosperity often happened at the expense of their parishioners and the result was to the detriment of the Church's mission. When rural distress was at its height the clergy seemed to be concerned with raising their own incomes, and as a result the Swing riots, which took place between 1830 and 1832 as a result of widespread economic depression, attacked the clergy. It was not only the clergy who were attacked as a result of the demand for higher rates of tithe collection. In Wales, the attempt of John Palmer Chichester, the lay owner of tithes from a third of Cardiganshire, to collect all the tithes due to him, including those of hay and milk which had not been paid to his predecessor, resulted in a widespread campaign of opposition. For a quarter of a century much of Cardiganshire was plunged into litigation, disputes and open rebellion against Chichester.[11]

Tithes were naturally unpopular among the dissenters, and especially so among the Quakers. Quakers held firmly to the belief that Christ's instructions to his disciples to 'freely receive' applied to the clergy. Their opposition to tithes led many Quakers to be imprisoned in the first half of the eighteenth century. Campaigns mounted in the 1730s and 1750s to remove tithe payment from Quakers were unsuccessful, but there were also campaigns against imprisonment of Quakers for non-payment of tithes in the 1770s, 1780s and 1790s. By the end of the century it was rare for Quakers to be imprisoned, though there was still restraint of property to ensure payment.

A Reformed and Unreformed Church?

The Church, before the Ecclesiastical Commission of the 1830s, has been portrayed as a Church in which slumbers were not 'disturbed by the sleeper's uneasy conscience'.[12] One of the most recent works on ecclesiastical history set the parameters of the 'age of negligence' as 1700 and 1840.[13] These views suggest that ecclesiastical reform is the chameleon of history: before 1830 the work of the Church to reform itself is overlooked because it is set against a backdrop of resistance to reform; after 1830 the reform of the Church has attracted attention because it occurred during a time of social and political reform. In fact there were significant measures of Church reform before 1830. Best concluded that after 1790 the wind of reform was blowing through the Church.[14]

The publication in 1808 of the second edition of *The Clergyman's Assistant* reveals the extent of church reform in the second half of the eighteenth century. The work – a guide for clergy – contained the texts of eight recent Acts of Parliament concerning the Church. The preface indicated that the second edition sought to provide the clergy and public with statutes which had been passed in the last few years, and with which the Church was bound to comply. Significantly, the volume also included two other items which the clergy were considered to require. The first of these was the royal proclamation 'for the encouragement of piety . . . and punishing of vice' of 1787. It was the fifth such proclamation by monarchs since 1694 and indicated George III's 'resolution to discountenance' vice, profaneness and immorality. It appealed to his subjects to avoid dice, cards and gaming on Sundays and charged ecclesiastical and civil justices with punishing immoral behaviour. The proclamation was required to be read in all churches in the land. Bishop Porteus of London (1787–1809) and the evangelical MP William Wilberforce acted on the King's example by setting up a society to promote the objectives of the proclamation. By 1802 the renamed Society for the Suppression of Vice was 'vigorous [in] warfare against brothels, fortune tellers, and obscene publications'. The second item was the Archbishop of Canterbury's letter to the bishops of his province issued in 1770. The letter, the contents of which were to be communicated to all the clergy in the dioceses of the province, contained thirteen injunctions. These focused on assiduously checking and examining candidates for Orders; they enjoined bishops to take care in licensing curates and granting qualifications for pluralism; and they sought to prevent non-residence and corrupt presentations. These two documents indicate that there was no absence of desire to develop and reform the Church and the people in this period.

The temporalities of the Church were the subject of a number of acts in the 'pre-reform' era. In 1777, Gilbert's Acts sought to increase clerical residence through the repair and provision of parsonages. The Act established a far wider role for Queen Anne's Bounty, freeing it from augmentation by lot in favour of targeting money in the form of low interest and interest free loans for parsonages. Those livings with an income of less than £50 a year qualified for loans of up to £100. The Act also placed punitive rates of interest on loans to non-resident clergy.

Whilst the Act was not fully implemented by Queen Anne's Bounty until 1811, it proved to be a great success thereafter. By 1825 about £250,000 in loans had been laid out and over 500 loans had been agreed. One of the first of these was the Revd Sydney Smith, who as rector of Foston borrowed £1600 to repair his parsonage, and repaid the loan at £130 a year. A series of Acts of 1803 released Queen Anne's Bounty from the Mortmain Act of George II's reign, which restricted gifts and bequests to endow churches, chapels, parsonages and glebes. Another Act required episcopal permission to be granted before a clergyman could farm land other than the glebe.

The most significant measure, however, was the Church Building Act of 1818. The Act was the brainchild of the Prime Minister, Lord Liverpool, and Nicholas Vansittart, the Chancellor of the Exchequer, acting on the prompting of the Hackney Phalanx, a group of clerical and lay High Churchmen. The Act allowed subdivision of parishes and provided £1,000,000 for the construction of new churches and authorised subscriptions for further buildings. Building of churches was targeted at new industrial towns. Altogether 218 churches were built with money provided by the government, and a further £500,000 was granted in 1824. Liverpool considered the Act the most important measure he had ever submitted to Parliament. The Act also required at least a third of all seats in the churches to be free from pew rents and was also the spur to dioceses to set up their own church building societies. The increase in the numbers of sittings provided by church building was remarkable. Between 1801 and

1851 the population of England rose from 8,892,536 to 17,927,609, yet the average number of sittings for each hundred people fell only marginally, from 58.1 to 57.0. The Church, though behind in its provision, achieved a striking feat in maintaining the level of church accommodation at the time of greatest population growth. Above all, the reform saw the Church taking the lead and drawing support from the State. From its example of commissioners to supervise the church building the Ecclesiastical Commission was set up to administer church reform in the 1830s.

The reform of temporalities was complemented by the revision of the position of clergy. The Stipendiary Curates Act of 1796 followed a number of earlier acts attempting to promote the interests of parish and curate. The Act allowed a bishop to authorise the employment of a curate if a parish was left without a resident clergyman for longer than eight months. Bishops were also able to award stipends to curates of up to £75 and an additional £15 for a residence. The Act relied perhaps too much on bishops and by its permissive nature did not achieve all that was expected. Parliament attempted to replace and amend it in 1805, 1808, and 1812. On each occasion the anxieties of peers and bishops prevented the passage but in 1813 a new Stipendiary Curates Act was passed. Even Virgin concedes that it was 'a decisive and, in many ways, radical piece of legislation'.

The 1813 Act replaced permissive legislation with mandatory elements: it laid down a scale of stipends for curates, based on the population of the parish, with a minimum of £50. Curates were required to be appointed in places where an incumbent was non-resident, whilst bishops were granted discretion to increase stipends. Significantly, the legislation had been inspired in part by the views of Bishop Porteus and Lord Grenville that curates as educated professional men deserved higher incomes. Perhaps the one reservation in the Act was that it applied only as each living fell vacant (an approach which was widely adopted in the Church reforms of the 1830s and 1840s) and this meant that its impact was felt rather gradually. The Clerical Residence Act of 1803 was also an attempt to restrain pluralism, by requiring each instance to be justified to the diocesan bishop, who was empowered to revoke licences. In addition, bishops were required to forward figures of non-residence to the Privy Council.

The reform of the Church in the period 1760 to 1830 was gradualist and has been criticised for a lack of radicalism. Yet the scale of the problems facing the Church at the time have been understated by historians, as have the nature of the solutions. The Church had managed to move the State from its policy of *quieta non movere* in the mid-eighteenth century to one of undertaking legislation to promote wider religious observance. The shift in attitudes is perhaps best illustrated by the assertion of the Secretary for War, Lord Liverpool, regarding the clergy in 1809: that 'it was highly incumbent upon the legislature to do all in their [sic] power to better the situation of a class of men, who, of all others, were the most serviceable to their country'. Such a statement represented a stark contrast to the policies of Walpole and Newcastle and was occasioned by different circumstances. As Best has indicated it was during this period that substantial results accrued to church reform. But more importantly 'the governing class's long-standing uneasiness about the state of society began to crystallise into clearer perceptions of what was wrong and what needed doing'.[15] Whilst the legislation that this attitude spawned was by no means perfect, it was the foundation upon which all later church reform was built.

The Church in Wales

The inheritance of the Church in Wales in the eighteenth century was an unfortunate one. The Reformation had in St David's diocese removed 58 per cent of tithe income, worth by the start of the nineteenth century £24,143 to impropriators. The Ecclesiastical Revenues Commission discovered that the Chichester family received an income of £6000 from the alienated tithes of thirteen Welsh parishes. As a result of tithe alienation, parishes in Wales in the eighteenth century were badly affected by the poverty of both the dioceses and the livings. Not only were the incomes of parishes and dioceses at the beginning of the century at a low base, but they were also subject to lower growth rates than England.

Brecon's clerical incomes grew by only 0.6 per cent in the eighteenth century.

Plurality was widespread, and necessarily so. Where there was sufficient money to employ a curate the stipend was often very low. In Llandaff diocese, in 1763, the average curate's stipend was just £15 a year. In one case, that of the parish of Bassaleg, the curate was paid 40 shillings, £2, for assisting at services once a month. By the 1830s the average curate's income in St David's diocese was £55 compared with a national average of £82. The same is true of the beneficed clergy: in St David's the average annual income in the 1830s was £137 compared with the national average of £285. As a result of such low stipends curates and incumbents had to become pluralists, serving more than one parish. An additional problem was that of non-residence. The 1828 visitation returns for St David's revealed 58 per cent non-residence. This was in part a reflection of the atrocious position of parsonages in the diocese. In the whole diocese only 10 parsonages were fit for residence, 78 were unfit and a further 221 parishes were without a parsonage at all. Only 17 benefices took advantage of the loans from Queen Anne's Bounty to build a parsonage.

As with England these circumstances produced two alternative interpretations. William Williams of Pantycelyn, regarded the Church's poverty as a factor in causing the sleep from which the Church in Wales suffered; a more recent conclusion is that in spite of such difficulties the Church strove to keep spiritual life alive.[16] This view is reflected in the fact that in 1828 the majority of rural churches in St David's had single services on a Sunday and most of those in towns had two services. Where popular piety was invigorated it was in part achieved through the work of the Welsh circulating schools. *Welsh Piety*, an annual report issued from 1738 to 1777, demonstrated the extraordinary commitment of the Welsh people to Christian education. The leader of the Welsh circulating school movement, Griffith Jones, laid great emphasis on the catechism and on prayers as part of the life of the schools. By 1760 the organisers of the Welsh circulating schools reported to the SPCK that there was a total of 218 schools educating 9834 scholars. The reports from the circulating schools often present an insight into the difficulties faced by the Church in the period. In 1771, the curate of Brongwyn commented that children in his school were too poorly clothed to go to church services. The circulating schools also indicate the advantages afforded to the Welsh people from provision of Christian education in their own tongue. Across Wales there were monoglot English clergy who could not minister to the needs of Welsh speakers. In Llandaff, five clergy were non-resident because their Welsh flock could not understand them. Occasionally, such churches had monthly Welsh services or sermons or the services of a Welsh-speaking curate. However, in some areas, like Anglesey (in many ways a model of ecclesiastical provision), English sermons and services were the exception. In St David's diocese also services in English only were in the minority; most parishes had Welsh, alternation between languages or separate services for English and Welsh.

The issue of language became something of a distraction for churchmen of the nineteenth century; they asserted that the problems of the eighteenth century were a result of the appointment of English bishops to Welsh sees. After John Wynne's elevation to the See of St Asaph in 1714, there were no Welsh speakers on the bench of bishops until Connop Thirlwall learnt it, after his nomination to St David's in 1841. There were also English bishops who sought to avoid staying long in a Welsh see, which often – through size and terrain – demanded the greatest exertion from the diocesans. In 1761, Lord Hardwicke commented to Newcastle that the income of St David's was so low at £900 a year and that without some 'tolerable commendam' it would not tempt Dean Green of Lincoln to accept it. In 1774, Dr John Moore was relieved to have 'escaped' St David's. But there were also English bishops who took great pains to struggle with the problems that confronted them. Bishop Moss's work at St David's has already been noted and Bishops Warren and Horsley accepted translations within Wales in 1783 and 1802 respectively. Horsley's episcopate at St David's began in 1788 with a blizzard of paper as he required all curates to exhibit their licences to their rural deans. The effect was to sweep away the numerous unlicensed curates who often received stipends as low as £5. Horsley licensed them, imposing a minimum stipend of £15. He also improved the standard of clerical education in his diocese and supported church repair. Bishop Thomas Burgess of St David's furthered Horsley's educational work with the creation of St David's College, Lampeter for the education of men training for Orders. W. T. Morgan's assertion that Thomas Burgess stood out as 'a shining exception' among the bishops cannot be supported, for while he was an excellent bishop he was not an exception.

The Church in Wales also faced the difficulties caused by the industrial revolution in South Wales. Even where the Church maintained its churches and clergy it was not able to keep pace with the massive population growth. The population of Glamorgan rose in the first half century after 1801 from 74,189 to 240,095. Bishop Herbert Marsh's visitation of Merthyr Tydfil in 1817 found that, in a town of 11,104 people, there were only forty communicants. Bishop William Van Mildert of Llandaff, and later of Durham, was able to claim in 1821 that the repair of churches had improved in his diocese, but their number could not keep pace with the populations of new towns. Only with the creation of district chapelries after 1844 could the Established Church try to catch up with the Nonconformists. But by that time the Nonconformist churches had achieved an impressive lead. The religious census of 1851 revealed that in the diocese of Llandaff nonconformist chapels outnumbered churches and attendance at chapel services outnumbered that at Anglican services by over four to one. Nonconformity flourished where the Welsh language was strongest, and chapels were the cultural and religious counterparts of the same problem. In Breconshire and Radnorshire, where there was a good level of church accommodation, the Church in Wales providing more than any other denomination, attendance figures were still low: only 21.7 per cent of the population attended Church in Wales services, compared with 62.3 per cent attending other services. In some parts of St David's diocese the 1828 visitation returns reveals church attendance falling below 10 per cent. In the wake of the Ecclesiastical Commission bishops – albeit Englishmen – like Alfred Ollivant and Thirlwall sought to advance the position of the Church in Wales. Funds to endow curates' stipends and church extension were developed across Wales in an attempt to retrieve the situation and to minister to the working classes.

2

CHURCH AND STATE, 1760–1830

The Church's Relations with the State: the American Revolution and the Abolition of Slavery

The relationship between Church and State which George III inherited in 1760 was principally one of cooperation. The Church's goal was to maintain the equilibrium between the forces in the constitution. The first 'Martyrdom sermons' of the new reign, preached on the anniversaries of the execution of King Charles I by Bishop Samuel Squire of St David's and Bishop John Green of Lincoln (in 1762 and 1763 respectively) emphasised the old Whig view that the monarchy was subject to limitations, and that the King should avoid entanglements with politicians who sought to expand royal power. It was a restatement of the early Hanoverian position of balances in the constitution between Parliament, Monarch and Church. Later in the decade the 'Wilkes and Liberty' campaign witnessed the Church ranging itself against the radical John Wilkes, and both the Oxford Assize and the Martyrdom sermons of 1769 denounced Wilkes's views and supported the King. As George III's reign developed the relationship between Church and State was maintained but it was also subjected to challenges. Two major issues threatened to unbalance the equilibrium: the American Revolution and the slave trade.

The American colonial revolt struck at the heart of the issue of government by the consent of the people, an issue on which the Church supported the State in upholding the principles of the

41

Glorious Revolution. The unrest in the colonies brought to prominence an issue which for some years had threatened to divide the Church from the State, that of the consecration of a bishop for the colonies. Successive bishops of London, in particular Gibson and Sherlock, had fought hard for a bishop for the plantations. The bishops supported the view that denial of a bishop for America would have grave spiritual effects, but the government was convinced that denial of a bishop was a lever which could be used against the troublesome colonists.

In the 1760s two proposals, one for a tour from an English or Irish bishop, the other for the consecration of a Canadian bishop, were blocked by the government. As time went on the bishops found themselves increasingly frustrated. In 1766, Bishop Richard Terrick of London appeared twice at meetings of the Board of Trade and openly expressed his opposition to government policy. In 1768, Archbishops Secker and Drummond waited on Secretary of State Lord Shelburne to recommend the appointment of a bishop for America but, as Secker recorded in his autobiography, they 'could make no impression at all upon him'. Secker privately indicated that he was frustrated by the government in his plans to send a bishop to America, and it is clear that Secker was providing substantial funds for the American Church. Secker maintained pressure on the government until his death later that year. His will contained the sensational bequest of £2000 to the Venerable Society to help the establishment of a bishopric in America. The call for an episcopate in America remained the cry of the High Churchmen, like Horsley, who feared that Dissent would gain an irreversible grip on America.

Perhaps the most forthright statement of the Church's anger with the government came in 1767 when Bishop Ewer of Llandaff preached the annual SPG sermon. Of the sermon one historian has written, 'no Anglican prelate of the eighteenth century committed as great an indiscretion as did John Ewer'.[1] Ewer scourged the ministry with the charge of 'scandalous neglect' of the colonists, and called for the establishment of an American episcopate. Ewer was attacked for his sermon in government organs including the *St James's Chronicle* and *The London Chronicle*, but he was joined in his views by Bishop Warburton.

42

The passage in 1774 of the Quebec Act, which granted toleration to Roman Catholics in the newly won colony of Quebec, whose population was estimated to be comprised of 150,000 Catholics and 400 Protestants, added a further religious dimension to the conflict with the American colonies. The New England Protestants were infuriated, and further inflamed by the landing of a Catholic bishop in Nova Scotia. Lord Northington, who had resigned in 1766 over the latitude shown to the Quebec Catholics, was joined by Lord Chatham who virulently opposed the Quebec Bill in the Lords. The bishops were in a difficult position: their natural conservatism led them to be suspicious of toleration of Catholics, but they also appreciated the government's need for stability to the north of the American colonies. Eventually the bishops were, claimed Chatham, 'traitors to their religion' and reluctantly voted with the government for the bill. In the wake of the passage of the bill, *The Royal American Magazine* and *The London Magazine* carried a print of four English bishops doing a minuet around the Quebec Act while Lord North, the other bishops and the Devil look on. The Act represented an important accommodation between Church and State, the bishops recognising that they had an ultimate loyalty to the government's policy in North America.

During the revolution itself the Church maintained little contact with the colonists. Earlier, in 1766, the Anglican bishops had apologetically explained that they could not achieve much for the colonists 'when you . . . [are] on fire about the Stamp Act'. They could do less in the 1770s as both sides slid towards armed conflict. However, at least one bishop, Jonathan Shipley of St Asaph, ruined his chances of promotion to Canterbury through his failure to support the government during the war. Other bishops spoke out on less significant issues but nevertheless provoked the government's anger. Archbishop Markham of York roused the ire of the moderate Duke of Grafton in 1776 when he treated the American Revolution lightly and Grafton's protégé, Bishop John Hinchcliffe of Peterborough, urged restraint on the government in its dealings with America in 1774. In 1778, Hinchcliffe again entered the lists, imploring the government to abandon the reprisals and scalpings that had been carried out in

America. Bishop Keppel of Exeter also opposed the government over the war with America. But these were, for the most part, lone voices rather than the concerted reaction of an episcopal bloc.

The natural sympathy of some bishops to the American cause was reflected in some wider national religious divisions. The old Royalist–Tory, and often strongly Catholic, areas of the country were strongly in support of the war with the colonies. Cumberland, Westmorland, Northumberland, Durham, Cheshire, Yorkshire and Lancashire sent numerous loyal addresses and petitions to London. In contrast those areas with strongly Protestant communities, East Anglia, Wales and Scotland, tended to oppose the war. Quakers, with close links with American Societies of Friends, collected signature for peace petitions. Suffolk, Essex and Wales together sent only four loyal addresses to London, and Scotland failed to send one. In Cambridge, the university sent an address only reluctantly. The strength of opinion of the clergy can be seen in Colley's discovery of a Staffordshire clergymen's comment in his register: 'to future ages it will appear to be an incredible thing . . . that these kingdoms should maintain (as they have done) a glorious, but unequal conflict for several years with the most formidable and unprovoked confederacy that should be formed against them'.

After the war the bishops as a whole quickly returned to a position of support for the Americans. As early as 1781 Bishop John Moore of Bangor recognised that the colonists' victory had changed church policy. By 1783 the leading American clergyman Samuel Seabury travelled to England, seeking consecration as a bishop, but he found the English bishops still unable to act independently of the government. Bishop Robert Lowth of London (1777–87) told Seabury that it would take an Act of Parliament to allow his consecration, and Lowth was able only to introduce one which would release deacons and priests destined for America from their oaths of loyalty. It was in 1787 that White and Provoost were consecrated by English bishops.

Whatever the relationship between the Church of England and the Church in America, the American Revolution threw light on relations between Church and State. The refusal of the government to concede an episcopal appointment for America had badly strained relations between the Church and the government. However, the absence, during the later years of the crisis, of determined champions of the colonists' cause, like Secker, prevented a broader gulf developing. Less forthright prelates found in the American Stamp Act debates an issue on which they wished to declare their independence from the ministry. Bishop Richard Terrick of London was, on this issue, 'absolutely unattached to any Man or Party of Men, but determined to act by his own Judgement on hearing the debate'. Even Bishop Thomas Newton, a government supporter, protested at the government's action because of 'the sacrifice of the honour and authority of Great Britain, and all the consequent troubles in America'. However, Terrick and Newton were not radicals, nor prepared to breach the Church's relationship with the State over the American issue, particularly when a war was in progress. Bishops protested at aspects of the government's dealings with America but they did not fundamentally question the justice of the British cause. The bishops embarrassed the government at a time when it needed national support for its actions. Some, like Shipley and Keppel, might have gone further if there had been stronger episcopal leadership. But the alliance between Church and State survived intact, while some bishops had asserted their independence. Bishop Warburton's *Alliance of Church and State* . . . had suggested that the civil governor, as a rule, had the Church 'wholly in his power'. This assertion cannot be maintained with regard to the split that dented the alliance as far as bishops for the plantations were concerned. As Greaves pointed out 'the alliance of church and state in England was in fact not one but many. An immensely variegated mosaic of customary accommodations between . . . bishops and ministers of state . . . , sometimes in harmony . . . , sometimes quarrelling – these were the realities which Warburton attempted to generalise in his idea of one alliance.'[2]

In England, it was Dissent which had been most vocal in support of the American cause, and after the Revolution many State legislatures, including Virginia, effected the formal disestablishment of Church and State. Thus, in spite of their sympathy for the cause of the American Church, as events unfolded the bishops in England could not help but associate the revolution with hostility to the form of establishment which they enjoyed. Radical change seemed to promote danger to the Church.

The second issue which affected the relationship between Church and State was that of the slave trade. The issue had caused disquiet among the clergy for years. In 1784, the Revd James Ramsay, vicar of Teston, published his essay on the treatment of slaves in the West Indies, calling for their emancipation. Ramsay may not have been alone: a recent study by Drescher suggests that there was widespread support for abolition among a number of religious and social groups. In 1786, Bishop Porteus of Chester discussed the slave trade with Sir Charles Middleton, and they agreed to write to the young MP William Wilberforce, suggesting that he raise the matter in the Commons. In 1787, the Society for the Abolition of the Slave Trade was established principally by Quakers, though with the help of Anglicans like Bishops Porteus and Watson, and Archdeacon Paley. Whilst the slave trade had been regulated before the society was set up, the State had made no further attempts to end it. After the American War of Independence the slave trade resumed, principally because the Prime Minister, Lord North, feared that Britain's European competitors would surpass Britain unless all forms of trade were restored. In 1787, Wilberforce introduced an abolition bill in the House of Commons, and when evidence was marshalled in the debate Pitt conceded a Privy Council inquiry to the abolitionists. However, the result was merely that an Act of 1788 restricted the numbers of slaves to be carried in each ship.

Occasionally clergy, such as the Revd Thomas Thompson, claimed that slavery was consistent with passages in the Bible, though Bishop Horsley swiftly despatched such views with a plethora of quotations. More frequent was the pragmatic view that it would be difficult to eradicate slavery. Dr Samuel Parr in 1800 claimed that emancipation of slaves was 'Utopian'. The primate, Archbishop Moore of Canterbury, indicated his support for the gradualist attitude of the State when he claimed in 1787 that 'it is a cursed trade, but too deeply rooted to be forcibly and at once eradicated'. Moore's view was waning, however; by the end of the eighteenth century every English bishop had condemned slavery. Such condemnation drew together evangelical, High Church, dissenting and humanist opinion. Above all, the condemnations were significant because of the violation of property rights that such views entailed. Bishops like Porteus were determined to maintain the pressure on the government. Indeed for Porteus the cause of abolition became a crusade. His biographer wrote that 'next to the great paramount concerns of religion, the Abolition was the object of all others nearest to his heart. He never spoke of it but with the utmost animation and enthusiasm. He spared no pains, no fatigues of body or mind, to further the accomplishment . . . In short, the best years of his life and all his talents and powers were applied to it.'[3]

In 1787, Porteus even ordered clergy in the West Indies to begin the systematic teaching of the Church's doctrine, or catechizing, of slaves. It was a radical step, and one which the SPG had rejected three years earlier. In order to avoid the censure of the State, Porteus founded his views on special pleading: slavery, he claimed, was the only case in which property might be appropriated from its owners. Bishop Horsley, speaking in the Lords in 1799, recognised that the anti-slave traders had been associated with the Jacobinism of the French Revolution. But he claimed that abolitionists put forward no vision of the equality of man or of the rights of man: 'we strenuously uphold the gradations of civil society: but we . . . affirm that these gradations . . . are limited'. Equally, Bishop Douglas of Carlisle supported abolition, though he claimed he did not understand the concept of an inalienable right. But voices still assumed that abolitionists were Levellers: Lord Westmorland in 1807 denounced abolitionists as men who would threaten titles and estates.

Ultimately, however, the abolitionists were shifting the concept of the State to one which guaranteed and protected mankind as well as property. Horsley, in 1799, argued that abolition advantaged the State by reducing civil conflicts, like the slave rising in St Domingo in the previous year. Others based their arguments against slavery on thoroughly paternalist grounds. Either way, in 1807 Bishop Porteus was able to rejoice at the abolition of the 'most execrable and inhuman traffic that ever disgraced the Christian World'. However, the principal reason for the failure to abolish slavery altogether was the association of the cause of abolition with that of the French republicans. Slave uprisings in French colonies terrified Pitt and Grenville and turned their faces from complete abolition.

Once the slave trade was ended the complete abolition of slavery itself, after 1807, remained one of the few issues on which the Established Church agreed with Dissent. In Liverpool, for example, the Unitarians and Anglicans were both in the forefront of the abolitionist campaign. It was the Methodists who saved Wilberforce from defeat in the York election of 1806 and in Leeds, during the election of 1832, Richard Watson, the leader of Methodist opinion, urged his followers to vote for Thomas Macaulay rather than for Michael Sadler, since Macaulay was in favour of abolition. In Parliament the dissenting lobby consistently worked with 150 MPs to promote abolition. Such contact with Dissent reassured the Church that even radicals like Granville Sharp accepted a hierarchy within society; although there were those like Bishop William Otter of Chichester (1768–1840) who believed that such collaboration between Anglicanism and Dissent could only benefit Dissent by granting it respectability. Yet abolition, like the cause of the American episcopate, was one on which Church and State agreed to differ without affecting the overarching principle of the alliance. The Church seems to have been given licence to disagree with the government, and bishops were admitted to the bench who supported abolition, because on the fundamental issue of the day, which affected the structure of society, the alliance between Church and State still operated.

The Impact of the French Revolution

The greatest challenge to both Church and State came from the French Revolution. At first, it was not clear that the Revolution would have profound implications: one of the subjects for the Latin prize at Cambridge in 1790 was whether the French Revolution might prove 'advantageous' to Britain. The principal advantage in the Revolution was that it brought men like

Edmund Burke to the defence of an Established Church. In 1790 he wrote 'religion is the basis of civil society' and indicated his belief that the Church consecrated the governments with both legitimacy and with 'high and worthy notions of their function and destination'.[4]

Provision by the Church for the exiled French Catholic clergy indicated the horror the public as well as the State felt for the consequences of abandonment of the Church in France. The Committee for the Relief of the Suffering of the Clergy and Laity of France Exiled in England was funded and supported by the government. The bishops were active in subscribing funds for their French Catholic brothers and in allowing public collections in their dioceses. Altogether these collections obtained £41,314 for the French exiles. The clergy, like the dean of Middleham, supported this effort by urging the view that republicans were no better than the Levellers of the previous century who had destroyed the Church and the monarchy. There was also episcopal mobilisation. The bishops stood firm against a motion, proposed by radical peers, in July 1789 to celebrate the French Revolution with a Day of Thanksgiving; and by 1793, as Britain engaged in war with France, there was an episcopal onslaught against the Revolution. Bishop Horsley's sermon in Westminster Abbey in 1793 reached its peroration with a cry against the revolution: 'Oh my Country ! Read the horror of thy own deed in this recent heightened imitation, and lament and weep that the black French treason should have found its example in that crime of thy unnatural sin.'

The whole congregation stood and remained standing until the end of the sermon. Bishop Pretyman Tomline's charge to his clergy in 1794 devoted nine pages to elucidating the need for religious principles in society. The government, over which Pitt, Pretyman Tomline's former student presided, proceeded to introduce Acts which outlawed seditious meetings and suspended habeas corpus.

The revolutionary wars intensified the Church's hostility to France. In 1794, Bishop Manners-Sutton of Norwich claimed that the war was a just one and a crusade against infidelity; by 1798 even Bishop Watson produced a vehemently anti-French charge to the clergy of Llandaff. Not even Napoleon's Concordat of 1802 with the Church allowed any cooling of tempers. Among the clergy the sorrow at what happened in France was indicated by Parson Woodforde's diary entry for 16 October 1789: 'sad news from France; all anarchy and confusion, the King, the Queen and Royal Family confined at Paris. The soldiers joined the people, many murdered.'

It was clearly advantageous to the government that the growth in clerical income, which placed many clergy into the landed class, coincided with a time of national crisis. If confirmation were needed, it reinforced the Church's support for the Establishment. The loyalist organisations set up in England and Scotland in the years after 1789 (the Association for Preserving Liberty and Property against Republicans and Levellers, the Anti-Jacobin Club, and the Crown and Anchor Club) all contained clergy among their most fervent supporters. John Reeves, of the Association for Preserving Liberty, circulated his literature to all the clergy since they were so firm against the Revolution. Many clergy volunteered as chaplains to yeomanry regiments. But it is easy to overstate the adherence to the State which the Revolution generated. In 1801, Wilberforce wrote:

> I am deeply hurt by the apprehension . . . that a rooted disaffection to the constitution and government has made some progress among the lower orders, and even a little higher; and when it is not quite so bad as this, there is often an abominable spirit of indifference as to our civil and ecclesiastical institutions, instead of that instinctive love and rooted attachment to all that is British which one used to witness . . . I myself have observed a calculating, computing principle, considering what would be gained and what would be lost if there was to be a new order of things.[5]

What worried the government, and the Church in particular, was the attempt by some to argue that religion was in essence revolutionary. Samuel Taylor Coleridge in Bristol, in 1795, emphasised the revolutionary nature of Christianity, speaking ominously of Christ as a reformer, and of the poverty of the apostles. Such views were rare among the Anglican clergy but were perceived as widespread in Dissent. For many Anglicans it became a popular view that, compared with Dissent, Catholicism was now ranged on the side of the State against republican forces. It was these views which eased the passage of the Catholic Relief Act of 1791. Equally, it was the identification of Dissent with republicanism that blocked the repeal of the Test and Corporation Acts for Protestant dissenters. Burke said in the 1790 debate on repeal of the Test and Corporation Acts that 'it was not the time to weaken the safeguards of the Established Church'. Similarly, in 1789, Archbishop Moore of Canterbury warned that 'unrestrained speaking, writing, printing and publishing of religious opinions' would cause terrible mischief. Even liberals like Wilberforce agreed. As Unitarians like Joseph Priestley discussed the nature of religious rights and civil liberties, and petitioned for what they clearly regarded as rights rather than privileges, Church and State saw spectres of revolution in their talk. The three days of rioting instigated by the Birmingham Constitutional Society in 1791, inspired by suspicion of Unitarians, seemed to confirm the government's worst fears. Even Methodists, who under Wesley were firm in their loyalty to the State, found themselves attacked as Jacobins.

By 1800 Bishop John Randolph of Oxford made clear his view that Unitarianism was as responsible for the French Revolution as deism. The Boyle lectures of Van Mildert in 1802–5 also suggested that Unitarians and Quakers were the modern embodiment of infidelity. The role of dissenters in the Sunday schools movement also raised the question of whether their interest in education was really in spreading Jacobin views. The ability to read gave the poor access to seditious pamphlets as well as to the Bible. This view was particularly strong in 1792 when Thomas Paine's *The Rights of Man* sold 200,000 copies. Dean Horne of Canterbury, who had warmly welcomed Sunday schools in 1785, suddenly saw them as a source of revolutionary contamination in 1791. Bishop Horsley openly denounced the Methodist schools and sought to destroy them where he could; he saw Methodist opposition to Pitt's anti-sedition legislation as proof of their treason. In 1798 he even asked that the clergy be mobilised into an armed militia for the final defence of the nation against any armed invasion from France.

51

The mobilisation of the Church against the threat from France was strongly appreciated by the State. In 1817, Bishop Sparke of Ely claimed that it was the clergy who had stemmed the torrent of seditious activity during the wars with France. Henry Majendie, Bishop of Chester and later of Bangor, also held the view that the clerical reforms of the early years of the nineteenth century were the rewards granted by the State in return for the defence the Church had mounted. It was equally the case that clerical reforms were inspired by the hope in government circles that a more effective Church, rid of pluralism and non-residence, would be an even greater barrier to revolution. This was certainly the view of Bishops Watson and Porteus. Porteus himself had written in a charge to his clergy that 'there never was . . . a single period in which the personal residence and personal exertions of the parochial clergy were ever more wanted . . . and expected and demanded by the general voice of the whole nation . . . in order to fortify the faith, and to sanctify . . . the people'.

The 1818 Act for the building of churches was in part inspired by the need for greater access by the Church to influence the people of the industrial centres. Richard Yates wrote in 1815 that the country had received a 'most awful and instructive lesson . . . written in blood and heightened by every human misery. We have seen that Law, Science, and Civilisation, Liberty, Wealth and Order may all sink under the want of Religious and Moral Principle.'

The horrors of the French Revolution and the wars go some way to explain why some conservative bishops viewed even clerical reform with suspicion. William Cleaver, Bishop of Bangor, held firm to the view that, in the light of what had happened in France, all change was dangerous and had the potential to destabilise society. Other bishops saw the pockets of decline in church attendance as evidence of the effectiveness of sedition and infidelity. As the Revolution and the threat of its counterpart in England receded, the Church recognised its role in resolving the conflicts which had emerged during the two decades in which it had occupied the minds of the country. In 1824 Bishop Ryder, in his charge to the clergy of Lichfield diocese, indicated that he saw the role of the clergyman as 'the cementer of social union, the organ of kindly communication between the rich and poor of the land. He is at once the object of respect and the friend to each.' Other clergy were more partisan in their diagnosis of which class needed to change in order for such social cohesion to be achieved. A series of books written by churchmen denouncing mining disasters, factory conditions and poverty was produced in the years after 1815. The Revd Arthur Wade even went as far as to demand that the burden that lay on the backs of the poor should be passed to those of the rich, though few other clergy agreed with him. For many clergy the French Revolution was an event which moved their thinking in different directions. The deep conservatism of Bishop Charles Lloyd of Oxford sprang from his memory of the French Revolution and Gladstone as a young man remembered the growth in piety among the wealthy and fashionable classes that arose from the fear of 'the horrors and impieties of the first French Revolution'.

The Tory Governments and Church Patronage, 1801–30

The governments during the years of the revolutionary wars drew deeply on precedent to ensure that bishops in the Lords were chosen from the ranks of those who would support the regime at a time of crisis. The series of short-lived Tory premierships between 1801 and 1812, lasting an average of only two years, adopted traditional strategies to ensure that the bench of bishops was sympathetic to the ministry.

Prime ministers like Pitt and Grenville ensured friendly support in the Lords by nominating their former tutors to the bench of bishops (Pretyman Tomline and Huntingford respectively). Prime ministers also obliged senior ministers by preferring their tutors: Samuel Goodenough, Joseph Allen and William Mansel received preferment since they were the tutors of the Duke of Portland, Lord Althorp and Spencer Percival. Indeed Portland recognised, when he wrote to the King asking for the appointment, that Mansel was less worthy than others but the political situation forced Portland's hand. Bishoprics had become a currency within the government, a system of compliments used for the maintenance of political support and credibility. They acted as bonds, tying ministers to the ecclesiastical and political patrons. George III was not, however, always impressed by such requests. In 1807, he denied Portland's request for a bishopric for Sparke, a nominee of the Duke of Rutland. In spite of the rejection, the basis for the application is evidence of the way in which he saw the power of Church patronage to create important bonds. Portland had supported the request with the claim of 'the great gratification which this benefice would afford to the Duke of Rutland, whose attachment to your Majesty was exemplifily [sic] manifested on a late occasion . . ., would impress the Duke of Portland with the most lively and lasting sense of devotion'.

Royal tutors also had a claim on government patronage and could usually be relied upon to reflect an establishment view. Pitt allowed both Richard Beadon and Henry Majendie to receive mitres as a reward for their tutorship to members of the royal family. Addington advanced John Fisher to Exeter as a reward for similar service to the Duke of Kent.

Political allies were also swift in demanding places on the bench of bishops for their nominees. Among the senior ministers obliged by the nomination of relatives to offices within the Church were Lord Bathurst, Lord Liverpool, the Duke of Athol, Lord Sherfield, Lord Chichester and the Duke of Buccleuch. Occasionally, prime ministers did not give in to such pressure. In January 1810, for example, the Marquess of Ely told Perceval that his price for continued support for the government was a bishopric for his brother. Lord Ely possessed two rotten boroughs which allowed him the nomination of two MPs to the Commons. The staunch evangelical Prime Minister, Perceval, however, was made of sterner stuff than some of his colleagues, and replied to Ely that 'I would rather be driven from my office tomorrow than purchase my continuance in it.'[6]

Other forms of political support were rewarded too. Addington nominated Thomas Burgess to St David's in 1803. Burgess was a schoolfriend of Addington's and was nominated by him 'though we have been separated almost thirty years'. Charles Moss Jr was similarly preferred to Oxford in 1807, by Grenville, because he was an old schoolfriend. William Harcourt's reward for switching his vote to Grenville in the Lords, on the day after the death of his patron Pitt, was the archbishopric of York. Grenville's church patronage was dominated by his desire for support from Oxford University. Grenville's pretensions to be Chancellor of Oxford University lay behind the preferment granted to Bishops Cleaver and Randolph and to Grenville's spy at Oxford, 'Carissime' Carey.[7] Regional influences also operated. In 1808, Portland translated Bishop Cornewall to Worcester to establish a strong Tory influence there. It was presented to the King as a matter of 'the state of political opinions in the County of Worcester'.

It would, however, be inaccurate to ascribe the worst motives to the dispensers of ecclesiastical patronage. Pitt received the advice of Wilberforce in 1797, 'let me entreat you, as I see another Bishop is dead, to consider well whom you appoint. I am persuaded that if the clergy could be brought to know their duty, both the religious and civil state of this country would receive a principle of new life. I call God to witness that for several years I have never named anyone to you for church preferment whom I did not believe, all things considered, the best man for the situation.'[8] Pitt followed this advice in promoting two bishops who represented the emergent evangelical wing of the Church, Manners-Sutton and Bathurst. Pitt also withstood the demands of the most unworthy clergy for preferment. He rejected Pelham for preferment, and replied to a bishop who asked greedily for the deanery of St Paul's as a commendam, 'I am willing to hope that on further consideration . . . there are parts of that letter which you would yourself wish never to have written . . . until that letter is recalled, your Lordship makes any further intercourse between you and me impossible.' Equally, Perceval has been praised for his exercise of church patronage.[9] But he did not always consider the best interests of the Church. Perceval allowed William Jackson, dean of Wells, to become bishop of Oxford (his brother had been tutor to George IV), in spite of being a notorious rake. Perceval also considered appointing his own grandfather to a bishopric.

Prime ministers had to accommodate the views and wishes of the King, George III and later of the Prince Regent. In 1805, the King denied Pitt's request for the primacy for Pretyman Tomline, instead he rode over to the house of Bishop Manners-Sutton and offered it to him without consulting Pitt. The incident brought the prime minister to the brink of resignation. But Pitt was not alone in facing such royal intrusion. Portland in particular had considerable difficulties with George III. His first two nominations were flatly refused by the King and under Portland the King was able to exercise more influence than under other premiers.

It was Liverpool's lengthy series of governments from 1812 to 1827 that allowed a significant reappraisal of the distribution of church patronage to be undertaken. One of the problems faced by Liverpool's predecessors was the pile of promises for church places they tended to accumulate, few of which could be fulfilled. In 1810, Perceval told the King that he had 'inherited from Portland the experience of the extreme embarrassment occasioned . . . by promises made at any distance from the time when they are to be carried into execution'. Liverpool abandoned the practice of making promises in advance of a vacancy. Indeed in 1824 he indicated to George IV that it was no longer acceptable to make such undertakings 'as events sometimes occur which renders promises of this nature particularly inconvenient'.

Lord Liverpool certainly recognised the social and political importance of church patronage, and was prepared to use it to advance his governments' causes. He rewarded Herbert Marsh's services as government adviser on economics during the Napoleonic Wars with the See of Llandaff in 1816 and he allowed Robert Carr's Toryism to weigh in his mind when seeking a bishop for Chichester in 1824. Political grandees were also accommodated, the Duke of Abercorn, Lord Eldon, Lord Sidmouth and Sir Robert Peel securing the elevations of Bishops Howley, Parsons, Phillpotts and Lloyd respectively. However, Liverpool was careful to establish limits to his willingness to make such accommodations: in 1819 he wrote to Lord Talbot 'it is impossible where pretensions are nearly equal, wholly to set aside all other considerations'. Indeed it was only where pretensions were equal that Liverpool allowed grandees to nominate clergy. In the case of Gerald Wellesley, brother of an important ally, the Duke of Wellington, Liverpool twice told the Duke that since his brother was estranged from his wife, almost to the point of divorce, it would not be possible for him to receive anything other than an obscure appointment. Liverpool also rejected requests for preferment for John Peel, Sir Robert's brother, and for nominees of Lord Harrowby, the Duke of Bedford and Prince Leopold.

In years of peace after 1815 Liverpool also abandoned the partisan nature of Tory church patronage. He recognised the qualities in Whigs like Charles Blomfield, James Monk, William Howley and William Van Mildert and preferred them into or within the episcopate. All four were modest reformers, Blomfield taking a leading part in the ecclesiastical reforms of the 1830s. Liverpool also relied heavily on Blomfield and Howley for nominations for the bench. As a result, widely admired divines like Christopher Bethell, Robert Gray and John Kaye were advanced to the episcopate. Liverpool's pluralist outlook also enabled him to accept those who were not of his own High Church kidney. Like Pitt he corresponded with Wilberforce and conceded in 1821 that he recognised the claims of evangelicals to high office in the Church. As a result moderate evangelicals like Henry Ryder, George Murray and Henry Law were preferred by Liverpool.

There was also a structural change in Liverpool's exercise of church patronage, and one which established a precedent for Goderich and Wellington. Liverpool, with efficiency and effectiveness to the forefront, systematically denied bishops commendams to hold alongside their sees. In 1813 Liverpool insisted that John Parsons give up his deanery of Bristol before he receive the see of Peterborough. Similarly, Edward Legge was asked to surrender all his other offices before accepting Oxford. Even the determined Carey, who struggled hard and long to keep his four pieces of preferment as well as the see of Exeter, had to concede all but one of them. By 1824 it had become expected that a bishop would give up most of his preferment when consecrated. Even John Wade, the radical scourge of church corruption, accepted that Liverpool's governments saw the numbers of commendams held by bishops fall dramatically. Liverpool, and Wellington, did not apply the rule inflexibly: bishops like Henry Law, with a huge family, and Burgess, at a great age, were allowed easier sees.

Liverpool also attempted to restrict the role of the monarch in church appointments, standing his ground on occasion to restrict a bad royal nominee. His successor, Goderich, even began the practice of sending three names to the King for him to choose, thus effecting a restriction of the power of the monarch. Wellington also tended to anticipate all the possible translations and moves a single vacancy could open, so that whoever received a translation Wellington always had a candidate to step into his shoes. It seems difficult to avoid the conclusion that Liverpool and his successors began to reform the system of church patronage in the period between 1812 and 1830, in the gradualist way which complemented the ecclesiastical legislation of the period.[10]

Church Parties: the Hackney Phalanx
and the Clapham Sect

The Hackney Phalanx was in essence a group of friends based around Joshua Watson, a businessman who had interested himself in the lot of the poor of Shoreditch and Hackney. Watson's brother, Archdeacon John J. Watson, was Vicar of Hackney and together with his curate, Henry Norris, acted as the focal point for the group's meetings. The Phalanx was a Tory and High Church group of clergy and laity who cooperated on charitable and religious projects. The Phalanx included men like Archdeacon Charles Daubeny, Thomas Sikes and Christopher Wordsworth who were zealous in asserting the apostolic succession of bishops. Wordsworth believed that even the dissenters should be regarded as offsprings of the Church of England, rather than separate from it. The High Church element in the Phalanx also rejected notions of conversion as unrestrained. The Phalanx took the view that matters of liturgy and faith were beyond their own judgement, and that salvation could only be obtained from the word of God given to man through a corporate Church. The evangelicals perceived the attitude as one of complacency, but it was essentially one which rejected personal religious experience in favour of quiet, less expressive piety. The Phalanx's Toryism led its members to reject parliamentary reform; Watson was so alarmed by the 1832 Reform Act that he moved much of his money to Louisiana. But it was principally the paternalism of

Toryism which found an echo in the religious views of the Phalanx's social action. Norris acted privately as an ecclesiastical adviser to Lord Liverpool who was, in the words of one writer, 'Hackney's ideal Prime Minister'.[11] Certainly he combined a judicious exercise of church patronage and subscribed to the evolutionary view of change in society.

Liverpool was not the only highly placed supporter of the Phalanx. Through Wordsworth, Archbishop Charles Manners-Sutton was introduced to Watson, and in time Watson became an adviser to the primate. Watson was also a friend and confidant of Van Mildert, Thomas Middleton, later bishop of Calcutta, and Hugh James Rose, the Cambridge theologian. In addition to the clergy, the Phalanx maintained contact with a wide circle of laymen and was drawn together by ties of family as well as the common outlook of its members. The Watsons seem to have been related, often distantly and by marriage, to many clerical members of the Phalanx. The principal organ of the Phalanx was the *British Critic*, a newspaper bought by Watson and Norris in 1812. It was in due course edited by Van Mildert and Middleton. The *British Critic* often took the field to defend the Church against its attackers, supporting the extension of the episcopate, especially in India and Australia, and adopting a suspicion of voluntary societies which were not officially sanctioned.

The Phalanx's first major project was in education. In 1811, Watson, Norris and John Bowles set up the National Society for Promoting the Education of the Poor in the Principles of the Established Church. Through the Phalanx's contacts, the Prince Regent was approached and agreed to act as patron and Archbishop Manners-Sutton took on the presidency of the society. Within a year £16,000 had been raised through the Phalanx's energetic fund-raising. The money was then used to encourage parishes to set up and run their own schools, rather than set up schools run by the society. By 1815 every diocese in the country was in contact with the National Society and 100,000 children were in its schools. Watson was a whirlwind of activity, acting as treasurer of the society, visiting schools and personally answering a huge volume of correspondence. However it was inevitable that the society could not succeed in funding and administering all the schools in the country, and yet the society denounced schools which were not established or run by the Church. Ironically it was the enormous success of the National Society that demonstrated the need for some form of state education. Watson tried to prevent the Whig grants to education in 1833 and the state regulation of it. Ultimately, however, the demand for Nonconformist denominational education and the need for mass education in cities overtook the National Society's hope that the Church could retain control of education. Elsewhere in education Watson supported Van Mildert's creation of Durham University, particularly since it was a church foundation, unlike the 'Godless' University College in London.

The Phalanx was also active in promoting church building. The stimulus came from John Bowdler, a High Churchman who sympathised with Nonjuror ideals. Bowdler was active in the SPCK and the National Society and with Watson approached both Perceval and Liverpool with suggestions and requests for money for church building. The campaign became broadened, with laymen like George Bramwell, Joseph Cotton and Sir Thomas Acland entering the lists. In 1817, Liverpool eventually granted his consent to the creation of the Incorporated Church Building Society. Having gained the support of Manners-Sutton and the Duke of York, the society was granted £1,000,000 by parliament in 1818 and a further £500,000 in 1824. Watson's business-like mind was exploited by the society, and he combined further fund-raising with devising rules for allocating the funds. The first report of the society laid down the form for building churches. Churches were to be built where there was a dense population, the maximum grant was to be £20,000, seats were to be free wherever possible – though pew rents were allowed – and the building was to be sanctioned by the bishops who would provide evidence of church need. By 1835, 212 churches had been built by the society and 208 had been aided by it. For the High Gothic apostles of the Tractarian Movement the churches were plain and dull, but the emphasis of the society was not on beauty but on function: on bringing religion to the people – only twenty inches were allowed for each seated person in the pews. The pew rents allowed were devoted to provision of curates for the churches. For Watson the problem of who was to minister to these churches became as great an interest as that of the building society itself, and in 1837 he began to work with Sir Robert Inglis and Benjamin Harrison in the Additional Curates Society. Watson initially gave £500 to the new society and £100 a year to it for the rest of his life. By 1851 the Additional Curates Society had raised £19,000 and had supported the incomes of over 300 curates.

The Phalanx's contribution to church reform was more limited in the area of administrative reform. The Phalanx supported the appointment of bishops by merit, the limitation of translations and a redistribution of ecclesiastical property. But it felt that change had to be undertaken by the Church, not thrust upon it by the State. The Whig governments of Lords Grey and Melbourne were less sympathetic to this view and ultimately it did not prevail. Watson and the Phalanx were tired and ageing by the 1830s, and though their supporters, like Bishop Blomfield of London, held high positions they were eclipsed by the demand for reform. Within the High Church movement the Oxford Tractarians felt that the Phalanx was too moderate to be of use in their work, and Watson's initial warmth towards Pusey and the Tractarians cooled fairly quickly.

One of the features of the Hackney Phalanx which has been neglected by historians is the way in which the Phalanx acted as a 'connection', a recruiting agency for the High Church clergy. One recent account has indicated that

> their talent-scouts spotted prospective protégés . . . middle-ranking brokers tried them out in temporary jobs, as preachers and writers . . . If they passed the appropriate tests, senior members of the Phalanx placed them with sympathetic bishops as chaplains . . . they moved onto archdeaconries and canonries . . . Then, as deans and bishops, they were in a position to act as patrons in their own right.[12]

One such clergyman was William Lyall who was spotted at Trinity College, Oxford by Phalangists. He went to a Hampshire curacy then, via a preachership at Lincoln's Inn and the chaplaincy of St Thomas's Hospital, to the editorship of *The British Critic*. This launched him into the centre of the Phalanx and to the attention of the Phalangist Bishop Howley. He was appointed archdeacon of Colchester, and when Howley moved to Canterbury Lyall went too, first as archdeacon of Maidstone and then to the deanery of Canterbury. Under Howley Canterbury's canonries and dignitaries were packed with Phalangists. One of the most exciting suggestions has been that the Phalanx consciously acted as an instrument of social mobility, rewarding merit and achievement. The Phalangists' connections, protégés and marriage partners were principally men drawn from the upwardly mobile business classes and professional middle classes. Not only were such men advanced within society to offices of higher rank, even the spiritual peerage, but their children became the university-educated establishment classes of the next generation. Even where nepotism occurred within the Phalanx and its patrons, there was a denial of office and places to the lazy and unworthy; only the most diligent relatives obtained the highest rewards. This interpretation indicates that within the High Church Phalanx most of the ingredients for the reform of the Church were in place before the Ecclesiastical Commission was set up in the 1830s.

Between 1800 and 1830 the Phalanx had addressed the issues of education and church building, they had opened the Church to a new breed of clergy dedicated to efficiency and they had promoted a spirituality which focused on social action. The influence of the Phalanx on the work of clergy working in parishes was undoubtedly smaller than they would have wished. In finding places from which they could influence events they overlooked opportunities to change the way in which the Church itself operated. But the achievement of the Phalanx was to establish, within a High Church context, the way ahead for the Church. They set the agenda for the future reformers in administrative changes and spiritual advance. Traditionally, the Phalanx has been seen as a sect that failed, but its failure lay in being superseded by reformers who accepted the diagnosis determined by the Phalanx, and who also accepted the treatment it determined. The difference between the Phalanx and the ecclesiastical reformers of the 1830s was simply one of speed and method.

The origins of the Clapham Sect lay in the appointment of the Revd Henry Venn to the curacy of Clapham in 1754. The village of Clapham was the home of a number of wealthy merchants who rejected Venn's 'disgusting earnestness'. Nevertheless Venn pressed on with his evangelical services and was followed in the incumbency of Clapham in 1792 by his son John. The parish of Clapham at that time had a newly built church and, in spite of bouts of ill-health, Venn made Clapham the home of evangelical theology. Perhaps the single most important event in the establishment of a body of evangelicals was the move to Clapham in 1792 of Henry Thornton who shared a house with Wilberforce on Battersea Rise before their respective marriages. Thornton introduced Venn to Thomas Scott, Lord Dartmouth and Lord Teignmouth who regularly worshipped at Clapham church in order to hear Venn's inspirational preaching. The Clapham 'sect', as it was derisively nicknamed, attracted evangelical laymen like Zachary Macaulay, James Stephens, Charles Grant and Thomas Gisborne. Indeed, by 1799 Clapham Common was home to nine leading evangelical families. Even after Wilberforce moved into London, Clapham retained a score of prominent evangelical residents and John Venn was succeeded as vicar of Clapham in 1813 by William Dealtry, another strong evangelical. By the first years of the nineteenth century a number of schools was set up in Clapham to take advantage of the spiritual climate.

The evangelicals at Clapham were always moderate in their views, avoiding adventist, pentecostal and revivalist opinions in favour of an individualism which ensured that they were never seen as a threat to the Church. Wilberforce's conversion in 1785 had also brought him into a circle of evangelicals who believed in conspicuous social action. The existing evangelicals tended to be focused on urban centres like Cambridge, Cheltenham, Hull, Islington and other districts and suburbs of London. The Clapham Sect's position in the evangelical movement emerged in 1799 when Venn took the lead in forming the Society for

Missions to Africa and the East, afterwards called the Church Missionary Society.

Undoubtedly Wilberforce, sitting for Hull in Parliament, was the leader of the sect. He, above all, was able to give a national voice to their social concerns. From 1784 to 1832 there were over a hundred MPs, principally Tories, who were identifiably evangelical in their views, of whom thirty were Clapham supporters, following the lead given by Wilberforce and as a result gaining the nickname of 'the Saints'. Wilberforce was also enormously successful in promoting the sect's views in print. His *Practical View*, which sought to contrast professed Christianity with 'real' evangelical Christianity, was published in 1797 and within six months 7500 copies had been sold. In the following twenty five years it ran through fifteen editions. The Clapham Sect's emphasis on conspicuous, practical works of the Gospel drew them into the attack on the slave trade, and their effort on this – though by no means alone – was perhaps the most consistent and energetic of the movement. One writer has described their contribution to the abolition movement:

> detailed information needed to be amassed, witnesses collected from all parts of the world, and opposing witnesses cross-examined to expose their false assertions. An endless succession of meetings were held and hundreds of pamphlets written in an attempt to educate public opinion. Committees had to be attended almost daily, petitions organised, deputations headed, Cabinet Ministers, newspaper editors and others interviewed and instructed. The work for such a small company of advocates was overwhelming. Others . . . were co-workers, but the bulk of the labour fell upon the Clapham group.'[13]

Their work also drew them into an enormously wide range of social issues including, schools, prison discipline, savings banks, tracts, village libraries, district visiting and church building, each for a time their favoured project. Within the sect 'every human interest had its guardian, every region of the globe its representative'.[14]

Thomas Babbington said 'this is the age of societies' and the sect, like the Phalanx, operated principally through societies. The Society for the Relief of Persons Imprisoned for Small Debts; the

Auxiliary Bible Society of Clapham; the Society for Bettering the Conditions of the Poor at Clapham; the Society for the Reformation of Prison Discipline; the Indigent Blind Institution; the Foundling Hospital and a mass of societies for foreigners in distress were all creations of the sect which sought to focus its attentions on the practical issues of the day. Indeed Ford Brown's list of evangelicals gives twelve resident at Clapham, who held between them 291 memberships of various societies.[15] Both the sect and the Phalanx studiously ignored the theological controversies of Calvinism and Millenarianism. These controversies were distractions from the real work of drawing men to God.

The society which undertook the chief work of the sect was the CMS. It stands out for two reasons. First, it drew together evangelicals of many differing hues, including Charles Simeon, the Eclectic Society, and the dissenters of the London Missionary Society. Second, it enshrined the deeply practical approach of the sect. Archbishop Moore refused to sanction the society but Bishop Porteus was more sympathetic and agreed to ordain clergy for its work. The society embraced Clapham laymen like Wilberforce, Thornton and Grant and its first sphere of activity was Sierra Leone, where freed slaves could find refuge and be converted. The colony was created as a result of a Clapham initiative to set up a company to develop Sierra Leone. Henry Thornton and Wilberforce invested large sums of money and in spite of difficulties the territory was eventually established. Zachary Macaulay's activity on behalf of the colony earned him its governorship. The CMS often took over from the older SPCK and SPG, particularly in Africa. Their work was focused not simply on conversion of indigenous peoples, but also on the ordination by English bishops of indigenous converts who could carry forward the evangelism more effectively. By the middle of the nineteenth century the CMS was responsible for the establishment of dioceses in West Africa, India, China and Canada.

The effectiveness of the sect's involvement in social issues was a result of its willingness to be active in the political sphere. Macaulay was 'always at hand while Parliament was sitting, and would be found either in the gallery of the House of Commons or below the bar in the House of Lords, able to furnish facts or suggestions to the leaders of his party, and ready to produce any Blue-books or State Papers required for reference, or to point out some quotation apt to the subject'.[16] As Boyd Hilton has shown the Saints were principally liberal social theorists who supported free trade and minimal government interference, rather than advocates of an interventionist or paternalist model of government. Thus the Saints opposed the Corn Laws and supported only modest factory reform; when factory reform became too radical they opposed it. Though they held influence over some of the liberal Tories in Liverpool's reconstructed ministry after 1822, the Saints seem to have eschewed the chance of directly influencing policy. Ultimately, the Clapham Sect's views on punishment and salvation were too heavily oriented towards the individual to try to advance national or institutional redemption by assuming the reins of government.

The work of the Saints has been criticised by Ian Bradley for their apparent and singular lack of concern for those suffering in their own country. The Clapham Sect, and evangelicals in politics, seemed to have an emotional response to issues like slavery and absence of the Gospel, but they lacked a coherent ideology which could embrace all the sufferings they witnessed. There was therefore no plan for the reordering of society and as a result Tories were as comfortable with the sect as were radicals. Indeed, it was Wilberforce who introduced the hated Combinations Act of 1799 into the Commons, failing to appreciate that in a later age a connection would be perceived between the slavery of the new world and the industrial bondage of the old. Later evangelicals like Lord Shaftesbury were to attack the sect for this weakness, Thomas Arnold accused the members of the sect of having 'infinitely little minds'.[17] The sect was too strongly populated with bankers, merchants and businessmen to see problems in the social order. Social inequality was, for Venn, Wilberforce and Thornton, a necessary element in the divine order.

In the sphere of religious liberty the Clapham Sect was remarkably intolerant, opposing Catholic Emancipation until fairly late in the day – though Wilberforce was converted to it in 1813. Equally, their attitude towards parliamentary reform was one of cautious disapproval, only supporting minor changes to purify the electorate of corruption, rather than extending the franchise. Thus for the most part the social actions of the evangelicals and the High Churchmen were no more than *ad hoc* responses to a series of problems, not a single response to a whole social system. Yet it is difficult to judge harshly men like Wilberforce who gave so freely of his own money (£3000 in one year) that at the end of his life had no house of his own, or Macaulay who effectively gave away a fortune of £100,000 and died a poor man. It is also impossible to gauge the impact of the Clapham activities on the generation of churchmen who followed the Saints. Samuel Wilberforce, for example, claimed that he was his father's son in remaining true to the teachings of the Clapham Sect. But other evangelicals found their brand of liberal reform of factories, education and poverty at variance with the views their fathers held.

The Church, Toleration and Emancipation, 1760–1830

Two issues between 1760 and 1830 directly affected the Church's relations with other denominations: the toleration of Dissent and emancipation of Catholics. Toleration of dissenters had been episodically significant throughout the century. The annual Indemnity Acts, which granted exemption from prosecution, were an indulgence rather than a right and stood against the background of the maintenance of the Test and Corporation Acts. These laws led occasionally to unacceptable practices. Until Lord Chief Justice Lord Mansfield gave his ruling against the practice in 1767 the City of London regularly nominated wealthy dissenters to City offices, and then fined them when they refused to take the test. However, the cause of Dissent was not uniformly treated with hostility by the Church and State in the late eighteenth century. The Feathers Tavern Petition, a request by over 200 Anglican clergy, including the Master and fellows of Peterhouse College, Cambridge and the Archdeacon of Cleveland, for relief from subscription to the thirty nine articles, and its replacement with a more general assent to the doctrines in the

Bible indicated the sympathy felt for Dissent. It was rejected by the Commons in 1772.

The government's position was broadly sympathetic to Dissent, but in 1772 George III indicated that he felt sufficient relief was afforded to dissenters by the regular writs of *Nolle Prosequi* which were issued to prevent overenthusiastic magistrates from initiating prosecutions. Nevertheless the 1772 petition paved the way for bills to relieve dissenting ministers and schoolmasters from subscription in 1772 and 1773, though both were defeated in the Lords. They passed the Lords in 1779, together with repeal of the Test Act for Ireland. In 1787, a meeting of bishops, called by Archbishop Moore at Pitt's request, advised Pitt that only Bishops Watson and Shipley were in favour of total repeal of the Test and Corporation Acts. Indeed, since 1779 Shipley had supported repeal of the Test and Corporation Acts and opposed 'the disgrace of the National Church', as he called the failure to grant toleration. Toleration certainly produced hostility from the less moderate Anglican clergy, like Archdeacon Balguy of Winchester. But support for dissenters was more widespread than might be supposed; besides Shipley it had adherents in Dean Tucker and Archdeacon Paley, who recognised that toleration would not undermine the necessary obligation of the Church to maintain social order.

There were motions for repeal of the Test and Corporation Acts in the Lords in 1787, 1789 (lost by 124 to 104 votes) and 1790 (lost by 294 to 105 votes). In the first of these debates only Bishop Shipley of the bishops voted for repeal, though Archbishop Cornwallis spoke modestly in favour of toleration. Even an attempt in 1792 to correct an Act of William III's reign regarding the position of Unitarians failed against the opposition of Pitt and Burke. The dissenters' campaign seemed to stimulate opponents as well as supporters, perhaps because the demands for rights for dissenters coincided with usurpation of rights in France. From 1794 to 1804 events abroad meant that Parliament did not provide opportunities for division on the issue of toleration. It was a period in which the dissenters recognised that the route to toleration lay in shifting the foundations of their case. They increasingly developed a case for toleration based on the issue of wealth and position rather than the less acceptable principle of rights. Such an argument (that dissenters were able to own property and accumulate wealth, and as such ought to be allowed relief) was one which found increasing support. Moreover, within the Tory party it became clear that toleration was an opportunity to draw out the threat from itinerant preachers and to regularise Methodist ministers.

Lord Sidmouth's Bill of 1811, which demanded the provision of testimonials before dissenting ministers could be licensed, is an example of the feeling that itineracy was a potentially dangerous issue. Once again, in 1811, the bishops and the Lords denied the passage of toleration. On this occasion the modest nature of the relief did not reflect the popular view that the State was being ungenerous to the dissenters, who, as Liverpool pointed out to Sidmouth, had not caused any divisions in the preceding years. The problem was that relief for dissenters remained one of the key issues which divided the Whigs and Tories. The Whigs, attracted to ideas of rights and liberties, saw in Dissent a model for a liberal response. Lords Brougham and Holland, both hostile to the Church, were instrumental in welding relief for dissenters into the mainstream of Whig policy. It was unsurprising, therefore, that the Tories had little commitment to relieving dissenters, or that the Whigs were expected to enact legislation which would improve the dissenters' position. In fact the Tory repeal of the Test and Corporation Acts was only undertaken to diffuse the threat of violence in Ireland.

Relief for Catholics had to overcome the smouldering embers of anti-Jacobite inspired opposition to Catholicism. Anti-Catholic feeling had the potential to flare up long after the Jacobite rising of 1745. In 1761 and 1776 new editions of Foxe's *Book of Martyrs* were published in cheap instalments that were enormously popular and could be found in even working class households. The growing access to cheap printed material seemed to thrive on common prejudice and popular hatred. Colley's view is that this gave working class Protestants an advantage and superiority over Catholics, who were reliant on the interpretation of printed material which tended to be in Latin. Equally Protestant feeling was fuelled by a foreign policy which relied on a series of attacks on Catholic foes. At the same time, there seems to have been a collapse of support for Catholicism among the old families of Essex and the north of England.

Catholic emancipation was thus in many ways more controversial than relief for dissenters. In 1778, a measure of relief was afforded by the passage of the Catholic Relief Act which removed life imprisonment penalties for Catholic bishops, priests and schoolmasters and abolished the reward of £100 to informers who secured convictions. The Act also laid down an oath of allegiance for Catholics who held such offices. The passage of the Act was eased by the growing sympathy of Lords North, Rockingham and Mansfield for the Catholic cause. Moreover, the threat from Catholics was reduced, and perceived as such, largely by the Thatched House Tavern Petition of loyalist Catholic gentry to George III. The King allowed a committee to be set up to consider the petition, to which nearly 200 Catholic gentry wrote supporting the terms of the Catholic Relief Act. Whilst the government had moved closer to recognition that Catholicism did not necessarily imply disloyalty, popular reactions were more emotive. The first reaction to the Catholic Relief Act came from Scotland, where it was said toleration could only be preached at the risk of one's life. Scottish Protestant Associations sprang up fermenting alarms among the working classes. Extravagant stories abounded, and in 1779 the Central Protestant Association claimed in its 'Appeal to the People of Great Britain' that popery did not simply curse the soul, it brought down the wrath of God on society. The subsequent Gordon Riots against the Catholic community, which were an attempt to intimidate Parliament, suggested that relief was not popular in society as a whole. It was impossible for the government to fail to respond to such pressure and, acting in accordance with the popular mood, denied any prospect of wholesale emancipation of Catholics.

The second attempt at relief came in 1789. The Catholic community maintained its links with the government and negotiated a measure which would relieve Catholics from penal laws. The Bill was drafted in 1789 and became effective from 1791. Perhaps the biggest stumbling block during the negotiations was that of the oath which Catholics seeking relief would be required to take. It was Horsley who broke the deadlock. His friendship with Joseph Berrington, a member of a Catholic family, allowed him to suggest that the wording of the oath was too contentious and instead he proposed that the alternative oath in the 1774 Irish Relief Act, to which the Catholic Vicars Apostolic did not object, be adopted for the Act. This intervention allowed the bill to pass. The new Act was in many ways a major step forward, it allowed (licensed) Catholic chapels to exist for the first time and sanctioned the Mass in buildings which did not contain a bell or steeple; moreover, after 1791 Catholics could enter the professions.

The horrifying events in France which unfolded from 1789 brought a measure of sympathy for the Catholic Church and particularly for French emigrés and emigré priests. Indeed, the assimilation of the French emigré priests went a long way to undermine the negative popular view of the papacy. However, as the French Revolution developed, Pitt felt that the time was wrong for further Catholic relief. Catholics ascribed this to the sinister influence of the intolerant Pretyman Tomline. Other forces which operated against Catholic relief were those for whom the Union of Britain and Ireland of 1800 posed a concern, but the Catholic community was reassured by Pitt's apparent support for some further relief in the Union negotiations. Nevertheless, a connection of cousins, Lord Chancellor Loughborough, Lord Auckland and Archbishop Moore, worked hard to deny Catholics widespread relief in the Act of Union and even wrote to the King, confirming his own prejudices. The apparent cause of Pitt's resignation in 1801, on the issue of the failure to achieve Catholic emancipation, has recently been challenged by Charles Fedorak. Fedorak suggests that Pitt used Catholic emancipation as a pretext for resignation, rather than the cause of it. Nevertheless, the Loughborough–Auckland connection was victorious and lasted until 1805, rejecting the Catholic petition of that year.

The King's refusal on grounds of conscience to consider emancipation, together with Liverpool's decision in 1812 to establish an embargo on debate on the issue because of the irreconcilable divisions it would create in his government, effectively denied any hope to Catholics in the opening years of the nineteenth century. During these years the central issue of relations between the Catholic Church and the State revolved around whether the King should enjoy a veto over Catholic episcopal appointments in England and Ireland. In 1808, Bishop John Milner, Vicar Apostolic of the Midland District, conceded that he would have no objection to such a veto. Whilst Milner later repudiated the idea, his fellow bishops in England and Ireland were won over to it and in 1808 the bishops agreed that it could be included in a bill. In this, as in other ways, the Catholic bishops were being led by the Catholic laity, who saw the veto as a useful concession to the government in reassuring it of the safety of further Catholic relief. By 1821, when a bill to allow a veto was debated in parliament, the laity again drove Catholic policy. Bishop Poynter reported to Rome, 'it is inconceivable how eager our Catholic noblemen and Gentlemen are to possess their seats in Parliament. It is impossible to stop them'.[18] Whatever the origins of the veto its informal operation in the years after 1810 reassured the government that the papacy was not hostile to the English State. During the 1820s, and even during the Wellington's premiership, the British government, often through its envoy in Parma, maintained contact with the Papacy and indicated secretly (since contact with the papacy was illegal) whom the government felt acceptable and unacceptable for Catholic sees in England and Ireland. For his part, Pope Pius VII expressed his willingness in 1815 to satisfy the English government and to ensure that the Catholic clergy did not meddle in politics. The reward for this growing rapprochement was the opening in 1817 of English army and naval commissions and chaplaincies to Catholics. For years, of course, as the Dublin MP William Plunkett pointed out, the Irish Catholics in the British army had sacrificed their lives on the battlefields of Europe in the war against Napoleon. It was an important claim, since it refused to accept that the Tory–Anglican coalition had a monopoly on patriotism. Support for Catholic emancipation grew accordingly, in 1819 it failed in the Commons by just two votes, and in the votes in 1821 and 1823 motions passed the Commons only to be defeated in the Lords. Thus by 1823 the barrier to emancipation lay solely in the Lords, the gradual erosion of opposition to emancipation in the Commons had been achieved largely because there was no longer a perception of a threat from Catholics.

From the 1820s onwards, the focus of the campaign for emancipation shifted to Ireland and the work of the Catholic Association. Few English Catholics entered the campaign, as they felt it would damage their own more modest undertakings. However the theoretical basis of opposition to emancipation had shifted significantly in the years that led to the Acts of 1828 and 1829. The view, held in the eighteenth century, that Catholicism was not merely a religious denomination but a political one also had been eradicated. The Ultramontanist threat had been circumvented by the oaths that Catholics had been required to undertake by the Relief Acts, by the admission of Catholics to military and naval commissions, and by the informal operation of the 'veto' on Catholic appointments. Thus in 1825 during a debate on the Catholic question Canning was able to ask whether Catholicism was incompatible with the duties of a good citizen. In his answer he suggested that Catholics were in many ways far better citizens than those who embraced a Calvinist creed. Of course, to men like Henry Phillpotts such arguments based on social ideas rather than theology were anathema, and doctrines like confession and absolution, claimed Phillpotts, opened Catholics to all sorts of moral and political dangers.

Jonathan Clark's opinion that the repeal of the Test and Corporation Acts, the passing of Catholic emancipation and the Parliamentary Reform Act of 1832 were separate elements in a single achievement is based on the assumption that the central element in these events was the breaking of the Anglican monopoly.[19] Clark's thesis is that the achievement of Emancipation was a far greater one than that of the 1832 Reform Act because the constitutional implications of emancipation were far greater than those of the 1832 Act. Emancipation implied principles of justice, civil rights, equity and liberty which were not present in the 1832 Reform Act. Above all, it alluded to a nation and constitution in which all people had a right to representation – something which the 1832 Reform Act cannot claim to have done. For the most part, of course, expediency and the fear of a conflagration in Ireland were uppermost in the minds of the ministers who advocated repeal of the Test and Corporation Acts in 1828 and of emancipation in 1829; those who opposed these measures confirm Clark's view. Van Mildert, for example, opposed the measures because they suggested abstract rights which he could not concede. It was this dilemma which confronted Peel in 1829: to stand with Van Mildert and Bishop Lloyd of Oxford, his old tutor, on the principle of denying the rights claimed by the Catholics and dissenters or to 'rat' and support the expedient line of pacifying Ireland. Faced with this problem Peel was doubtless affected by Sydney Smith's view that 'the only argument which has any appearance of weight is the question of divided allegiance; and generally speaking, we should say it is the argument which produces the greatest effect in the country at large'. Yet Smith himself felt that divided allegiance was a nonsense since the papacy lacked real power and possessed only a 'wax-work pope'. With the religious argument lost, Peel 'ratted' and Catholic Emancipation followed hard on the heels of the repeal of the Test and Corporation Acts.

Catholic relief was not achieved silently, however, 3000 petitions were received from across Britain against emancipation. This was perhaps the last echo of the anti-Catholicism of the 1770s. The huge immigration of Catholics from Ireland, which reached 580,000 by 1831, may paradoxically have both fuelled and calmed reactions. The working people of large cities like Liverpool, Manchester and Glasgow found themselves undercut by the cheap labour of Irish Catholics and this may have prompted a stronger reaction against emancipation. However, the increased contact of the British with Catholics may explain why the reaction was principally in the form of petitions and not riots and unrest. In some areas the opposition to Catholic emancipation reflected a throwback to the folklore of earlier generations. In the West Country this was apparent in the propaganda rehearsing the 'martyrdom' of the West Country-men during the Monmouth rebellion. Colley's view is that people perceived Catholic Emancipation as an erosion of a major pillar of

British success, the Protestant character of the country. However, this was principally a working-class view. Among the commercial and professional classes Catholicism was not the threat it had been in 1745. Moreover, there had been no Catholic foe abroad since 1815 and thus the resources of government propaganda had not been turned against Catholicism.

3

RELIGION AND SOCIAL CHANGE

Methodism and Politics: the Halevy Thesis

Historians have been concerned about the issue of Methodism and
politics since Lecky and Halevy suggested that revolution in
Britain in the 1790s was averted by the influence of Methodism.
For Halevy, Methodism was a stabilising influence in British
society, making Jacobin propaganda unpopular and unacceptable to the people. Methodism not only taught religious doctrines
of loyalty and submission to the State, but also inculcated the idea
that the liberties of Englishmen were in direct opposition to
revolutionary principles. From the French Revolution onwards
and through the wars that followed, asserted Halevy, Nonconformity – and especially Methodism – caused 'an uninterrupted
decline in revolutionary spirit'.[1] The Halevy thesis found support
in most subsequent works but found its strongest and most recent
supporter in E. P. Thompson.

Thompson's *The Making of the English Working Class* developed
the view that Methodism consistently developed social and
psychological attitudes which promoted acceptance of the established order. Methodists were expected to report religious failings
to their minister; laymen and preachers were expelled for
unorthodox views; Methodist preachers taught the virtue of an
inner compulsion to discipline and they emphasised the inade-
quacy of good works compared with the elevating power of grace.
The creation of such an organisation working for cohesion could
not fail to avert upheaval. For Methodists, waiting patiently to

receive grace from God had a direct counterpart in secular affairs in the patient wait for an improvement in their political and economic fortunes. Methodists were encouraged to cast their material cares into their prayers rather than into direct action. Quoting the scientist Andrew Ure (1778–1857), Thompson called this 'the transforming power of the Cross'. It was administered through emotive images of damnation and rigorous pastoral work. Thompson emphasised that the Methodists' concentration on breaking the proud spirit of the flesh had a useful social message for the State. It raised 'a pitiless ideology of work' and in the emotive violence of its preachers it offered a 'chiliasm of the defeated and the hopeless'.

It was not surprising then that Sir Robert Peel's father wrote in 1787 that he left the management of his Lancashire works in the hands of the Methodists, or that Methodists were allowed their own services in the Royal Navy. For Thompson, 'the leaders of Methodism . . . weakened the poor from within, by adding to them the active ingredient of submission . . . Methodist theology, by virtue of its promiscuous opportunism, was better suited than any other to serve as the religion of a proletariat whose members had not the least reason, in social experience, to feel themselves to be "elected".'[2] Even when confronted by Methodists who took part in the Pentridge rising, the Tolpuddle martyrdom, the Plug plots and Chartist activities, Thompson denies that Methodism was an important factor, suggesting that because some people rebelled religiously by rejecting the Established Church, and also rebelled politically by rejecting the social Establishment, this does not mean there was a causal link between the two. Thompson's view that Methodism operated on a subtle, psychological level is supported by John Rule's study of Cornish tinners. In Cornwall, the tinners' irrational and superstitious folk beliefs were not eradicated by Methodism, but were absorbed and transformed by Methodism into religious activities. Revivals, hymn festivals, watch nights and love feasts took over from less acceptable superstitious folk traditions. In South Lindsey, too, Methodism absorbed popular cultural features and matched its own practices to those of popular superstitions.

Obelkevitch's study of South Lindsey, however, challenges

some of the assumptions of the Halevy–Thompson thesis. It contends that Methodism was not simply a religious mechanism working against social change, indeed Obelkevitch suggests that in South Lindsey Methodism was an instrument for modest social change and modernism. Methodism brought greater contact between urban and rural life, as preachers and ideas circulated; it also brought modern attitudes to work by breaking down the parochial boundaries of people's existence. People were encouraged to develop self-expression and to take responsibility for organising their work and leisure time. However, while Methodism was socially progressive, the evidence from Obelkevitch's study does not fundamentally undermine the Halevy–Thompson thesis. Obelkevitch was writing about Methodism more than one generation later than the period which Halevy and Thompson examined. Moreover, Obelkevitch makes clear that by the 1850s Methodism was promoting middle class values, just as it had earlier promoted those of the industrial elite. Nevertheless, in politics the Methodists were fairly evenly divided between Whig and Tory, though there was a strong correlation between Tory landowners and Methodist tenants who voted Tory.

A recent study of Nailsworth in Gloucestershire by Albion Urdank suggests that the structure of land ownership promoted Dissent. Land ownership in the Nailsworth valley was widely dispersed and this tended to reduce the authority of local gentry and institutions. As a result Dissent was able to flourish more effectively in the valley than elsewhere, but this did not threaten the social equilibrium. The Whig gentry chose to cooperate and ally itself with the growing numbers of dissenting landowners rather than stand against them. Urdank also suggests that Dissent offered a model of self-expression for working-class consciousness. In the Stroud valley in the 1820s, for example, militant workers established union associations with elders and all the hierarchy drawn from dissenting chapels. Some even maintained their secrecy with an oath.[3]

The most effective accommodation of the Halevy–Thompson thesis has been produced by Jonathan Clark's work on English society. Clark advances the view that Wesleyans and Anglicans shared a common heritage rooted in the desire for social respectability. It is clear that Wesley was a convinced Tory who preached non-resistance and argued against religious support for political parties. After Wesley's death the Methodist Conferences in 1791–9 continued to propagate his views; indeed in 1792 the conference officially indicated that it would be wrong to speak irreverently of the government, and by 1797 it ordered expulsion of members who 'propagate opinions inimical to the civil government'. Clark suggests that Methodism specifically directed itself towards the poor, leaving the gentry and higher social groups to evangelical Anglicanism. Nevertheless, Clark extends the Halevy–Thompson thesis to include the Church of England, arguing that it preached to a far larger congregation and for a far longer period than Methodism. Compared with the Methodists the clergy of the Church of England were more active in undertaking militant forms of anti-revolutionary feeling, of which John Venn's membership of the Clapham Armed Association is an example. The Church's publications also tended to have a wider circulation than those of the Methodists. Hannah More, for example, wrote fifty works for the Cheap Repository Tracts series, which by 1796 had sold over 2 million copies. All her works stressed the need for submission.

Clark concedes that Methodism and Nonconformity tended to support opposition to the government at the polls, and that locally the national system of Wesleyan orthodoxy was often ignored by radical preachers. Unlike Thompson, Clark recognises that individual Methodists who were involved in direct political action were expressing defiance in both religious and political terms. Though for the most part Clark concludes, like Halevy and Thompson, that Methodism formed part of the Establishment's cultural hegemony of the unreformed era.

The most satisfying response to the Halevy debate is to be found in a denial that Methodism can be described as a single monolithic movement with a single political theology. This view, advanced most recently by David Hempton, incorporates the fact that Methodist leaders were from the 1790s onwards uncertain of their position regarding the State. They faced the paradox that however conservative they claimed to be in social issues, they could not escape the fact that their very existence challenged the monopoly of the Church of England and thus the basis of authority in the State. Hempton suggests that older Methodists, who laid the emphasis on saving souls, were not concerned by issues of politics; whereas younger and better educated Methodist leaders felt that stability and order were important concerns.[4] Jabez Bunting is an excellent example of the latter. Bunting tried to maintain that his support for order and authority were not political. Few Methodists followed official conference policies to the letter and as result paradoxes and inconsistencies arose. Methodism found itself strongly supporting the campaign for the abolition of slavery, but equally strongly opposing Catholic emancipation. Wesleyanism thus seems to have spawned many 'Methodisms'. Methodism was a broad church which embraced many avenues including the Methodism of the reactionary Irish, who in 1799 supported military suppression of a rebellion; of the Sheffield Methodists who supported parliamentary reform; of the folk Methodism of Cornish tinners and of the respectable petty bourgeois of the Midlands. 'Methodism . . . was a living religious movement, which changed and was changed by the social contexts in which it took root.'[5] It is undoubtedly the case that across the country there were areas in which Methodism promoted radical change. In Durham, for example, in 1811 the radical and Methodist John Ward wrote ferociously militant letters and pamphlets against the intolerant laws and aristocratic government of the country.

Thus Methodism did not exist as a single entity, uniformly promoting the authority of the State. Its pattern of provision across the country undermined the notion that it touched the lives of many factory workers or urban poor; in many places factories and urban workers were left untouched by Methodism. This is the thrust of the views of Ian Christie and Eric Hobsbawm. Certainly, numbers of Methodists were small: in 1781 they numbered 37,000 and by 1801 there were 87,000. As late as 1850 the registered membership of the Wesleyan Societies of England and Wales was no more than 340,000; even if the members of the other Methodist sects are added the total numbers of Methodists did not exceed half a million in a population of 18 million. Even so, Hobsbawm suggests that periods of greatest popular agitation coincided with periods of increased Wesleyan recruitment. Thus people may well have found an outlet for their grievances in Methodism. Hobsbawm's interpretation is that this indicates a link between Methodism and radicalism, though it may of course equally support the Thompson view that Methodism provided a dramatic substitute for action.

Further evidence that Methodism was a denomination which embraced many different varieties emerges from an examination of its social composition. In 1796, the correspondents of the Methodist secessionist Alexander Kilham in the north of England included merchants, bankers, farmers and factors as well as shoemakers, hosiers, potters, coopers and plumbers. The evidence from Gilbert's analysis of the social composition of Methodism suggests that, between 1800 and 1830, 63 per cent of Methodists came from the artisan or skilled working class, and a further 24 per cent came from the class of unskilled labourers. Given that many artisans enjoyed modestly comfortable incomes, it seems likely that Methodism included a wide spectrum of society. Moreover the affluent members of the Methodist societies bore a disproportionate influence over them. Many wealthy Methodists owned the title deeds of the local chapels and exercised subtle influences over the tone and form of Methodism. As a result, Methodism was as frequently the resort of those with a sense of aspiration as it was of those with a sense of despair. Moreover statistical evidence on church growth raises doubts as to whether Methodism was the resort of the despairing. Indeed periods of economic dislocation, like 1799–1800 and 1816–19, were periods of low and falling recruitment to Methodist ranks. In other words, people did not turn to Methodism when they needed food. Paradoxically 1793 and 1832, years of political unrest, were years in which Methodist recruitment grew.

Challenges to these developed and synthesised versions of the Halevy–Thompson thesis have tended to concentrate on Methodist thinking. Bernard Semmell's view is that Methodism was a strong force for change, and that it was from their theology that Methodist leaders developed a view of society which assumed such dramatic social changes that Methodists were in effect revolutionary. The most recent challenge to the Thompson–Halevy thesis has emerged from James Bradley's study of radicalism in English cities in the eighteenth century. Bradley concludes that Dissent and Methodism were strongly associated with political opposition and that urban radicalism was inextricably linked with Nonconformity. Throughout the 1770s and 1780s, asserts Bradley, Methodism and Dissent posed consistent challenges to the established hierarchy of Church and State. Above all, the preaching of the Nonconformists, Methodists amongst them, represented a challenge to the social order, opposing deference and inequality. In Nottingham in 1770, for example, the dissenting pulpit produced a corporation split between the Anglican supporters of the government and the dissenting supporters of the American colonists. It was a scenario repeated in Bristol, Newcastle, Coventry and other boroughs in a plethora of local and national issues. The most recent analysis of the social composition of Nonconformity suggests that Congregationalists and Baptists, as well as Wesleyans, attracted the lower orders. For Bradley 'nonconformity functioned as a midwife to radical political behaviour among the artisans'.[6]

Support for Bradley's view can be found much later in the circumstances of the Northumberland and Durham miners' strike of 1844, during which Parliament was told that religious feeling was bound closely to militancy. Primitive Methodist preachers were instrumental in promoting the strike, offering prayers and invoking God's blessing on the strikers. Miners recognised that they found political strength and solidarity in attending Methodist meetings.

Bradley's explanation of the failure of this radical nexus to achieve revolutionary change does not lie in the nature of Nonconformity, rather it lies in the government's reaction to them. Throughout the 1770s and 1780s the government's tolerance of Nonconformist publications, and the judicial tolerance of Nonconformity, drew the sting of political agitation. That dissenters could vote 'provided a safety valve of unparalleled importance'. For the lower orders the right to petition provided a similar outlet. The government's astute handling of the Nonconformists allowed them to present a face of sympathetic tolerance to the public while privately menacing popular agitators.

A further explanation for the failure of religious radicalism is advanced by Robert Hole. Hole asserts that between 1760 and 1832 a fundamental shift occurred in the context of the political debate. In 1760 the fundamental questions were about the origins of government and society and of political obligations and rebellion. These were intimately religious questions concerning divine sanction for the State and obedience to it. By 1832, claims Hole, the debate had become wholly secular, political obligation resting not on God's will but on people's view of the benefits to be achieved from it. Those who used religion to advance ideas of hierarchy and social order were a dying class. The churches, including Methodism, withdrew to other social missions, like education. Thus radical change was declining as a religious issue and the churches moved their involvement with the people to other social areas.

Perhaps the most significant political impact of Methodism in the first half of the nineteenth century lay not solely in preventing a revolution but in the legacy Wesleyanism bequeathed to the Victorian era. Traditional assumptions about Wesley's Toryism have been reconsidered. John Walsh's work on Wesley's message for the poor emphasises that Wesley's social views were in some ways markedly different from his political opinions. Wesley argued for the sharing of goods and property and the duty of denying materialist urges. Thus Wesley's sermons expounding the virtues of thrift and hard work were not directed to the same goal as the Protestant work ethic, but to a more radical one. This formed the taproot of the Liberal Nonconformist Conscience. Methodism initiated and developed some of the social views that formed the weft of Liberalism. In particular, involvement in local and civic government after the 1830s grew significantly.

Patterns of Religious Practice, 1760–1850

One of the difficulties in determining the patterns of religious practice in England before 1850 is that many people did not think of themselves as simply 'Anglican' or 'Nonconformist' in the way that later generations did. As late as 1861 the Revd Benjamin

Armstrong, vicar of East Dereham, confided to his diary that although membership of his congregations generally rose throughout his tenure of the parish, when dissenters put on a 'Love Feast' his congregation temporarily thinned.[7] Indeed, the nineteenth century was the period in which adherence to one church or denomination developed into strict membership. As Armstrong discovered, there was a clear danger in regarding attendance as the same as affiliation. The occasional decisions of both established and nonconformist clergy to compete by holding services at times which would clash with each other, thus forcing the people to choose between them, reflected the growth of exclusive affiliation. Sometimes clergy would refuse to bury Methodists, as the *Stamford Mercury* reported in February 1838 and May 1839. Elsewhere it was possible to find an accommodation like that in Lindsey, where as late as the 1850s Wesleyans left their services in time to reach the parish church. Indeed, the Revd F. C. Massingberd of South Ormsby believed such double attendance to be useful, claiming that he could woo the Methodists to Anglicanism by offering the parishioners the calm dignity of his services to compare with those of the Methodists.

The statistical evidence suggests that the number of communicants in the Church of England declined between 1700 and 1850. In a sample of Oxfordshire parishes between 1738 and 1811 communicants declined from 911 to 755, and other evidence is marshalled by Currie, Gilbert and Horsley from the diocese of York to support this conclusion. It is possible to exaggerate the slip of support from the Church of England. Gilbert claimed that between 1740 and 1830 the Church suffered a disaster, falling from virtual monopoly to virtual religious minority. Both the Anglican monopoly before 1740 and the decline up to 1830 fail to acknowledge that church attendance – and in particular figures for communicants – do not reveal the full picture of individual piety or levels of faith. The prejudices of the people towards taking communion may make reliance on such figures dangerous. Moreover, Bishop Samuel Butler's discovery that in Lichfield and Coventry diocese in the 1830s few churches had free pews reveals part of the problem in identifying and correlating attendance with piety.

Nevertheless, the Nonconformist churches were attracting people away from the Church of England. While the Catholic population fell before 1800, the Protestant Nonconformist bodies grew. Between 1770 and 1810 the Wesleyans grew fivefold and Baptist and Congregational denominations both quadrupled. Yet the burst in support for the Methodists did not continue uniformly; in 1770, the annual growth rate of members was 4.5 per cent of the total, by 1870 it had fallen to 1.5 per cent though the actual numbers of new members were greater. At its peak in 1841 Methodist members were 4.5 per cent of the adult population, compared with 1.6 per cent in 1801. Moreover, the annual recruitment level fluctuated wildly between 1776 and 1850. It seems impossible to avoid the view that political and economic factors affected such fluctuations. Growth in Nonconformist membership coincides with periods of domestic economic stability and prosperity. Paradoxically, turbulence in foreign affairs also seems to have stimulated membership. Thus it may well be that the abnormally high recruitment of 14 per cent in 1793–4 may have been a product of the war with France. Certainly the years of the Napoleonic Wars saw six years of abnormally high recruitment to the Methodists.

It is clear that some external factors affected church membership. The influx of French emigrés and Irish immigrants after 1790 strengthened the Catholic population of England which probably increased threefold in the half century before 1851, when attendances at Catholic services on census Sunday stood at 383,630. A similar influx from Scotland into England effected a rise in membership of the Presbyterian church in England. Domestic demography had a great impact too: in some areas the growth of large factories after 1835 reduced the numbers of skilled manual workers, who were often members of the traditional Nonconformist churches, and increased the numbers of unskilled workers, among whom there was often not a pattern of membership of Nonconformist churches. There is no general rule that factories produced Nonconformist communities: large factories in Leicester, Lancashire, West Yorkshire, Durham and South Wales were witness to comparatively low numbers of Nonconformists among the unskilled workers. Once established, however, Nonconformist communities often remained after factories declined, as happened in Gloucestershire. Either way, there was a decline in the membership density of Methodists in society after 1841. The introduction of a large scale industrial society also created a new class of white collar workers who looked to the Church of England to provide them with respectability and social advantages. Thus the Church of England's membership grew during the mid and late nineteenth century.[8]

Recruitment of members by churches was comparatively easy during the early years of the Industrial Revolution. Mobility of labour allowed individuals or families to be recruited by the Nonconformist churches and new communities sprang up which might be recruited as a whole. Often a religious disposition or affiliation already existed which was supplanted by new forms of religious provision. However, these fresh fields for Nonconformists to plough lasted for only a few years. After the first major wave of industrialisation recruitment focused on children rather than adults. The rationale behind the Sunday schools which so many denominations adopted was the promotion of an attachment of the young to a church. As society became increasingly secularised recruitment had to take more subtle forms. In the Methodist circuits, like those in Lindsey, this included the introduction of preachers noted as 'major stars' who visited chapels and drew often huge crowds. Anniversaries, like those commemorating the foundation of the chapels, were developed as important occasions, drawing in large congregations. As the High Church Anglicans found, ritual and the paraphernalia of Anglo-Catholic worship was also effective in recruiting among the poorest and the most deprived communities. Benjamin Armstrong steadily introduced more saints' days and other festivals into his calendar at East Dereham to attract greater attendance – sometimes even from neighbouring villages. He also involved himself in a number of societies and organisations which gave him greater access to the people of the parish. But he conceded that the population of the village was declining. With every death or departure the Church lost a member who was not always replaced. Loss of members by the churches happened not only from the circumstances of mortality or mobility but on occasion resulted from expulsion of a member by a church. The Nonconformist, particularly the Presbyterian, churches were particularly anxious to avoid social or religious views which conflicted with their own orthodoxy. Moreover, just as church growth was affected by economic and social factors, so also was decline in membership. Falls in Nonconformist recruitment correlate to periods of high food prices, high unemployment and economic dislocation, suggesting that membership was, to some extent, affected by a 'fair weather' element.

Another feature of religious practice after 1800 was the gradual shift of religion from the primary function of the head of a household, and thus a male gender role, to the function of both men and women. In pre-industrial societies the attendance of the community at services was the model which drove worship. But frequently husbands attended services as representatives of their households. Certainly, men seem to have received Communion more frequently than women, and they dominated the choirs. However, during the first half of the nineteenth century changes occurred in the role of women in religion. In part this was due to the shift, effected by industrialisation, to individual religious commitment, which required attendance by each family member at services. It was both a cause and effect of the changes in religious observance: in South Lindsey, for example, women and girls dominated the Sunday schools, as both teachers and prizewinners, and women steadily came to dominate the choirs and confirmation classes. Outside the established Church Nonconformists, by separating the sexes, created leaders among the women. Women could be preachers or stewards but were more frequently missionary collectors and organisers of festivals and events. A survey of obituaries in *The Primitive Methodist Magazine* indicates that women were mentioned almost as frequently as men. These were the foundations for the official recognition of a role for women, albeit a subordinate one, in the Church of England in the second half of the century through the creation of the Mothers' Union and the women's temperance societies. Equally significant is that the churches were one of the principal factors in the attention that was increasingly focused on children. Sunday schools, catechising and a plethora of children's activities, which bound the young to the Church, were the first institutional expression of a youth culture.

Perhaps the most significant form of change in religious practice is that to be identified among the newly emergent classes of the nineteenth century. In 1780, the aunt of the Revd William Jones told him that 'all the lower class of people, who pay any attention to religion, in general follow the Methodists'.[9] Certainly, the first priority of the Wesleyans, Baptists and Congregationalists was the conversion of the poor who had been neglected or forgotten by the Church of England. In South Wales, the poor and depressed were the particular target of the Baptists and elsewhere there was a sense among the Methodists that the Church of England could be left to deal with the professional classes and above. Indeed the Duchess of Buckingham told Lady Huntingdon that even Calvinist Methodism was much at variance with rank and breeding. Between 1800 and 1837, 59.4 per cent of Nonconformists came from the artisan class, compared with only 9.3 per cent from the lower middle class groups of farmers and shopkeepers and a mere 2.2 per cent from merchants and manufacturers. In spite of the Nonconformist drive of the late eighteenth century, by the middle of the nineteenth century both ends of the social spectrum were underrepresented in Nonconformity. Among the middle and upper echelons of society only 'old Dissent' featured alongside the Church of England. The Quakers and Unitarians may not have grown at the same rate as the newer denominations, but they held on to their members among the wealthy mercantile, professional and manufacturing classes. Among those at the lower end of the social pyramid Primitive Methodism achieved greatest penetration, particularly among the miners and colliers.

It would be a mistake to ignore the role of Anglicanism among this class. From the 1840s onwards the Church's role among the poorest increased. Anglican clergy were instrumental in supporting friendly societies and persuaded them to abandon their rituals in favour of a religious service at the start of their meetings. The Church also involved itself in the Cooperative Movement and the slum priests worked hard to absorb lay assistants at their services. Nevertheless, the identification of Anglicanism with the Establishment was perhaps too great to be easily overcome. It took many years for the people to forget that the magistrates who read the Riot Act at the Peterloo débâcle were Anglican clergy. The higher clergy represented a wide spectrum of social attitudes from Bishop Barrington's generous charity and Dean Ryder of Wells's soup kitchen for the poor to extreme Tories who rejected the need for palliatives – like the thirteen bishops who voted against a motion for a select committee to investigate the conditions of the poor. After 1840, however, a new class of bishop emerged, represented by Bishops Thirlwall, Longley, Lonsdale, Lee and Wilberforce, and above all by Bishop Blomfield.[10] Blomfield's knowledge of his diocese led him to espouse social reform. He was a strong factory reformer and supported the work of Edwin Chadwick on both the Poor Law and on public health and sanitation. In 1839, he called for a full examination of the health and sanitation of the poor. Blomfield's period of greatest activity coincided with the premiership of Peel, with whom he was on good social and political terms. As a result the bishop was able to promote the cause of the 1846 Bath and Wash House Act as well as a plethora of improvements to other public health legislation.

The Urban Church and Industrialisation

Bishop Cornwallis's memories in the 1770s of visiting a 'great trading town' (Birmingham) included his 'curiosity to inspect the manufacture carried on'. He was surprised to hear that the factory employed 500 men and that all of them were in the clutches of a debauched troupe of visiting players. Such reactions speak volumes about the Church's response to the changes industrialisation visited upon England.[11] The historian W. R. Ward has suggested that the Church's response to industrialisation was the reaction of an ancient social institution unable to relate to the changes it faced. The towns, argued Ward, represented materialism, dissent and change whereas the Church was essentially rural, paternalist and conservative. It was therefore no surprise to Ward that the bishops in the House of Lords did not support factory and mining reform. Whilst there is much evidence to suggest that many churchmen greeted urbanisation and industrialisation with such a response there were other reactions.

For some clergy industrialisation was welcomed because it met the growing need for increased clerical income. In Rochdale, Bury and Manchester Acts of Parliament in 1763 permitted the lease of the glebe for industrial use, and by the time that the Ecclesiastical Commissioners examined the income of Rochdale one estimate put its income at £5000 a year, raised principally from its leased glebe. In other parishes there was a cooperative response to the challenges of industrialisation. In Manchester, the creation of the Sunday school system in 1784 was a collaborative effort, with Anglican, Nonconformists and Catholic clergy serving on the committee which arranged fund raising, preaching and agreements on forms of worship to be used. Schools were often the focus for ecumenical activities. In 1821, Lancaster marched the Catholic, Methodist and Nonconformist grammar school children through the town together to celebrate the coronation of George IV.[12]

For the most part, however, the problems generated by industrialisation outweighed their advantages. The principal difficulty was that of church provision for new industrial towns. In some areas new chapels were built to accommodate more parishioners but, as at St James's Rochdale, some were full with appropriated pews by the time the building was completed and had no extra accommodation for the poor. In such circumstances the vacuum was filled by Nonconformity. In Rochdale, for example, by 1818 eighty-nine Nonconformist preachers and clergy held sixty-six services a week, while the five Church of England clergy maintained six services a week in three churches. The massive population growth experienced by England and Wales after 1770 was a phenomenon which the Church could not respond to within its existing model of parish provision. In 1816, it was calculated that in larger towns there was a population of 5.2 million and accommodation for one million. In eighty London parishes only about a ninth of the population could be accommodated in churches. The Midlands and Leeds were particularly lacking in churches, in the latter there was accommodation for

3400 out of a population of 67,000. In the face of such enormous multiples even the strenuous activities of the Church Building Commission and diocesan building societies were unable to resolve the problem. In some cases local clergy viewed church extension with suspicion; some felt it drained support from the parish church, others saw it as a prelude to parochial division. The issue of pew ownership also presented problems. In Sheffield, where St James's church was built in 1788 it was designed to hold over 600 people, and was paid for by shares of £50 each which entitled the shareholder to a freehold of the pew. One tenth of the new church was thus appropriated from the needy poor of the parish. By 1801, the parish of Sheffield contained 45,758 residents, most of whom could not be accommodated in either Anglican or nonconformist services. At the same time as a church accommodation crisis existed, the ties of social control appeared to loosen. An unruly mob in the half century after 1770 regularly rioted and disturbed the peace, and in 1791 destroyed the home of the local magistrate, the vicar of Sheffield.[13] By 1821 there were fewer than 300 free sittings available for the 60,000 poor of the city. It was the Act of 1818 which stimulated a burst of church extension in Sheffield, resulting in the opening of St George's in 1825, Christ Church, Attercliffe in 1826, St Phillip's in 1828, and St Mary's in 1830. By 1841 there were thirteen Anglican churches in the city accommodating 15,000, compared with the thirty seven nonconformist chapels accommodating 25,000. A Royal Commission report on conditions in Sheffield in 1843 testified to the energy of the clergy 'it is not for want of exertion on the part of the clergy if the churches and chapels are unfilled . . . a population has arisen without the habit of observing the Lord's Day, and so without any conscientious restraint on the subject'.[14]

In consequence of this the Church was unable to meet the Chartist threat as successfully as it would have wished. In 1839, Sheffield Chartists started imitating the Methodists with their own class meetings. They tried to force the vicar of Sheffield to preach on a text of their choice and filled the parish church, excluding pew owners. When the vicar and curates preached on texts which offended the Chartists they caused disturbances. After a month of such unrest the police, armed with cutlasses, admitted only the respectable to the Church. It is naive to assume that all the social and religious problems of Sheffield would have been solved by more churches, but it was a significant ingredient in the resulting social dislocation. It was a prospect which Bishop Cleaver of Chester had anticipated in his charge to his diocese in 1799, when he suggested that declining church accommodation would lead to a dangerous decline in the support of the Establishment. However, Cleaver was a comparatively rare voice in this regard; few bishops before the 1820s appreciated the danger which was fast coming upon them. The government, distracted by the Napoleonic War, was unwilling to dismantle any structures at home. Bishops were therefore obliged to fall back on the willingness of the wealthy to provide proprietary chapels for their workers, as Barrington urged in Durham diocese in 1797. Bishop Watson's proposal to build large churches in urban areas in the diocese of Llandaff exclusively for the poor with government money fell on deaf ears.

In Leeds the High Church vicar, Walter Hook, elected by the trustees in 1837, adopted the solution which seemed most practical: wholesale church building. His own parish saw twenty-one new district churches built during his vicariate, and by the middle of the century the parish of Leeds was almost regarded as of equal importance to a diocese. It was, however, division of parishes which was increasingly regarded as the best solution to the problem. Parochial division was permitted by the 1818 Church Building Act and by six further Acts before Peel's District Churches Act of 1843. In 1835, Sidney Herbert, Secretary to the Board of Control, had pressed Peel to allow division and union of parishes 'as seems best'. But parochial division was fraught with problems. High Church bishops like Van Mildert feared that new parishes would be manipulated to become centres for evangelicalism. Incumbents felt their income and surplice fees were an important obstacle since the parish's income had to stretch over the two new parishes. Moreover, the supply of curates and clergy was often not sufficient to meet demand, and as Alan Haig has suggested, this may well reflect the perception that clerical work in the northern urban parishes was more burdensome than in the rural southern parishes. Certainly clergy educated at Oxford and Cambridge were scarcer in the northern towns than in those in the south.

Parochial division did not, therefore, always solve the problems of the urban church. Where the Church responded most effectively to the challenge of industrialisation it did so as a result of changes in its conception of itself. The most successful urban clergy were often those who abandoned the rural pattern of paternalist association with the gentry, replacing it with an identification with the urban poor. Trollope commented in his articles on the clergy that the 'country parson is all but the squire's equal . . . the town incumbent . . . in the estimation of many of his fellow-townsmen is hardly superior to the beadle'. Similarly, the *Guardian* in 1856 claimed that the clergy exercised great power over the aristocracy and rural labourers but had lost its hold on the urban classes.[15] Those clergy who willingly accepted urban parishes, claims Brian Heeney, were often of a lower social class than their rural brothers. But recruitment of sympathetic clergy was not in itself a solution to the problems of the industrial city; it was a prerequisite. The resolution lay in the changed conception of the parish system. Wilberforce commented in 1838 that the traditional parish system in urban areas was 'wholly obsolete' – it was a view which was shared by Lord Shaftesbury, Hook of Leeds and Bishop Fraser of Manchester.

From the 1830s onwards a new model of parish operation emerged. One important element in the model was the maintenance of large historic parishes, rather than subdivision of parishes. The legislation between 1818 and 1843 eased the way to division of large parishes, and from 1840 to 1876 1727 churches were built as part of this policy. However many churchmen argued that division was not an appropriate response to huge population growth. They preferred large centralised parishes. Such large parishes could offer the sound financial base denied to small divided parishes; they avoided the isolation of the poor and of 'slum priests' in separate parishes and allowed for large teams of clergy to invigorate a parish under the management of a senior cleric. By the mid-nineteenth century a corps of London clergy, including Bryan King of St George's-in-the-East, John Kempe of St James, Charles Eyre of Marylebone, Henry Mackenzie of St

Martin-in-the-Fields and William Cadman of Southwark all argued in favour of the benefits of large city parishes. In such large parishes, which included Leeds, Sheffield and Southwark, incumbents allocated areas of their parishes to curates and delegated schooling, preaching and visiting. The mother church retained a focal role for the parish, often used for large festivals and parades and the curates found other accommodation for district services until a chapel could be established. In Southwark, as in most similar parishes, the rector or vicar retained control over finance, and as with Mackenzie this allowed for economies of scale to be exploited. The Revd Robert Gregory, vicar of Lambeth, saw the incumbent's role in such an urban parish as that of supervising and directing his staff, not undertaking direct pastoral responsibilities.

It was these clergy with a new managerial model of the Church's role who were most active in recruiting lay helpers. From the 1830s onwards the growth of organisations to promote lay helpers in the Church reflected their importance in urban parishes. The London City Mission, the Church Pastoral Aid Society and the Church of England Scripture Readers' Association were all formed before 1850. Robert Bickersteth, the evangelical bishop of Ripon (1857–84), regarded lay helpers as 'pioneers', forming a link with the clergy of the parish. In Leeds, for example, where the knifegrinders were commissioned to seek out unbaptised children, they brought 400 to the churches to be christened. As the use of lay helpers grew, it embraced the middle and upper classes, becoming particularly an occupation for genteel ladies. In 1850, 13,000 visits were undertaken by the ladies in the Park Chapel district of Chelsea. In some cases the gentrification of lay parish work might have alienated the poor who were the object of their attentions, but it might also have effected some element of reconciliation and charity. Hand in hand with the gentrification of lay work went the emergence of Tractarian and High Church slum priests, like Lowder, Mackonochie, Stanton and Dolling, who added a sacerdotal flavour to the worship in inner cities. It was unsurprising that the majority of clergy imprisoned under the Public Worship Act of 1874 were ritualistic city clergy.

Trollope claimed that the existence of large parishes containing numerous curates were an example of supply and demand entering the Church; a curate responsible for a district church in a large parish was dependent upon the pew rents and fees from his parishioners. 'Those who want him will come and pay him . . . If he can fill his church we will live well.'[16] Thus the large urban parish became a more democratic element in the Church than perhaps any other, responsive to local demands and needs rather than to an institutional view of pastoral care.

In some areas the existence of large parishes managed by clergy with a reconstructed system threw the traditional system into sharp relief. In Salford the evangelical rector, Hugh Stowell, though a politically controversial cleric in other ways, used the new model in his parish. Besides undertaking an enormous volume of services, sermons, lectures and catechising, aided by two curates, Stowell employed volunteer lay workers. These parish workers visited the poor of a particular district in their homes. A similar group of volunteers ran ragged, Sunday and adult schools. There was a refuge for fallen women, clothing clubs and libraries. The district visitors and volunteers had a meeting with Stowell once a month for advice. Standing two miles away, Salford was compared favourably with the lethargy of the wealthy collegiate church of Manchester. Lord John Russell, speaking in Parliament, said he was so exasperated by the absence of pastoral care in Manchester that he took the opportunity of the creation of the new See of Manchester to indicate that the improved oversight of the parish should be charged to the collegiate church, even though it claimed, like other cathedrals, not to be responsible for the cure of souls in the parish.

A further problem for the Church was the inability of the bishops to recognise that the nature of diocesan oversight needed to develop to encompass the new industrial cities. Bishops like John Kaye of Lincoln, Monk of Gloucester and Phillpotts of Exeter were particularly unable or unwilling to recognise the shift that had taken place and remained woefully ignorant of the needs of the urban church. However, Bishop Blomfield did much valuable work in drawing the needs of urban parishes to the attention of his brethren, and some like Bishops Howley, Ryder of

Lichfield and Coventry, Maltby of Durham and Short of St Asaph were able to see that urbanisation had changed the role of the Church.

From the 1820s onwards the new conception of the Church produced a new type of bishop. Blomfield's appointment to London owed much to his experience of an urban parish gained during his incumbency of St Botolph's Bishopsgate. Before the middle of the nineteenth century bishops like Jackson, Longley, Lonsdale, Otter, John Pelham, Powys and Shirley were appointed with an eye to their success in presiding over large urban parishes, a stark contrast with the dominance of the bench by men with experience of rural parishes at the start of the century. These 'new model bishops' strove to inculcate a new approach to parochial duties among the clergy of their dioceses, and gradually effected a shift in the pastoral leadership of the Church. As Alan Haig has indicated, by the early Victorian era the Church cannot be accused of ignoring the towns.

The Church's Wider Social Missions

The Church's reaction to economic change included the development of new social missions, many of which were responses to the circumstances of the new industrial economy. The principal development was the enlarged role of the Church in education. Education had always been in practice an ecclesiastical monopoly, and it operated as such in the institutions of the grammar and public schools and the universities. Many curates in the eighteenth century survived on the meagre sums they were able to earn by taking in scholars, as canon law explicitly permitted. As R. A. Soloway has indicated, those who justified the Church's privileges on the grounds of its utility for the State could point to the Church's role in education as a valuable illustration. Recent research by Brian Heeney suggests that the Church did not merely teach the people; it taught the people about their duties. The charity schools of the eighteenth century were a significant attempt to address the problem of the education of the poor, but as industrialisation developed they were clearly inadequate to the task.

The evangelical Gloucester journalist Robert Raikes recognised this in 1780 when he set up the first Sunday school. Within seven years Raikes claimed that the Sunday schools were educating a quarter of a million children. Nevertheless, Sunday schools were viewed with some suspicion by the Church of England, as they were often set up by Nonconformists or evangelicals. Hannah More encountered considerable opposition from local landowners when she attempted to set up her schools in Blagdon. Some sympathetic bishops, like Lewis Bagot, Barrington and Porteus, supported and promoted schooling of the poor. But during the French Revolution bishops like Richard Hurd, Horsley and Horne feared that teaching the poor to read was akin to giving them guns. It was the bishops who were instrumental in blocking Samuel Whitbread's 1807 bill, which sought to place education in the hands of magistrates and to fund it from the rates. Whitbread intended that it should remove controversy from the education of the poor by placing it on an equal footing with the administration of the Poor Law. However the proposal coincided with a decline in the support for the Poor Law, and its spiralling costs for the ratepayers. Moreover, the Church saw this as an attempt to remove education from its control by creating a national system of education sponsored by the state. Led by Archbishop Manners-Sutton the bench of bishops attacked the bill for its usurpation of education from the hands of the parish clergy and the proposal foundered.

In the absence of a national system of education it was voluntary schooling that won the day. The establishment of the National Society for Educating the Children of the Poor in 1811 by the Hackney Phalanx demonstrated the effectiveness of the voluntary system. Within three years there was enough money for 360 schools; by 1824 there were over 3000 schools educating half a million children. The Church could reconcile itself with mass schooling by the National Society because it was administered and operated on a diocesan basis, placing itself squarely in the hands of the Church. But it was this feature which attracted radical opposition to the society's schools. The Radicals Joseph

Hume and Francis Place argued that the society schools were part of the Tory landowner's armoury against the poor. The society's attempt to suggest that it sought to educate the poor to be responsible workers, thereby eliminating the need for heavy reliance on the rates, was a vain attempt to ingratiate its schools with the Whig Utilitarians. In 1828, Bishop Blomfield argued that the National Society schools were so effective in reducing juvenile crime that the government should support them on the basis of that argument alone.

The development of the education system relied almost exclusively on the clergy. By 1839, when the government established grants for elementary education, it found that most parochial schools were in the exclusive hands of the clergy. In 1851 the census revealed that of 10,595 schools receiving state aid, 8170 were church schools. For High Churchmen like G. A. Denison and Edward Munro this was as it should be: clergy ensured orthodoxy and were educated sufficiently to enable them to undertake the correspondence, financing and staffing of the schools. Many clergy also taught in schools from the best motives. The Revd W. H. Lyttelton's schools in Hagley sought to 'cultivate human nature as a whole . . . bodily, mental and spiritual'. Equally, there were those like the Revd E. J. R. Hughes, a Yorkshire cleric, who admitted that arithmetic and writing was the pretext he used to impress them with religious truth for a fraction of the time he had with them. These clergy regarded schooling as an extension of parish evangelism; another tendril into the community. For some it was important to reach into the community, but Samuel Wilberforce was anxious that teaching, and particularly the onerous fund-raising to support the schools, should not lead the clergy away from their spiritual calling to a more secular role. Teaching, argued Wilberforce, could be embraced by the clerical profession if it retained a clearly sacred objective, but not if it appeared to ignore it.

Book clubs promoted by the clergy were dominated by Christian literature; parish lectures (even when they were biographical or technical) tended to have a religious message and W. W. Champneys even 'salted' his Mothers' Meetings with expositions of what the Christian wife should do. Adult classes, like those held by the clergy of Lambeth parish, which focused solely on the skills needed by the students without a covert evangelical motive, were rare. The more usual educational function embraced by the clergy was catechising the children prior to confirmation. This took on a new importance in the nineteenth century as membership of the Church was no longer assumed to be as automatic as in the eighteenth century. Admission to the Church, and positive recruitment, required more rigorous induction which catechism became. Samuel Wilberforce's confirmation classes took place on both Sunday and Wednesday afternoons and Walter Hook saw it as the keystone of parish work.

Within the clerical profession the legitimacy of teaching as a single 'ministry' had been restricted to the universities. But this changed as clerical schoolmasters reached deaneries and bishoprics from headships of schools. Queen Victoria disliked schoolmaster-bishops, but by the end of the century the headship of a public school was referred to as a 'stepping stone' to a diocese. Certainly, it was for men like Tait, Temple, Butler, Benson and Prince Lee. Among the parish clergy the legitimacy of teaching was recognised by a rash of handbooks which indicated that it could be an integral element in parish life. John Sandford's clerical guide was entitled *The Church, the School and the Parish*. Men like Nathaniel Woodard recognised that the Church had a valuable role in providing sober and genteel education for the middle classes, and founded a string of schools, dominated by the clergy, from Taunton to Lancing. Elsewhere the institutions for the poor such as the Working Men's College and the People's College in Sheffield were founded by clergy of various denominations. Nevertheless, in the long term such efforts proved ineffective in educating the masses, for which by the end of the century the government assumed responsibility.

In addition to their role in education, clergymen fulfilled a significant part in promoting the health of their parishioners. It, too, had been a traditional role of conscientious clergy. Anthony Russell has shown that George Herbert, Richard Baxter and Gilbert Burnet were all commended as amateur physicians. Throughout the eighteenth century the medical role of the clergy remained, particularly in rural parishes. James Woodforde of Castle Cary undertook veterinary work and Sydney Smith at Combe Florey equipped an apothecary's shop at the rectory. The clergy were often among those who arranged for inoculation of the children of the parish, and clergy frequently visited the sick to provide both comfort and to be vigilant to the need for further medical care. Hospitals relied on the clergy for fund-raising and for administrative support. Vestry meetings to administer the Poor Law could employ physicians to attend the poor but many were content to try the parson's remedies. Clergy also played a significant role in supporting the 'sick clubs', informal assurance societies. At times of cholera or other epidemic disease it was to the parson that the people looked for aid.

In this role in promoting personal health the work of the clergyman expanded, but it was in the area of public health that the clergy developed a new role in the late eighteenth century. The response of the clergy to industrialisation was, in part, a concern for the physical well-being of their flock. Nonconformist clergy preached retribution for the misery visited upon the working classes. Ward's view was that the Anglican clergy were far less impressive in their reaction to physical industrial conditions. Unitarian, Swedenborgian, Wesleyan and Baptist clergy were prominent in Lancashire and Yorkshire in opposing poor factory conditions. Parson Bull in 1833 argued that from among seventy clergy of all denominations in Manchester only two were public advocates of the factory reform movement.

At a higher level, whilst there was no widespread episcopal support for the issue of public health and factory reform, Bishop Majendie – whose diocese of Chester contained many factories – promoted the 1802 Health and Morals of Apprentices Act, asking clergy to make a special effort to work with magistrates to enforce the Act. It was only with the appointment of Blomfield to London that a significant episcopal push developed for resolving the problems of public health in towns. In 1839, Blomfield collaborated with Chadwick in calling for an enquiry into the health and sanitation of working people. When the report was complete Blomfield also supported the radical proposal that the government should take responsibility for constructing model sanitary housing, a proposal which even Chadwick opposed as destructive to the free market. Blomfield supported subscriptions for wash-houses and the work of the Society for the Improvement of the Conditions of the Labouring Classes and the Association for Promoting Cleanliness. Blomfield was joined by bishops like Stanley, Lee, Longley, Lonsdale and C. R. Sumner in his labours for improved sanitation. After the 1849 cholera epidemic it was increasingly difficult for other bishops to remain silent. Blomfield and the progressive bishops ascribed the epidemic solely to physical conditions and made no suggestion that moral or religious factors affected it. The encouragement from such bishops was that opportunities for self-improvement were divine gifts to be grasped.

Many clergy saw involvement in public health as important acts of charity and a social duty for men of rank. This combination of the secular and spiritual underpinned the work of the Revds William Butler and Edward Elton on the water supplies at Wantage and Wheatley. Vaughan Thomas, Rector of Yarnton, was even chairman of the Oxford Board of Health in 1853. At Bilston in Staffordshire the Revd William Leigh assumed virtually sole responsibility for the health of the area, chairing the board of health and numerous other meetings, marshalling medical help and even arranging for supplies of coffins during the 1832 cholera epidemic. Bishop Durnford of Chichester recounted in 1874 his experiences earlier in the century as an incumbent in an area devoid of gentry or squires. He was obliged, as the parson, to take the lead, acting as chairman of the commissioners for roads, gas and drainage.

Relief of poverty had traditionally been a significant role undertaken by clergymen. The clergy were frequently the first resort of the poor for charitable support; they administered parish charities, dole and alms bequests, and they often appealed to the wealthy on behalf of the poor. Relief of the poor by impoverished clergy encompassed such practical help as soup kitchens, coal, blanket, shoe and clothing clubs. The 1837 enquiry into the Poor Law in Hampshire heard the report of the curate that at West Meon, 'there is a clothing club in which there are 50 poor people . . . there is a clothing club in the school of 30 members, [a] Men's

Provident Society, 15 members . . . There is a sick agricultural club, with 90 members . . . and I have started a fuel club at which I sell coals and faggots at half price.'17

The Revd Stephen Demainbray of Broad Somerford even arranged for the provision of allotments for the poor of his parish. The 1834 Poor Law Commission found that allotments arranged by the clergy were almost universal in Northampton-shire. Bishops Law and Blomfield even entered this field, providing allotments in their dioceses. These functions, through an implicit condescension, served to raise the status of the clergy in the esteem of their flock. Involvement with the Poor Law had also been an important role for clergymen. The Elizabethan Poor Law was administered through the vestry, and the parish administered its finance. Where parishes or parish unions had permission to build their own poorhouses the clergy were usually directly involved in their administration. It was therefore a system dominated by the Church which came under extreme pressure at the end of the eighteenth century. The dramatic expansion in pauperism in the first two decades of the nineteenth century raised questions about the clerical administration. As Soloway has shown, the Church at the end of the eighteenth did not yet view poverty as indicative of sin or moral turpitude. Bishops like Samuel Horsley and Lewis Bagot viewed the poor as the objects of providential poverty, not authors of it and thus worthy of charity and pity. However, this view was under threat from the evangelicals and the Nonconformists, for whom outward distress was mistaken for a sign of inner corruption. It was also threatened by the apparently uncontrolled spiralling of the cost of the Poor Law, which in 1818 reached £7.8 million and stimulated Malthusian responses.

In the years after the Napoleonic Wars, Anglican clergy mounted a spirited defence of the Poor Law. Edward Coplestone and Thomas Courtenay both argued that there was no link between the law and the burgeoning levels of poverty. As the Whig solution to poverty crystallised into the Poor Law Amendment Act of 1834 Bishop Phillpotts mounted an attack upon it. Phillpotts abhorred the idea of removing the pauper from direct contact with the ratepayer, which the old Poor Law enshrined. By establishing boards of guardians it both secularised the system and removed it from the hands of the community. Workhouses would also become centres of institutionalised poverty. But Phillpotts and old Tories were becoming isolated, even Blomfield – who had chaired a relief effort for distressed weavers – was convinced that charitable relief was insufficient to meet the demands of the poor. Whilst nine bishops opposed the harsh bastardy clauses in the Lords which proved unworkable, only Phillpotts signed a protest on the passage of the Act.

The new Poor Law detached the vestry from the administration of relief, but many clergy entered the debate on the Poor Law after 1834. Some, like Edward Duncombe, rector of Newton Kyme, George Bull and Walter Hook resolutely opposed the Act, supporting petitions and demonstrations against the workhouses. Many clergy with similar views continued their work with the poor, attempting to help them avoid the workhouse. Others committed themselves to the new Poor Law, like John Ballard, vicar of Cropredy in Oxfordshire who was chairman of the Board of Guardians of Banbury Workhouse from 1840. Kitson Clark was able to recount ten other such cases of clerical chairmanship of boards of guardians. Clergy remained prominent in giving evidence to the various parliamentary committees and commissions enquiring into the working of the Poor Law, in 1847, forming a quarter of all witnesses. For Kitson Clark this willingness to participate in the new Poor Law suggested 'the masterful assumptions' of the clergy of an earlier age, and suggested a magisterial role. But it might equally reflect the clergy's high view of the pastoral responsibility they discharged. In the transformed industrial world the clergy accepted responsibility not just for the souls of their flock, but for their physical well-being too.

Few clergy who gave evidence to the various parliamentary committees were committed to the principle of less eligibility. Some allowed their commitment to the poor to spill over into politics. Parson Bull became a mainstay of the Ten Hours Movement, writing tracts and pamphlets. The vicar of Warwick, Arthur Wade, led a procession of 50,000 people to protest at the treatment of the Tolpuddle Martyrs, whose actions were principally motivated by a desire to escape the workhouse. In some cases, the clergy showed evidence of organisation as a pressure group, as when they came forward to give evidence to the 1843 Poor Law Commission on the immorality caused by the mixing of sexes in the gang system of working in the countryside. Clergy like Henry Moule of Fordington and Lord Sydney Godolphin Osborne of Durweston were fearless in writing letters to newspapers and national figures on issues like sanitation and rural poverty. Chartism, whilst in many forms hostile to the Church, attracted those clergy who contemplated direct action. Birmingham and West Bromwich were both strongholds of Christian Chartism, with Chartist meetings opening with prayers and hymns. Preachers like the Primitive Methodist Joseph Capper brought Methodist organisation to the Chartists, with classes, walks and processions. Even orthodox clergy like Hook of Leeds maintained cordial relations with his Chartist churchwardens.

There was equally a move to distance the clergy from the relief of poverty. Bishop Kaye in his diocesan charge of 1846 argued that this was no longer a role which clergy should fill. By the middle of the Victorian era Canon Champneys advised curates to leave poor relief to the district visitors, allowing clergy to focus solely on spiritual matters. Ashton Oxendon argued that the clergy would be judged only on their ability to relieve poverty, not on their religious function, if they continued to distribute alms. Thus, just as the clerical role was separated from that of doctor, magistrate and teacher, so it diverged from that of relieving officer as the century progressed. Kitson Clark's view was that the nineteenth century saw the State emerging as a new Leviathan, taking over the secular functions of a new industrial society to which the Church felt less commitment. In the eighteenth century the Church was so closely associated with secular society that there was no question that it was appropriate for it to undertake educational, charitable, and other pastoral functions. But the new industrial society did not appear overnight, as Kitson Clark implies. As it evolved so did the Church's perception of its own role. Until the end of the nineteenth century the Church undertook a major role in secular affairs efficiently and gladly. The numbers of people whose lives were improved and ameliorated by the work of the clergy with a strong pastoral commitment were legion.

4

THE CHURCH AND THE REFORMS
OF THE 1830s

The Church and the 1832 Reform Act

As Jonathan Clark has shown, the 1832 Reform Act was a hurried and unplanned consequence of Catholic emancipation. If the repeal of the Test and Corporation Acts in 1828 initiated the breach of the alliance between Church and State, the divisions over the Reform Act of 1832 were evidence of the breach. As many as 250,000 dissenters were expected to obtain the right to vote as a result of parliamentary reform, and this represented a massive erosion of the Establishment of the Church. The Church's particular difficulty was that the leading churchmen ranged themselves on the side of the Tory Ultras, against reform. In doing so the Church had miscalculated the mood of the people; most people felt that reform was necessary, and were prepared to break with the Church to achieve it. At Cricklade, for example, the election occasioned by the failure of the first Reform Bill saw an unprecedented alliance of High Church and evangelical clergy oppose the reform candidate. But the electors defied the clergy and voted him in.

Lord Brougham, well aware of the mathematics of the House of Lords, said in 1831 that if the Lords rejected reform 'the bishops will be made to bear the blame . . . the roar and fury will be directed against the Bench and I foresee the very worst consequences'. It was a threat that was not lost on the bishops. The High Church Bishop Van Mildert was convinced that the Whigs would impose reform on the Church whether or not they supported parliamentary reform. Bishop Edward Coplestone of Llandaff claimed that if parliamentary reform was achieved it would be like a sop thrown to a surly dog; he would soon return with a more ravenous appetite to the Church. G. F. A. Best claims that this is exactly the achievement of the 1832 Reform Act: it unleashed anti-clerical feeling which successive governments used as a lever with which to initiate Church reform. The opposition to parliamentary reform was exactly the same among the evangelicals, who since the days of Pitt, Perceval and Liverpool had been ranged on the sides of the Tories, and who were aghast that the Whigs had insisted on Sunday sittings of the Commons. The instinctive agnosticism of many of the Whigs was a further feature of the campaign for the Reform Bill. Whigs like Lord Holland and even – it was rumoured – government ministers like Brougham were agnostics who shared no attachment to the Church, or to any religion.

The technique of identifying the clergy and bishops, and by implication the Church as a whole, as the culprits in opposing parliamentary reform worked to the particular satisfaction of the radical Whigs. Although the second Reform Bill was lost in the Lords by forty one votes, the twenty-one episcopal voters against it were blamed for the loss; only two bishops, Maltby and Bathurst, voted in favour. Holland privately conceded that the bill would have been lost anyway but this did not prevent a popular surge of anti-clerical feeling. At a meeting in Regent's Park, Hume was handed a placard which read 'Englishmen remember it was the bishops, and the bishops only, whose vote decided the fate of the Reform Bill'. In the debate on the bill itself Grey had appealed to the bishops to 'set their houses in order', suggesting that he saw their opposition as particularly reprehensible. The loss of the second Reform Bill in the Lords was met with three days of riots in Bristol during which the bishop's palace was burnt down, and that at Exeter was saved only by armed intervention. Abusing the Church was not new, but abuse of the Church on such a scale and with such violence was. Clergy were subject to widespread attack. Blomfield cancelled a preaching engagement after word that the congregation intended to walk out in protest, and Howley's carriage was chased out of Canterbury during his visitation. Sydney Smith, though he appeared on a pro-reform platform in Taunton, even went to the extreme of buying a blue coat to avoid looking like a clergymen. It was a technique the rector of St Martin's Birmingham might well have adopted: he was attacked in the street. The bishops of Carlisle, Lichfield and Coventry, Llandaff, Bath and Wells, Durham and even the innocent Roman Catholic bishop of Cork were among those menaced. Worse still, political threats existed too: Brougham wrote to Lord Durham 'the Bishops have done for themselves, and that they begin to feel already. They will not vote on many more bills'. In Coventry a placard urged people to punish the bishops for their votes by refusing to pay tithes and church rates.

These were chastening experiences. By coincidence the abolition of tithes in Ireland was debated in the Lords in February 1832 and it passed without episcopal opposition. Moreover the establishment of the Ecclesiastical Revenues Commission before the final reading of the third Reform Bill held a sword of Damocles over the bishops. Lord Eldon said, 'I attribute much to affright and fear of mobs.' By the second reading of the third Reform Bill twelve bishops shifted their votes to support it. Grey had worked hard to bring pressure on the bench. William IV had failed to persuade the bishops to support reform and Grey had to fall back on personal approaches. Harcourt of York and Carr of Worcester conceded, but the principal prize was Blomfield, who agreed to make a declaration in support of the bill when it reappeared in the Lords in March 1832. Blomfield was one of the prime movers in effecting the shift in episcopal votes on the Reform Bill, and worked behind the scenes to persuade his fellow bishops to vote for reform, collecting ten votes for it. He wrote to Bishop Monk that the bishops would have to be careful to judge the bill both by its contents and by the majority it obtained in the Commons. He was even able to divide the episcopal brothers Charles and John Sumner. Blomfield's principal argument was that reform could bring the people closer to their ancient institutions. It was not widely known that he held this view; for the general public the bishops' opposition to reform was too well known. Those who fully embraced reform like Archbishop Whately of Dublin were threatened by the mob along with the other bishops. Clergy like Thomas Arnold, who supported the bill, did not attract public support. Neither did Sydney Smith, who even proposed names to Grey of men whom he thought would make suitable peers, if he had to resort to mass peer-creation to force reform through the Lords.

A study of poll books during the 1831 election, however, suggests that it is easy to overstate the opposition to reform among the parish clergy.[1] In Northamptonshire, a majority of the clergy voted for the Whig Lord Althorp and at Cambridge a third of the clergy supported Palmerston, the reform candidate. The subtle arguments of Howley – who claimed that moderate reform with bi-partisan support would have gained his vote – were lost on the people. Indeed, Howley's own proposal for modest reform of pluralities was introduced into the Lords in June 1831, but was regarded as too limited. A second Howley Bill, to allow ecclesiastical corporations to augment their poorer livings, was passed, and it allowed Van Mildert to unload £1000 a year to help poor clergy. Those bishops who changed their minds were unable to gain any credit for their switch to support for the Bill. It was clear that they were only grudging and expeditious suppor-ters. Harcourt was perhaps the most cynical; voting for the bill in 1832 he claimed that only diocesan business in Yorkshire had prevented him voting for it on earlier occasions. Bishop Kaye voted against the bill in 1831 on pragmatic grounds; the same grounds convinced him to vote for it in 1832. There remained determined episcopal opponents, like Phillpotts who entered into print against the bill but who was careful to avoid visiting his diocese of Exeter where he was burned in effigy. To the end he maintained a vitriolic duel in the Lords with Lord Durham against the bill, agitating particularly for the vote to be kept from the hands of the town dwellers who were more likely to be nonconformist.

For these die-hards the final blow was Wellington's inability to form a government in April 1832, after another bill was lost. It provoked a further outburst of venom directed towards the bishops, during which Bishop Ryder was mobbed in a church he was visiting. Wellington, recognising that the Tory die-hards had failed, used his influence to prevent further opposition. In the final vote on the third Reform Bill the twelve prelates who had voted against it were prevailed upon to abstain, allowing the bill to win a majority of eighty-four. Bishop Monk claimed that it would usher in an era of 'perpetual change'.

The reform campaign coincided with the 1831 cholera epidemic which closed theatres and caused fashionable society to avoid the towns. Apocalyptic preachers emerged from the independent evangelical congregations claiming that the warnings in the Book of Revelation were about to come to pass. Even Hurrell Froude wrote from Devonshire in 1831 that 'things are in a bad way down here . . . I have made up my sage mind that the country is too bad to deserve an Established Church'. Spencer Perceval Jr, son of the former prime minister, lectured the House of Commons on the pestilence soon to be loosed on it. The bishops had been taken to the precipice and shown the prospect. The historian Soloway, like Best, holds that the trauma of 1830–2 was perhaps a painful, but useful, one for the Church. It attracted leaders like Blomfield, and even Howley, to moderate reform and left the High Tories relatively isolated. Even the chapter of Durham, anxious at the huge income its coal fields earned, founded Durham University to mollify public opinion.

Once the initial shock of the Ecclesiastical Commission was overcome, Blomfield recognised that disestablishment was not the goal of the Whigs. Grey did not believe in disestablishment or in removing the Church's property. Blomfield also saw that much could be gained from cooperation with the government. Hook bemoaned the episodes of 1830–2 as a lost opportunity to gain the support of the people. But the apparent loss of the government's support was more momentous: the radicals in the Whig ministry turned their guns toward the Church. The threat to the Church of England was made indirectly, through the legislation enacted in 1833 to remodel the Irish Church with fewer bishoprics. Moreover, 1833 saw the decision of the government to provide money for education to both the Anglican National Society and the dissenting British and Foreign School Society. Dual funding encouraged suggestions that the Establishment was under attack. A year later there was a motion, ironically from the devout Lord Henley, to remove the bishops from their seats in the Lords. With the Tories reduced to just 150 MPs after 1832, the Church had no shield to defend it against the attacks of the radical Whigs. *Fraser's Magazine* concluded in August 1832 that 'we see the clergy represented . . . as proud and indolent, and enemies to freedom . . . their property is designated a burden upon the state'. J. S. Mill argued that the reform of the Church's property was a necessary corollary to parliamentary reform, and that the State had a duty to reform the Church's finances. In Parliament petitions supporting the views of John Roebuck that Church property was the property of the people gained currency.

Newman's *Tract No. 1* responded to these views with an assertion of High Church doctrine. Newman claimed that Parliament might claim supremacy over the Church's property, and might appropriate it. But this did not imply that Parliament exerted supremacy over the Church's mission or its usefulness to society. Newman called on the Church to consider its spiritual message at a time when it was exclusively focusing on its temporal position. Between these two positions lay that of the moderate reformers, like Peel and Blomfield. Blomfield's view was that reform of the Church's property was acceptable, as long as the reforms were made in cooperation with the Church and the property was still devoted to the Church and its purposes, and not alienated to the State. Thus a new criteria for Church property emerged: its utility for the people. It was a direct product of the Reform Act which had raised up the principle of public utility. Blomfield's view gained ground with bishops like George Law of Bath and Wells and Whately of Dublin. Even the Tory–High Church *British Critic* recognised that the people were the source of the Church's future, 'the people must be gained, or all is lost'. Blomfield seemed to be moving even closer to the reformist position when his 1834 *Charge* denounced pluralities as an inheritance from papal dominion. He also conceded that reform should come from outside the Church, since nothing the Church could do would satisfy public opinion.

The Church and the Ecclesiastical Reforms of the 1830s

The focus of writers like John Wade, the editor of the extreme *Black Book* who took advantage of the 1830–2 attack on the bishops to promote his views, was on the huge incomes of the Church. His view was that for such huge sums the people gained little advantage. In its edition in 1832 Wade's attack claimed that the Church of England was unreformed compared with the · Catholic Church. At the core of Wade's lengthy attack was the suggestion that Church property was public property, and that it had been appropriated by churchmen for their families through the system of plurality and non-residence. For 183 pages Wade ploughed through example after example of (often inflated) estimates of Church incomes and expenditure. The family of Bishop Sparke of Ely were amongst those identified as the most nepotist and most rapacious. In total the family's income from the Church was calculated at £40,000. Rumours were repeated that London diocese was worth £100,000. It was an attack that received encouragement from the passage of the Reform Act. What allowed this mud to stick was the absence of any figures that could be relied upon to refute it. In the face of such claims moderate churchmen agreed that a commission to establish the facts would be a bulwark against dangerously radical change. Watson was able to talk Van Mildert into supporting a commission which would be exclusively made up of churchmen. As Owen Chadwick has asserted in a recent essay, the success of the Ecclesiastical Commission was in part founded upon its ability to make changes occasioned by the perception of an emergency.[2] It found support from Wordsworth and Howley, and Blomfield was even sympathetic to including laymen.

When, in June 1832, Lord Grey announced the creation of the commission its members were principally conservative in complexion. The commission comprised the two archbishops, the bishops of London, Durham, Lincoln and Bangor and Sir Robert Inglis, the Tory who had beaten Peel at the Oxford election in 1829. The brief of the commission was simply to ascertain the extent and amount of church property. It turned out to be an onerous duty which necessitated renewal of the commission in

1833 and 1834. It also operated against a blizzard of proposals for church reform. Many of these were from hostile critics of the Church; others like those from Archdeacon Berens, Lord Henley and Dr Burton came from supporters of the Church. Blomfield's experience on the commission led him to the view that the Church needed a body of laity and clergy who could provide the leadership in reform. When, in 1834, Peel briefly took the reins of power, a long interview with Blomfield and Howley produced the creation of a new Ecclesiastical Commission to enquire into and recommend changes to Crown and episcopal patronage, the efficient discharge of pastoral duties and equal distribution of episcopal duties. Peel had already stated in the Tamworth Manifesto that he could not countenance the alienation of church property, and he ensured that the commission was comprised solely of supporters of the Church and Establishment. Its membership included the two archbishops, the bishops of London, Lincoln and Gloucester, Lords Lyndhurst and Harrowby. Peel included himself together with Goulburn, Charles Wynn, Hobhouse and Sir Herbert Jenner. There was some criticism that the lesser clergy were not represented on the commission, but this was principally the desire of the archbishops.

The commission met at Peel's house and by March 1835, after eight meetings and a number of committees, it published its first report. The haste of the commission was a response to the precarious nature of Peel's administration, and the need to prove that a commission sympathetic to the Church could achieve significant changes. The report was in effect a plan of the lines along which the Church's incomes and structures could be remodelled. Two new sees were to be founded at Manchester and Ripon and the bench was to be reduced by two seats by uniting Bristol with Llandaff and St Asaph with Bangor. Geographical changes would be made to the dioceses of Carlisle, Chester, Bristol, Lincoln, Ely, London and Rochester to reduce the size of the larger dioceses. The incomes of bishops were also to be equalised at between £4500 and £5500 for all but the leading five prelates. A few weeks after the report was issued Peel's government was defeated on the issue of redirecting the Irish Church's income to educational purposes, and the government resigned.

Historians like Chadwick, Brose and Best have followed the views of Blomfield that the brief Peel administration set the second Ecclesiastical commission in the direction which best served the interests of the Church. Its focus was on redistribution and equalisation rather than on appropriation and sequestration. Perhaps this view fails to appreciate the support that the moderate Whigs felt for the commission. Melbourne was happy to continue with the work of the commission in the same form and gave Howley the reassurance he sought that the government would not propose any reform of the Church without the approval of the bishops. The commission was advantaged also by the neglect of the politicians whom Melbourne appointed to it. Unlike Peel, who attended all the meetings, Melbourne, Lansdowne, Cottenham, Russell and Spring Rice rarely attended, leaving the commission in the hands of the clerical members.

Nevertheless, the commission knew it could not neglect its task. In March 1836, its second report addressed the problem of the need for parsons and money in the large towns and cities and the surplus in the cathedrals. It was to give effect to the concerns Blomfield found in his walk around his diocese – from St Paul's where he imagined Sydney Smith comfortably in his canonry, to north London where a vast mass of people could find no accommodation in their churches and no resources for effective pastoral care. It was also to respond to the vague feeling, expressed by the MP Edward Horsman, that the clergy in cathedrals were lazy men who had allowed the growth of Dissent. Surprisingly the report revealed that only seventy-six clergy received very large incomes (exceeding £2000 a year) of whom sixty held some cathedral dignity. At the other end of the spectrum, 15.6 per cent of English clergy received less than £100. A common fund was to be established to equalise clerical incomes taking money from cathedrals to augment the poorest benefices. There were also hopes that the government would contribute funds; Blomfield suggested a 2d tax on coal, but none was forthcoming.

It quickly became established that Blomfield, together with Charles Knight the commission's secretary, was the dominant force in the commission. One bishop commented that until

114

Blomfield arrived the commissioners sat around fiddling with their pens and talking about the weather. Blomfield attracted much abuse for his work, some called him the 'Right Reverend Utilitarian' others claimed he was the 'ecclesiastical Peel'. Blomfield was also attacked as the government's 'pope', just as Bishop Gibson had been in the eighteenth century. Much of the abuse arose from the commission's willingness to consider options without consulting the clergy and laity concerned. The diocesan changes to Bangor, St Asaph, Bristol and Llandaff were eventually rejected through widespread opposition. Attempts to abolish Gloucester and Bristol as separate dioceses were opposed and the plan to unite Sodor and Man to Carlisle also provoked opposition, even though the clergy would have shared the bishop's stipend. For whilst the commission asked for information and facts from the clergy it rarely sought their advice or opinions. The commissioners doubtless felt there was not enough time for consultation; action was important to avert direct interference from the Whig government.

Two further reports emerged in quick succession in May and June 1836. The former suggested that the commission be made permanent and also that its work in future be effected by the use of Orders in Council, thus avoiding the need for damaging debates in Parliament. The work of the commission was enshrined in three Acts: the Established Church Act of 1836, the Pluralities Act of 1838 and the Ecclesiastical Duties and Revenues Act of 1840. The Established Church Act of 1836 abolished commendams, equalised bishops' incomes, authorised the new sees of Ripon and Manchester, set up seven new archdeaconries, and established the permanent commission. It also established the principle that the changes which the commission introduced would take effect only as each diocese or living fell vacant. As one recent study of the changes effected in the chapter at Winchester has shown the changes were completed only in the 1860s and 1870s.[3] The last prebend to be suppressed under the 1840 Act was that of Wiveliscombe in Wells Cathedral, which fell vacant in 1891. The Pluralities Act limited the number of livings a clergyman could hold to two, which must be within ten miles of each other and together must not have a population exceeding 3000 or an income exceeding £1000. A dispensation was still required and bishops were also empowered to require two Sunday services and residence. The Dean and Chapter Act of 1840 suppressed most non-resident prebends and sinecure rectories and equalised the number of resident canonries at each cathedral. The incomes of the deans and chapters were to be vested in the commission and all deans and canons were to be nominated by the Crown and bishops respectively. Equally importantly, the 1840 Act made all the bishops members of the commission together with the Lord Chief Justice, five judges, the deans of Canterbury, London and Westminster and six laymen.

The work of the commission in parliament was represented as the work of a joint effort by Church and State. But the changes were by no means revolutionary. In terms of patronage the power of the bishops was increased. The decision of the commission to become permanent was also a product of the gradualist approach to change. No huge stipends were reduced, no pluralities abandoned, no sinecure suppressed until the death or resignation of the holder. Thus the commission needed to remain in existence to decide how best to redistribute the money as it became available. Moreover, the commission by its very nature seemed to support the view that, rather than representing change, Erastian control was being reasserted. How else could the Crown's assumption of appointments to deaneries be explained? The commission extended the alliance between Church and State that had prevailed in the eighteenth century rather than overturned it.[4] That the changes in the Church were perceived as conservative was confirmed by the Whig opposition to the use of Orders in Council for further proposals from the commission.

On the other hand the commissioners had turned deaf ears to the pleas, especially strong from the cathedrals, that they could reform themselves. The chapter of Durham claimed, with some justification, that it was already augmenting benefices and allocating its large income to worthy causes. The commission also ignored the pleas of the High Churchmen like Manning, who argued that the very existence of the commission subverted the nature of apostolic government. Manning claimed that the commission had established a new order in the Church: rule by government. The testimony of the two moderate reformers on the original commission (Bishops Monk and Kaye) was significant in answering these criticisms. Monk recorded his view in 1838 that the commission was faced with solving practical problems, failure to do so would have been taken by the government as evidence of the Church's inability to reform itself, and draconian measures would have been taken. Kaye's position was even more instructive to his fellow bishops. He was the bishop of a largely rural diocese with, he admitted, no conception of the needs of the Church in the industrial areas. He denounced any man who opposed the commission without viewing the evidence it had examined; he also asked whether the Church could claim to be fulfilling its duty in the northern towns. In the final debates on the 1840 Act, the commission drew together a remarkable alliance of Whig and Tory supporters: Howley, Blomfield, Peel, Russell and Melbourne. The opposition led by Gladstone, Inglis and Phillpotts was only able to protest at the changes.

The implementation of the changes established by the commission, and its legislation, was not without problems. The redrawing of diocesan boundaries was fraught. A successful campaign was launched to prevent the union of Bangor with St Asaph by Lord Powis in 1843. The union of Bristol with Llandaff was rejected on closer examination and substituted by the union of Gloucester and Bristol. This was agreed only when the bishop accepted both cities as his sees, and the arrangement lasted less than seventy years. The proposed union of Sodor and Man with Carlisle was also scuppered by popular protest in 1836. Thus the commission abandoned any attempt at limiting the episcopate and agreed that whilst there could only be twenty-six bishops in the Lords, who must include the five leading bishops, there could be more bishoprics. As a result some lords spiritual would have to wait for their seats until one of the twenty-six became vacant. There were bishops who resented and blocked the work of the commission. C. R. Sumner of Winchester refused to cooperate in transferring patronage to the commission. More reprehensible was the attitude of the chapter of Manchester Collegiate Church. The chapter asked the commission to believe that its total income was only

£4025. There was an outburst of disbelief from Joseph Brotherton, the MP for Salford, and from the *Manchester Guardian*. Even Bishop Prince Lee, the first bishop of Manchester, subsequently rebuked the chapter for lying to the commission.

There were also problems with the equalisation of episcopal incomes. An Episcopal Fund was set up to be the instrument for equalisation, but it proved difficult to calculate and anticipate the bishops' incomes accurately. In 1851, Sir Benjamin Hall challenged the income of Bishop Thirlwall of St David's, who had received a windfall from some episcopal mines. Thirlwall only narrowly escaped the suggestion of impure motives from the episode.[5] It was decided that wealthier bishops would make contributions to the fund to support those bishops whose incomes fell below the £4500 minimum. Bishop Allen who was translated in 1836 from Bristol to Ely found himself required to find £4000 for the fund. His openly published reply was to threaten to place the diocesan finances in the hands of the commission and merely claim from them his stipend. However, the commission, by settling on £4500 as the minimum for a bishop, created problems, since many bishops could not survive on the sum. Maltby claimed that he could not afford to come to London without his Lincoln's Inn preachership. The effect of this may well have been to exclude those from the poorest backgrounds from the highest reaches of the Church.[6] Whilst the numbers of aristocratic bishops declined as the nineteenth century progressed, the numbers from middle class backgrounds grew significantly. This could cause difficulties, as Best wrote, 'a bishop of the reformed era, if he lacked private means, was bound to be a needy man'. The commission also ran into difficulty in the provision of residences for the bishops. The public perception was that the commission was being lavish in buying Riseholme for the bishops of Lincoln for £52,000, and a parliamentary committee investigated the issue. New palaces cost a further £15,000 for Ripon, £23,000 for Gloucester, £19,000 for Manchester and £30,000 for Rochester. Repairs and other changes were made at a further twelve palaces, partly paid by loans from Queen Anne's Bounty and the sale of properties.

The Common Fund for parishes set up by the commissioners

was also beset with problems. The commissioners established, as the major priority, the augmentation of large populous parishes – those with more than 2000 inhabitants – which had incomes below £150. In all, there were over 300 of these parishes. After some deliberation they abandoned the system of augmentation favoured by Queen Anne's Bounty, in most cases in favour of annual stipends. They also needed to retain some money for building parsonages. The drawback with this system of augmenting annual stipends was that it did not provide for the long term endowment of churches at a time when church building was growing. Best suggested that this was a short-sighted policy which left many of the new churches and parishes without endowments which they sorely needed. To meet the huge demands for augmentations the commissioners contracted a loan from Queen Anne's Bounty which also precluded the Bounty from making its own augmentations for endowment. The system was unable to cope with demands for augmentations, and in 1844 a temporary halt was called until more funds became available. It was only in 1856 that the accounts of the Ecclesiastical commission came into credit.[7]

A further problem which arose after 1840 was the lack of continuity of attendance at meetings by the members of the enlarged commission. The chairman of the commission was always the most senior member present, which led to shifting the chairmanship as the various members missed meetings. At one meeting in April 1845 the chairmanship of the meeting changed five times as members arrived late and left early. There was a bewildering network of committees and the secretary took on enlarged importance as a result of the confusion of business. All these failings were revealed painfully in the parliamentary committee which investigated the commission in 1847–8.

Not all the achievements of the commission were negative, however. One of the most significant outcomes of the Ecclesiastical commission was the close relationship it generated between Peel and Blomfield. With Peel's return to power in 1841 Blomfield took on the principal role in ecclesiastical affairs, becoming Peel's unofficial ecclesiastical minister. There were few appointments which were not referred to Blomfield for an opinion including most major livings, the Mastership of the Temple, and that of Trinity College, Cambridge, professorships, the deaneries of Peterborough and of Westminster and the dioceses of Ely and Lichfield. Had it not been for Howley's recovery from a bout of illness, Blomfield would have been archbishop in 1842. Blomfield guided Peel through the dangerous straits of appointments at Oxford which could inflame either Tractarian or anti-Tractarian feeling. Together they ensured that the principle of appointment of men of moderation was applied as often as possible. They pressed forward the eradication of pluralities among the older clergy and members of the bench, and determined only to advance men of activity to the highest positions. Blomfield also supported Peel's emphasis on the subdivision of parishes pressing it forward in Barnet, West Ham and fashionable West London parishes. In short, the relationship between Peel and Blomfield demonstrated that in spite of church reform the relationship between Church and State was as effective as it had been in the eighteenth century. There were disagreements, Blomfield for example was unable to persuade Peel to release building land in London for churches; but for the most part Warburton's alliance reasserted itself after reform.[8]

The commission also achieved a relatively smooth transition to a more developed system of ecclesiastical organisation. An Act of 1850 established permanent commissioners and created an Estates commission. The Act recognised that the large commission made up of all the bishops and other amateurs was ineffective. The Church needed a smaller professional body to deploy its finances. The experience of the commission in the 1840s was a series of lessons that had to be learnt before the system could evolve. The Act of 1850 also allowed for the creation of delegated powers, confirming that the commissioners had established the correct lines for church reform.

The regularisation of leases on land was also brought under the commissioners' control (particularly endowments from the suspended canonries). The commission established a formal system for church lessees. Properly calculated systems for renewal of leases were developed, rather than relying on the short-term advantage gained from renewal fines. Rack rents were introduced to increase the yield from lands whose incomes had often not been calculated with any care. By 1845 there were even general rules for leases and renewals. Gradually as the century drew on these systems became standard throughout the Church and became the model for the management of other church incomes. By 1860 the commissioners had established a reputation for financial probity which led to Parliament entrusting all capitular property to their hands.

The greatest achievement of the commission, however, was the shift it signalled in the aims of the Church. The accumulated legislation of the period from 1760 to 1818 had suggested ways of reforming the Church in each parish: increasing the incomes of curates, building more churches and reducing pluralities. Such piecemeal reforms laid out the agenda for change, but did not address the larger issue of the structures of the Church or the institutional changes that were needed. The Ecclesiastical commission was able to redefine the mission of the Church by changing structures. Edward Horsman went further than most in claiming that the reformed Church was now able to address the problem of the poor. Speaking in the Commons in 1845, he claimed, 'it is for the poor that our Established Church exists. The revenues of that Church are the heritage of the poor.' Not all bishops and clergy would have agreed with him; nevertheless, after the work of the commission, the Church could care for the needs of rich and poor alike with more efficiency. The acid test for this view, Chadwick argues in a recent essay, is the conversion of Horsman. In 1848, having earlier been an ardent critic of the commission and its work, Horsman paid tribute to the commission, claiming its work had 'been followed by results which their most sanguine supporters could not have anticipated; there [is] a new race of clergy; and the Church has been raised to a usefulness and a popularity unknown before'. Two historians have recently confirmed this view of the value of the reforms. R. Brent and J. Parry have suggested that the reforms consciously fostered a 'Liberal Anglican' style in the direction the Church of England set for itself. As a direct result of this change the Church could become a mechanism for the reduction of social tension between different sects and classes.

The Church and the Whig Reforms of the 1830s

It was neither the aim nor the achievement of the reforms generated by the Ecclesiastical commissions of the 1830s to divide the Church from the State. Their aim was simply to render the Church more effective in the discharge of its duties. Nevertheless, reforms were considered and undertaken by the Whigs during the governments of the 1830s which had profound effects on the relationship between Church and State, perhaps more so than the legislation of the Ecclesiastical commission. The Municipal Corporation Act of 1835 was a direct response by the Whigs to the demands of dissenters. By extending the principles of reform from Parliament to the borough, the administration threw open local government, which had previously been a major sphere of clerical activity. Perhaps the greatest impact was the way in which the Municipal Corporation Act eased the way of dissenters into local government in a far more widespread way than that of their admission to Parliament by the repeal of the Test and Corporation Act. Some boroughs like Northampton and Leicester continued to be predominantly Anglican, but others saw dissenters enter councils and influence them. A Unitarian mayor was elected in Liverpool, and Leeds' mayors from 1835 to 1845 were dissenters. Chadwick listed thirteen boroughs in which dissenters were elected in 1835.[9] Almost without exception these dissenters were Whigs or radicals. During the passage of the Act Phillpotts had warned that it would have the effect of handing corporations over to men without a deep attachment to English traditions. This was a particular concern to the Church in boroughs where the corporation exercised ecclesiastical patronage, like Bristol where the corporation owned the advowsons of eight parishes. Blomfield denounced the implications of the Act, suggesting even that dissenters would deliberately appoint ineffective clergy to parishes to discredit the Church. Eventually, it was agreed that corporations would be forced to sell their advowsons. The effect of the sale of advowsons was certainly to keep the dissenters away from Church patronage, but it also divorced the Church from corporations. Those corporations with close relations with the parish churches, like Oxford, Norwich, Beccles, Bedford and

Helston were obliged to abandon them. It thus became easier for the new corporations to effect more profound changes. Liverpool corporation – a piebald corporation of Anglicans, Nonconformists and Catholics – decided to prevent the teaching of the Anglican prayer book in schools and the new dissenting mayor of Chester refused to attend services in the cathedral. By 1836, some corporations were planning to use corporation money to finance Nonconformist schools. In 1839, the *Eclectic Review* claimed that the 1835 Act had effected the most significant advance for dissenters of all the reforms of the decade.

The Whigs also pursued their traditional eighteenth-century policy of relief for dissenters. In 1833, Quakers and Jews received legislation confirming the legality of their marriage ceremonies, but attempts by both Russell and Peel in 1834 and 1835 to legalise all dissenters' marriage ceremonies were rejected. Finally, in 1836 a Marriage Act allowed dissenting ministers to apply for a licence to celebrate marriages. A registrar was appointed for each area who was required to be present at marriages (Anglican parsons were automatically able to act as registrars). The registrar could also solemnise civil marriages. The effect was dramatic; by 1845 14,228 marriages had been celebrated outside the established Church. At the same time, moreover, Anglican marriages also grew in number.

The Marriage Act was, in part, a product of the desire on the part of the government to effect clear and accurate registration of births marriages and deaths. However, the Act was greatly to the benefit of dissenters and hostile to the Church's traditional role. A series of administrative regulations arising from the Registration Act of 1836, such as that requiring a certificate from the registrar before burial could be undertaken by a clergyman, reduced the clergy to the level of mere bureaucratic functionaries. The Registration Act of 1836 also separated baptism from the registration of birth, and many clergy regarded this as a far more damaging effect than the break in their monopoly over marriages. Clergy like John Burgon feared that civil registration of births would lead to people regarding the sacrament of baptism as superfluous. However, Anthony Russell concludes that the separation of civil registration of birth from baptism achieved a rise in the status of the rite. Baptism became a purely spiritual observance.[10] But at the same time the separation meant that fewer people undertook to baptise their children. Ignorance and superstition about baptism continued: in 1867, the Revd J. H. Blunt found that some women in his parish confused baptism with vaccination. Some clergy found that a spirit of opportunism prevailed after 1836, with parents bringing their children to be baptised purely to qualify the baby for clothing and burial clubs. Moreover, the clergy found a further labour imposed upon them, that of searching out unbaptised children. There was the sense of a market into which the clergy were thrust; parents could take their children to a 'cheaper' parson for baptism. This also encouraged the view that the clergy merely dispensed a social service.

As expected, the Whigs concerned themselves with education. Here too the traditional goal of the Whigs was to relieve the lot of dissenters. From 1833 the Treasury paid £20,000 a year to the National Society and the British and Foreign Schools' Society, the two voluntary Anglican and Nonconformist societies. The money was initially directed to be spent on the building of schools and was to be paid in direct proportion to the sums raised by the two societies. The greater resources of the National Society, which could take advantage of the diocesan organisation which it had developed, allowed it to gain seven tenths of the sum over five years. In 1839, Russell expanded the grant to £30,000 a year and extended it to allow dissenting and Catholic schools to apply direct for a grant. A committee, under Kay-Shuttleworth, was established to distribute the grants to schools. The Whig brief to Kay-Shuttleworth was to encourage Nonconformist schools as much as possible, and as a result the committee was entirely composed of laymen. Archbishop Howley was outraged by the blatant attempts by the Whigs to inject money into the nonconformist schools. A boycott of the grants committee was undertaken by the Church, and in 1840 a compromise was agreed which allowed the Church the right to control its inspectors of schools. This concession won the cooperation of the Church with the grants committee. In fact the Church gained a great deal of money from the new committee for its own schools which applied directly for grants. It was a minor victory. In education, as elsewhere, the Whigs achieved their goal of breaking the Church's monopoly. Education was set on a path which led to greater secularisation. It was a long and winding route. In the 1840s Peel attempted to restore a predominance in education for the Church, believing that disestablishment would be achieved by equal grants to the various denominations, but the proposal did not succeed. The Nonconformist conscience, once inspired, could not be easily dampened.

This applied to higher education too. One of the disabilities under which the dissenters laboured was the religious test imposed by the universities. Oxford required all members to subscribe to the Thirty-nine Articles; at Cambridge there was no general test, but most colleges required students to attend compulsory services in their chapels and graduates were required to subscribe. Those few Catholics or Jews at Cambridge colleges were also affronted by the need to subscribe to the Act of Supremacy on graduation. The effect was the same, dissenters felt unable to matriculate at the universities. The view that the universities should be Anglican monopolies provoked a strong response in dissenters' demands for entry. The Duke of Wellington, in 1834, argued that admission of dissenters would split the union of Church and State asunder. The government's support for the admission of dissenters was indicated by Grey's presentation of a petition to the Lords in 1834 calling for the admission of dissenters to Cambridge. The petition was followed in June 1834 by a bill to admit dissenters. Its sponsorship by a Unitarian, G. W. Wood, provoked the opposition of the Tories in the Lords who rejected it. Within the universities support grew for the admission of dissenters. Thirlwall was sacked from his tutorship at Trinity College, Cambridge in 1834 for his advocacy of the admission of dissenters. The heads of houses at Oxford experimented with a resolution to remove the subscription, but resolved to keep it in 1835. Relief for dissenters came from leverage exerted by the foundation of establishments which did not require a religious test. St David's College, Lampeter; and later King's College and University College in London, and Durham University were all founded between 1822 and 1836. In spite of the strident opposition of Oxford University the Whigs insisted that London University should be allowed to grant degrees. Another bastion of the Church's defence by the State had fallen.

The finances of the Church were addressed by the 1836 Tithe Commutation Act, which sought to translate all moduses, tithes and compositions into a single commuted payment. The collection of tithes had for years been a difficult matter which frequently brought the parson into conflict with his congregation. In order to attempt to safeguard clerical incomes the tithe level to be converted into a cash sum was to be averaged over the seven-year period prior to 1836. Tithes were also to be linked to future cereal prices, to avoid allowing the agricultural depression of the 1830s artificially to reduce clerical incomes. A commission was set up to administer the commutation of tithes and the anticipated disputes which it would throw up. In all 7147 tithe commutation agreements were made voluntarily, but a further 5263 were made by compulsory awards determined by the Tithe commission.[11] The process took until the 1860s, in part because of the appeals to law and also because the Act only allowed the commission to work on an *ad hoc* district basis, rather than on the national system of tithes. In some cases, the clergy gained from commutation; the income they received was based on their former tithe entitlement, rather than their receipts (which were often lower than their entitlement). Peter Virgin argues that, taken together with the 1838 Pluralities Act, the commutation of tithes left a significant dent in the incomes of some clergy. The commutation of tithes also raised questions about the nature and legitimacy of clerical incomes. Clergy expressed the view that substituting a payment legitimised by Parliament for one legitimised by scripture weakened the position of the clergy and added to a diminution of their status.

A further issue which twice threatened to divide the Church from the State was that of church rates, the sums raised on ratepayers to repair parish churches. Rates were voted by a parish meeting, and dissenters were liable to pay if the parish agreed to raise a rate for repairs. Dissenters were also liable to punishment by the courts if they refused to pay the established rate. The law of 1818 which extended church building also extended this system to the new churches established under the Act. Defenders of the rate suggested that, since it had to be voted by ratepayers, it ensured the responsiveness of the Church to the ratepayers. But it also generated a great sense of injustice among dissenters, who sometimes found themselves paying a rate to two churches: one to the parish church and another to a new church built under the 1818 Act as well as to their own chapel. In cities where there were large dissenting populations the vote on a rate could be a source of friction. In Birmingham, in the early nineteenth century, it was only with the utmost difficulty that church rates were voted in. At Bradford and Dewsbury in the 1820s the church lost votes to strike a rate for repair of the parish churches.

The Whigs were confidently expected to abolish church rates. In Ireland they were abandoned by the 1833 Irish Church Act. Nevertheless, the moderate Whigs saw the rates as a cornerstone of the Established Church and however much the Whigs were portrayed as hostile to the Church, they had no intention of damaging it. The Chancellor of the Exchequer, Althorp, unlike the radicals, declared that the nature of an Established Church was one in which the State undertook the defrayment of the costs of repairs. However, the Whigs were under extreme pressure from dissenters to abolish rates, and petitions bombarded Parliament. In 1834, a Church Rates Bill was introduced by Althorp which proposed to divert a slice of Land Tax receipts to repair of churches. In fact the bill aroused more opposition than the existing church rates. Dissenters found a rate that could be opposed by a local vote far more acceptable than a national tax, which could not be evaded. In Manchester, the radical dissenters asserted that there would never be a resolution of the rates issue until there had been a 'collision' in the Lords over the establishment of the Church. But this was not part of the Whig's agenda. There were other problems – Scottish Land Tax payers petitioned the Commons denouncing the suggestion that they should subsidise the English Church. To the embarrassment of the Whigs the bill, which seemed to strengthen the State's responsibility for the Church, was supported by Peel and by Ultra Tories. This was too much and the bill was quietly dropped.

The Melbourne government also wrestled with the problem of rates, but its dependence on the radicals excluded any revival of the Althorp plan. Indeed, for Brose, the issue of church rates was symptomatic of the Whig dilemma: balancing their desire to respond to radical and dissenters' demands with their anxiety to maintain the establishment. Spring Rice, the new Chancellor of the Exchequer, suggested that more effective management of church leases might yield the money to replace the rates. It was hotly opposed by the Ecclesiastical commission, which felt it could not continue if the government was to interfere with its work in this way. Indeed, Blomfield warned Monk that the commission would break up if the government pursued the suggestion. It also roused the anger of the primate; Howley wrote to Peel pointing out that the bill showed that the dissenters were determined to effect the disestablishment of the Church. Blomfield and Howley spoke against the bill supported by sixteen other bishops. Again the plan was dropped. The problems occasioned by church rates rumbled on. Men of conscience, like John Childs and the celebrated John Thorogood, were condemned to gaol for refusing to pay the rate and they stayed there for two years before a special Act allowed their release. Dissenters were disappointed that the church reform acts of 1836–40 did not contain mention of abolishing rates, and local votes continued to generate civic unrest. In Manchester, the churchwardens were sworn in to the accompaniment of the diocesan chancellor warning that they must enforce the payment of rates to avoid 'the separation of the State from God'. In towns like Braintree, Wakefield and Portsea the rate continued to be a major source of distress. Chadwick calculated that between 1833 and 1851 there were 632 votes across the country, of which 148 were lost to the Church. In many parishes the clergy concluded that the division caused by rates was unacceptable, and abandoned them, relying instead on voluntary contributions. It was to be 1868 before rates were abolished.

The Whigs and Church Patronage, 1830–41

The Parliamentary Reform Act of 1832 and the reforms of the 1830s established the Whigs as the brokers of social and political reform and laid out the path of ecclesiastical reform for thirty-five years. Nevertheless, in Parliament the Whigs relied on the constitutional features of the pre-reform era. Even before the crisis of 1831–2 was upon the government, Grey talked of preparing the House of Lords. He certainly tried to arrange the bench of bishops so that it would be less hostile during the storm of 1831–2. After the reform Act the Whig governments of Grey and Melbourne resorted to an Erastian relationship with the Church that resembled the Hanoverian regime. Moreover, having determined to reform the Church, the Whigs nevertheless distributed Church patronage according to the tenets of the 'unreformed' Church.

After 1832 the nature of the establishment was re-evaluated by the government and church. Best emphasised that this meant in effect closer political relations between the Church and the State. The government was forced to respond to its own agenda of reform with techniques of Church patronage which were designed to entrench its political interests in the House of Lords. Before they assumed office the Whigs had the reputation of hostility to the Church. In 1828, Bishop Lloyd of Oxford scathingly referred to the Whig leaders as dominated by an atheist (Holland), a Unitarian (Lansdowne) and a deist (Brougham). Melbourne also indicated that the Whigs were unsympathetic to the Church when he commented that he saw no difference between Anglicanism and Roman Catholicism. Moreover, it had long been a Whig view that religion and politics were distinct and separate things. In 1832, at a meeting in Leeds, Macaulay expounded this view. Nevertheless, the Whigs believed that the State had a duty to regulate and reform the Church. This was one of the principles which lay behind the work of the Ecclesiastical commission. Henry Bathurst, himself the son of a bishop, wrote in 1833 that 'the state has a right to re-model the Church as to its internal arrangements with a view to its efficiency'. Lord John Russell shared this view. Some Whigs believed that the bishops were even subject to state control. George Pryme, a Whig MP, called them 'public functionaries'. But these views were simply reflections of the theory upon which Whig principles were based. They stemmed from the ideas on Church and State of Warburton,

Blackstone and Burke in the eighteenth century. Once the reins of power fell to Grey, and subsequently to Melbourne, the Whigs faced a dilemma. Were the Whigs to effect their ideals on the separation of politics and religion, and to promote a Church reformed of abuses and one conforming to Benthamite ethics of efficiency? Or were they to exploit the Church – and particularly its patronage – to further Whig ambitions in domestic reforms?[12]

It was clear that the Whig ministries of the period 1830–41, dominated by pragmatic Whigs like Grey and Melbourne, opted for a compromise. As a result the Whigs found themselves in the paradoxical position of promoting the end of abuse and inefficiency in the various Acts of the 1830s – measures that Melbourne described as 'to go at the Bishops'. But the same governments exploited the opportunities offered by the State's relationship with the Church, and strengthened this relationship, by advancing partisan (and perhaps unworthy) men to the bench of bishops in the House of Lords. Indeed, one of the government's own supporters referred to Melbourne's nominees to the bench of bishops as 'artful and rapacious' clergy.

Lord Grey in 1830 faced a serious problem. He inherited a bench of bishops comprising Tory appointees for the previous twenty years; most were Ultra Tories. Grey realised that, if he was to succeed with the Reform Bill, he would have to introduce and strengthen Whigs on the bench of bishops. In 1831, he tried to promote the pro-reform Whig Bishop Bathurst with the offer of the archbishopric of Dublin. The bishops themselves sensed that they were under pressure from the Whigs to vote for reform. In the light of this concern, Grey's first nomination was a surprise; he translated Robert Carr to Worcester. Carr had acted as a political agent in the Chichester election of 1818 in the Tory interest. The advancement was an act of loyalty by Grey to King George IV who had asked Grey to do this before he died. However, the advancement of Carr was very swift, so that he could take his seat and vote in the Reform debate in the Lords. Grey hoped that the appointment might put Carr under some obligation to support the government on the Reform Bill. But, in the light of the Reform Bill controversy, the three remaining appointments effected by Grey were predictably partisan. Maltby, who was the nominee of the staunchly Whig Russell family, was advanced to Chichester. He was an avowed Whig, who supported both Catholic relief and parliamentary reform. The second appointment, that of Edward Grey to the see of Hereford in 1832, caused a great sensation as he was the prime minister's brother. Grey's preferment of his brother cannot be seen as other than a doubly partisan appointment. The new Bishop Grey surprised everyone by supporting the Tories on many issues. As a result, ironically, he was refused preferment to Durham in 1836 by Melbourne. The last of Grey's partisan nominees was Joseph Allen, advanced to Bristol after the reform crisis in 1834. It was an unpopular decision as Allen was an ineffective cleric and an appalling preacher, nevertheless the Whigs could rely upon him because he had been tutor to Althorp.

The Whig governments, after 1832, felt confirmed in their determination to advance the cause of reform; and the Church felt that it would be the first sacrifice to the mob. The Church braced itself against the impact of hostility which the Whigs were expected to unleash onto it. Indeed, the hard-line Tory bishops felt under even greater threat than they had during the Reform Bill crisis. In February 1833, Van Mildert wrote of the king's speech, the new Parliament and the chance of church reform, that 'the great evil is that the ministers seem purposely to keep us in the dark as to their intentions so that it is impossible for us to be prepared for them'. However, the experience of passing the Reform Act had exhausted Grey, and the government did not directly challenge the establishment of the Church. Perhaps, moreover, the government saw the advantage of a corps of voters in the Lords whose composition could be influenced by the distribution of patronage.

After Grey's resignation in 1834, Melbourne's patronage was as notorious as Grey's for its partisan nature. Dr Lushington recorded a conversation with Melbourne about a candidate for a mitre:

' "Is he a good man?" Melbourne asked.
"An excellent man; he is a most accomplished theologian and is truly beloved throughout his district."

"Aye aye, I understand all that; but is he a good man? Is he a Whig?" '

Melbourne, determined that the bishops would not obstruct his legislation, established a system which enabled him to filter out unacceptable men, specifically those who would not support his government in the Lords. In considering Stanley for Norwich in 1837, Melbourne mused that 'all that can be said against him is, that he has upon some occasion attended public meetings and spoken at them; but I have never heard his speeches accused of either violence or impropriety'. So Stanley was advanced to Norwich. It was Melbourne's practice to tell a man that he intended to appoint him to a diocese, and then ask him about his political views. The prospective bishop either pledged himself to Melbourne in a moment of gratitude, or if his reply was disappointing, was quietly promised that he would be considered for future appointments as they arose. However, this system did not always work to Melbourne's advantage. In 1836 Longley, the new Bishop of Ripon, voted against the government's Irish Church Rates Bill in his first session in the Lords. Melbourne wrote to him to say that he felt it 'was politically the most hostile [course] that could be devised and . . . was neither civil nor considerate . . . If your conscience disapproves the measure, you cannot support it. [But] the disadvantage of your not doing so will fall solely upon me.' In fact Longley had warned Melbourne that he disagreed with the government on some church affairs and would oppose the government in the Lords. Melbourne had nevertheless agreed to advance him. Subsequently, Longley replied that he regretted voting against the government. However, it was not that in appointing Longley Melbourne chose a man of known political independence; Longley's appointment was obtained through the influence of Sir Henry Parnell, one of Melbourne's ministers.

Of the thirteen bishops nominated or translated by Melbourne, ten were Whigs. This suggests that the Whig government was only interested in the eradication of abuse in the Church if it did not reduce the powers of the State. Some of these bishops, like Musgrave and Bowstead, were otherwise undistinguished. In their cases it seems that Whiggery was the prime factor in their appointment. In 1836, Musgrave and six Cambridge Whigs wrote to Lord Melbourne complaining of the lack of Whigs from Cambridge on the bench. As a result Melbourne nominated Musgrave and Bowstead to the bench. Other appointees were deserving Whigs who had been denied a mitre during the preceding Tory era. In 1836, for example, when Butler was made Bishop of Lichfield and Coventry, Melbourne wrote: 'I am sorry that unavoidable circumstances have so long delayed your elevation to the bench but have this day directed the necessary steps to be taken for creating you bishop.'

In 1837, Melbourne enquired of Christopher Wordsworth: 'Are his opinions entirely Liberal, and could you learn for us whether he would go with us on the Church Rate question?' A number of bishops were, like Longley, advanced through the traditional network of political influence and aristocratic interests that, under Liverpool, had waned in importance. Grey had been embarrassed by the Lord Chancellor's agreement to the appointment of the son of Bishop Sparke to the living of Wisbech, worth £2000 a year in 1832. Sparke was a notorious nepotist and the appointment was seen as the Sparke family milking more money from the Church. Another interesting political appointee was Connop Thirlwall, who was advanced to St David's in 1840. Thirlwall was a controversial clergyman, who had provoked a storm by advancing the view that dissenters ought to be admitted to Cambridge. He had been forced out of Cambridge and had been given a living by the Lord Chancellor. Thirlwall's appointment was made in order that he could exercise his much needed oratory in the Lords in the Whig interest. Higher up the ladder of preferment the Whigs were equally influenced by family and social ties. Bishops Pepys and Shuttleworth were nominated through the influence of Whig grandees. Such was Melbourne's reputation for nominating the relatives of political colleagues that in 1835 Peel said that it would not surprise him if Melbourne nominated any future son of Lord John Russell to the bench of bishops. It is not surprising, therefore, that some of Melbourne's bishops were socially well connected, and this is certainly true of Longley, Shuttleworth, Stanley, Eden and Pepys. But three of Melbourne's bishops came from the classes that were the rarest in the ministry: Musgrave was a tailor's son; Butler was a draper's son and Bowstead from a poor Cumberland family.

As a result of these appointments the young Gladstone noted that Whig church patronage was highly partisan. Melbourne's bishops, if predominantly partisan, were not necessarily 'bad'. Robert Eden, advanced to Sodor and Man in 1847, and by no means a Whig, was an outstanding pastor and diocesan. Thirlwall, a strong reforming bishop, is another good example of the principle that political appointees were not of necessity bad bishops. Otter and Denison were both scholars and men of impressive learning.

In the men whom Melbourne kept from the bench there is further evidence not merely of partisan attitudes but also of the motives that stood behind them. In refusing a mitre for Dr Arnold of Rugby, against the advice of influential supporters like Archbishop Whately and the Lord President, he commented, 'what have Tory churchmen ever done for me that I should make them a present of such a handle against my government?' Bishops' seats in the Lords were undoubtedly the most important ecclesiastical issue for Melbourne. Longley of Ripon had repaid what Melbourne saw as his misguided patronage with betrayal but the prime minister had no intention of allowing a deliberate repetition of the affair. This was particularly important in the light of the Whigs' programme of reforms. Here Melbourne's radical colleagues came into conflict with the prime minister. Faced in 1837 with the proposal to exclude bishops from seats in the House of Lords, Melbourne followed the pragmatic path. His government voted to maintain the bishops' privilege – though a number of radical Whigs voted for the motion. Opponents like Graham assumed that the government was attempting to avoid the accusation of dismantling the Establishment. But the reality of the situation was that Melbourne's interests militated in favour of retention of his growing Whig corps of supporters in the Lords. By the end of the 1830s Melbourne had appointed a number of bishops who were energetic supporters of government proposals in the Lords. Among them were Ryder and Longley who strongly supported factory reform. Thirlwall was also a model of a reforming Whig bishop in his attitude to education and continued to be so well into the century. Indeed, a token of the Whigs' opinion of the usefulness of bishops was Grey's appointment in 1832 of Blomfield and Sumner to the Royal commission on the Poor Law.

Melbourne, however, was generally unsympathetic to the Church as an institution. When Peel set up the second Ecclesiastical commission in 1835 he allowed it to be more clerical in flavour than Melbourne would have liked. In 1837, Melbourne reneged on a bargain he accepted from Peel's short ministry which agreed that no bill would come before Parliament which did not have the support of the Ecclesiastical commission. In 1837, for example, the Church Rates Bill violated this convention. There can be little doubt of Melbourne's contempt for the Church; on one occasion he remarked to the archbishop of York, 'you bishops are sad dogs'. And to Queen Victoria he said, 'Bishops should be young, else they go off directly and don't learn anything.'

Melbourne also displayed a marked bias toward Cambridge men; he was a Cambridge graduate himself. Ten of his thirteen bishops were Cambridge graduates and four came from Melbourne's old college, Trinity. Melbourne defended his actions by saying, 'Trinity produces ten able men, when any other seminary produces one.' Moreover, Trinity was in many ways a nursery of liberal Whig divines of varying shades. In 1837, Melbourne told Howley that he found it almost impossible to find suitable Oxford divines; by which he meant clergy without a taint of Toryism or Tractarianism.

Melbourne was also forced to abandon the practice of doubling the credit available to a premier by shuffling vacancies. In the previous administrations premiers tended to advance 'junior' bishops to vacancies in senior sees and then appoint a new junior bishop, thus making two appointments for one vacancy. The process had the advantage of gaining more support for a prime minister in the House of Lords. Melbourne, however, was denied this advantage. The regularisation of episcopal incomes in the 1836 Established Church Act removed the ladder of preferment and eroded the episcopal hierarchy. There were no longer junior, middling and senior sees (other than the primacies and prestigious sees like London, Durham and Winchester). Melbourne was thus obliged to appoint directly to sees in a way unthinkable when dioceses carried different incomes. Davys went directly to Peterborough; Denison to Salisbury; Musgrave to Hereford; and Stanley to Norwich. Possibly Melbourne's attitude toward this arose also from the fact that he found the exercise of Church patronage distasteful and could generate little enthusiasm for it.[13] Church patronage was irksome to him. On one occasion he said, 'Damn it, another bishop dead! They do it to vex me.'

Four years after Melbourne left office, Prince Albert expressed a Whiggish view when he suggested to Bishop Wilberforce that 'a bishop ought to abstain completely from mixing himself up with the politics of the day, and beyond giving a general support to the Queen's government, and occasionally voting for it, should take no part in the discussion of State affairs'. It might have been expected that this would have been the achievement of nearly a decade of Whig rule. Yet Whigs like Archbishop Whately were disappointed by the governments of Grey and Melbourne. In 1831, he had started his archiepiscopate in high spirits. He had strong views on the reform of the Church. Before his appointment to Dublin he had advocated radical parliamentary reform and church reform on a scale that placed him firmly among the radical Whigs. His plan included the proposal that the bishops should have no place in the House of Lords, and that clergy be eligible for election to the Commons. Before long he was urging Grey on to effect changes. In 1832, he proposed 'the appointment of commissioners to devise, digest and submit' plans for new church government. But the radical reform of the Church he sought did not appear. By 1836 he was reduced to asking Bishop Copleston why the bishops did not agree to present some proposal to the government. But by 1839 Whately had withdrawn from attendance at Parliament and had clearly become disillusioned by what his Whig colleagues had achieved. Whately's disillusionment was a product of the divergence of the Whig principles from their self-interest. Their principles led them to radical reform, but their self-interest caused them to turn about and adopt traditional patterns of patronage. Thus the product of a reformed Church was promoted by outdated methods of patronage.

Reform and the Oxford Movement

One of the achievements of the reform crises of the 1830s was to act as a clarion call to High Churchmen. As Perry Butler has pointed out, the threat of democracy took on an apocalyptic aspect to men like Gladstone. It effected a major transformation in attitudes to the State. After 1832 Gladstone was committed to the service of the Church and of Christianising the social order. However the Reform Bill crisis of 1830–2 did not simply generate High Church feeling; it provided it with a focus. Newman and Froude had been active at Oxford, quietly developing their High Church views during the 1820s. In 1829, the issue of Catholic emancipation drew together an alliance of High Churchmen who voted Peel out of his seat at Oxford in favour of the Ultra Tory and High Anglican Robert Inglis.

The attack unleashed on the Church in 1830 provoked a High Church defence of episcopacy. Newman wrote articles in the *British Magazine* attacking the Whig policy for parliamentary and ecclesiastical reform. By 1833 other High Churchmen like Keble, Rose and Palmer had responded to the call to the defence of the Church. In July 1833, Keble's assize sermon denounced the government's reform of the Irish Church as sacrilegious and warned of 'National Apostasy'. There was no homogeneity between the High Churchmen. Froude, for example, disliked the relationship between Church and State and wanted the Church to elect its own bishops; whereas Palmer and Rose were committed to the Establishment. All of them agreed, though, that the debate on reform had been a political one, and had neglected the spiritual and doctrinal issues at stake. Indeed, spiritual explanations were provided for the circumstances of the 1830s; Newman's view was that political troubles were a reflection of the spiritual weaknesses of the people. The *Tracts for the Times* were an attempt to correct this by placing emphasis on the apostolic nature of church government, and on divine rather than parliamentary authority. Apostolic succession neatly promoted the disenfranchisement of dissenters and gave an authority to the Church wholly within its control. It was a defiant response to reform. Many comparisons were made between the bishops and

Whigs and the apostles and the Roman government of Judea. Newman wrote in *Apologia pro Vita Sua* that his study, in 1833, of the fourth-century Christians produced a useful comparison with his own age: 'with the Establishment . . . divided and threatened . . . I compared that fresh vigorous Power of which I was reading . . . her triumphant zeal . . ., the self-conquest of her Ascetics, the patience of her Martyrs, the irresistible determination of her Bishops . . . I said to myself, "Look on this picture and on that"; I felt anger for my own Church.'

The initial impact of the Tractarians was not, as they had hoped, among the general public. Indeed, the tracts were largely circulated among like-minded clergymen. The Tractarians also worked hard to support a declaration to the archbishop, made in February 1834. The declaration deprecated the reform of the Church and reasserted deep attachment to the apostolic succession. Its presentation, by ten archdeacons and leading Tractarians, achieved little. But the nation-wide campaign to obtain 7000 clerical signatures for the declaration achieved an element of reassurance for the Church at a time when Reform seemed to threaten. Writing a decade later Palmer claimed:

> we knew not to what quarter to look for support. A Prelacy threatened and apparently intimidated; a Government making its powers subservient to agitators who avowedly sought the destruction of the Church. The State, so long the guardian of the Church, now becoming its enemy and tyrant . . . And worst of all – no principle in the public mind to which we could appeal.[14]

The Oxford Movement thus took on the form of a reactionary rearguard defence of episcopacy and apostolic government because of the threat that faced the Church in the 1830s. With Catholics and dissenters qualified to sit in Parliament it was impossible to argue that the Church's authority rested on parliamentary writ. Tractarianism also took on aspects of its traditional inheritance from the Church: Toryism, hostility to Dissent and the duty to uphold ancient tradition. These were the touchstone of reaction; novelty and innovation were regarded as corruptions of the apostolic tradition. Keble, who Newman described as 'the true and primary author' of the movement, strongly asserted the rights of the Church that establishment guaranteed. Such a reaction to the events of the 1830s produced a particular view of the Church's duty. The image of pastoral care most highly valued by the leaders of the movement was that of the rural parson, not of the industrial parish. Indeed, Edward King, the Tractarian bishop who did most to promote High Church pastoralia later in the nineteenth century, was without any experience of urban church life. It was a feature of the Tractarians that lost them support from potential friends: Hook was one such, who recognised that in the urban industrial north only cooperation with the State could achieve the mission of the Church.

The Tractarian image also contained an assumption about the Church in the new circumstances. It assumed that the Church would no longer retain the support of all the people. The Tractarians had a message which would not be palatable to all, and the clergy could not expect all the people to respond to it. The Tractarians' belief that they were right and that they represented the repository of church tradition was more important than their desire for popularity. In the short term, therefore, the clergy would have to reconcile themselves to emptier churches, and to winning back gradually the people to the true traditions of the Church. Whatever the truth of the situation, this assumption reassured the clergy, for whom the events of 1828–32 had created the fear of a popularity contest with the forces of Catholicism and Dissent. It was an optimism which the young Gladstone felt and expressed in his *Church Principles considered in their results* in 1840.

The Tractarians also asserted a paradoxical response to the eighteenth century Church. They reaffirmed their belief in the Establishment: 'Church and King' was a popular cry. But they also placed heavy emphasis, through patristic scholarship, on the more ancient traditions of the Church. Keble, for example, compared the teachings of the Church in the early nineteenth century with that of the apostles, and found the former wanting. In particular the eighteenth century Church placed emphasis on rationalism and efficiency, whereas Keble supported the ancient reliance on the mysterious and miraculous nature of revelation and the Church's teaching.

Mystery also lay at the heart of the High Church promotion of ritual. The foundation in 1839 of the Camden Society at Cambridge was not intended to be other than the creation of an undergraduate antiquarian society. But it promoted enormous interest in church restoration. Popular ritualism and gothic architecture quickly became an outward sign of the Oxford Movement's spiritual and doctrinal ideals. The Camden Society, principally through its journal *The Ecclesiologist*, promoted the return to earlier forms of architecture, decoration, ritual, and by implication, doctrine. The Tractarian ideas of the mystery of the Church's revelations found a comfortable home in the decoration of churches which raised sacraments to a higher status. But ritualism did not have a healing influence on the Church. By the end of the 1840s Blomfield had left the Camden Society and denounced ritualism in a charge to his clergy. In Exeter there were surplice riots, and from 1845 onwards the ecclesiastical courts were full of cases of clergy or laity hostile to ritualism. Tory Churchmen found themselves in a dilemma; they supported the reaction to the reforms of the period, but found themselves appalled by the doctrinal changes implied by ritualism. Phillpotts, one of the die-hard bishops who had refused to support the Reform Act, also undertook the prosecution of ritualists. Accusations that the Additional Curates Society, founded in 1837, was establishing Tractarian priests across the country led to a cooling in support for its work by a number of bishops. The Tractarians were as much authors of exclusivity as victims of it. They did not subscribe to the view that the Church of England was a broad church, able to accommodate all views.

Their intolerance was most visible in the attack on Hampden's appointment as Regius Professor of Divinity. Newman, Keble, Pusey and Golightly disliked Hampden's advocacy of the admission of dissenters to Oxford, but they denounced his appointment on the grounds of his heretical views. Parliament was bombarded with petitions and protests, bishops lobbied the King, MPs raised the matter in Parliament and dons threatened to refuse to allow their students to attend Hampden's lectures. Hampden sought to resign the nomination to the post rather than face an orchestrated campaign against him, though Melbourne forced him to accept it.

The orthodox High Church clergy also responded directly to the Whig's church reforms. In 1845, Bishop Denison of Salisbury told his clergy that the association of the Church with secular policies, like the Poor Law, would create social friction. Many preferred the revival of the offertory, which collected alms for the poor in a sacerdotal rather than a secular atmosphere. Equal weight was placed on education as a result of the Oxford Movement. Education was advanced as a route back to the Tractarian ideal. The threat of secular schooling or inter-denominational schools was one which the High Church move-ment tried to oppose. The high view of the priesthood, which the Tractarians promoted, denied a role for the State or laity in Church schools. Many bishops, even those sympathetic to the High Church movement like Samuel Wilberforce, recognised that the Tractarians had an 'unbending rigidity' in their views. Blomfield feared that mystery, ornament and ritual would create confusion in the minds of the uneducated members of the congregation. He was quite wrong, as the slum priests showed; emphasis on ornament and mystery often generated popular attendance at church.

Assessments of the Oxford Movement have tended to emphasise its success. Virgin claimed it was a 'movement of the mind' and as such it was a great success. After the 1840s there were increasing numbers of priests who adhered to High Church principles. The model of pastoral work the Tractarians advanced, in common with the evangelicals, found assonance with the enlarged system of parish management promoted by the ecclesiastical reforms. By the end of the nineteenth century there were few towns and villages where Victorian gothic had not appeared in some form, where there was no heightened ritual or where there was no increase in the frequency of celebration of the sacraments. Armstrong of East Dereham, in December 1872, recounted to his diary the details of the procession of the Guild of St Nicholas. A gold cross, an effigy and full eucharistic vestments were used; 'who would have thought this possible in Dereham?' asked the euphoric vicar. Many such clergy suffered from abuse and attack, particularly after the secession of Newman, Manning and Robert Wilberforce to the Roman Catholic Church. Riots broke out at St Barnabas Pimlico in 1850 and at St George's in the East in 1859 over Charles Lowder's Tractarianism. But the High Church movement survived these squalls to become one of the principal strands of the Church of England. In this sense the Oxford Movement was a success.

The movement was also a striking failure. Its founders had a specific objective in the 1830s. They hoped to be able to sweep away the Ecclesiastical commission and restore authority in the Church to the bishops through the revival of an apostolic view of church government. In this goal the movement signally failed. There never was a widespread reaction to the control exercised by parliament over the Church. Parish clergy up and down the country may have possessed some of the *Tracts for the Times* or Keble's work on the Christian fathers, but far fewer subscribed to the zealous assertion of church government by apostolic episcopacy. Those clergy with experience in the urban industrial parishes saw the logic and necessity of reform. Moreover, before 1850 the Oxford Movement was too radical and controversial to develop mass support within the clergy. The turmoil of 'Papal Aggression' was sufficient controversy for the clergy, without contending with further fears from within. The conversion of Newman, Manning and Robert Wilberforce may in itself reflect the frustration of the Tractarians at their own failure to achieve this specific objective. Perhaps also a feature of the Oxford Movement which might be held to have contributed to its failure was what a recent essay has called the doctrine of reserve. 'Tractarian spirituality disliked all that was flamboyant. It shrank from religion in the market-square. It was not fond of seeking publicity.'[15] The Tractarians might dislike publicity but they could not succeed without it, as they found to their cost.

A further factor in the failure of the Tractarians was the bilateral decision of Whigs and Tories to embargo the appointment of any cleric tainted with Tractarianism. This denied the movement leaders of status in the Church. Not only were Tractarians *personae non gratae*, but avowedly anti-Tractarians attracted preferment. This, in part, explains the reluctance of Melbourne and Palmerston to appoint Oxford divines. A. T. Gilbert's appointment to Chichester in 1842 by Peel was interpreted as a direct reward for opposing Isaac Williams in the contest for the Professorship of Poetry at Oxford. Peel was also responsible for the appointment of the stern anti-Tractarian Thomas Turton to the deanery of Westminster. The appointments of Prince Lee and Graham to dioceses also seemed to be a reward for virulent opponents of Tractarianism. The only Tractarian to reach the bench, Hamilton, received his nomination as the result of a terrible mistake by the incompetent Lord Aberdeen.[16] In such circumstances the morale of adherents of the Oxford Movement was lowered. For a clergyman with an eye to the future the message was clear, and those who were supporters by conviction were marginalised. They had only a minor role to play in determining the policy of the Church.

5

RELIGION AND SOCIETY OUTSIDE THE ESTABLISHMENT

Roman Catholicism and 'Papal Aggression'

The removal of Catholic disabilities in 1829 played a part in the reversal of the decline in Catholic numbers which the eighteenth century had seen fall to 80,000 by 1780. The increase in numbers had begun before 1829: by 1800 numbers had risen to an estimated 129,000 and by 1840 to 371,500. However, the movement towards Catholic emancipation did not cause this increase; it acted as a political context within which other factors operated. The principal factor was Irish–Catholic immigration, particularly into the industrial cities which had a need for cheap labour. The Irish agricultural crisis also promoted migration from Ireland. Against this flood, the numbers of ancient Catholic families and the mid-century converts from High Anglicanism were a minority. The Catholic Church thus had to contend with massive expansion in numbers as well as a significant shift in the class and social composition of its supporters. There was some extensive church building: 1841 saw the building of St Chad's, Birmingham, and seven years later St George's, Southwark, was completed. Bishop Ullathorne's episcopate at Birmingham (1848–8) saw the establishment of forty-four missions (as parishes were called) and sixty-seven new churches. However, by the 1840s, most Catholic clergy were still by definition slum priests, using small rooms or meanly built churches. In Liverpool in 1850 the Pitt Street area was described as 'to a great extent Irish, & of course Popish; and the neighbourhood has become proverbially poor, squalid, noisy and every way uninviting'.[1]

Few Catholic seminarians, educated in the traditions of Douay or other genteel establishments, were prepared for the life of priest to Irish navvies. In this situation the vicars-apostolic faced a dilemma in the provision of clergy (which had always been problematic); they might try to import Irish priests for the large congregations, but such priests would not be likely to attract English converts. Attempts to use Italian and other foreign priests were not a satisfactory solution either. Above all they fuelled the Wesleyan view that Catholicism was essentially disloyal and un-English. In these circumstances, most vicars-apostolic were resigned to an inadequate supply of priests, and resorted to 'galloping priests' serving more than one church. There were additional problems for the priests, in particular the divergent views of how 'Roman' their worship should be. Some laity felt that the Catholic church needed to be as English as possible to gain popular acceptance, others, particularly Irish Catholics, felt that ultramontanism was a purer approach to faith which they should cling to. Naturally, the clergy tended towards one view or other, but when a priest was moved from one congregation to another he might often find a different mood prevailing.

The vicars-apostolic of England and Wales, who in 1840 were increased in number from four to eight, were largely dependent upon their congregations for funds. This meant that they were largely poverty-stricken, if not bankrupt, and hostages to the fortunes of the laity. For the most part the vicars-apostolic lacked financial acumen, and their investments were frequently bad, in one case causing Bishop Ullathorne to spend ten days in Warwick gaol. They were also beset with problems with Rome, and particularly the Congregation of Propaganda which controlled the 'mission' to England, and which seemed to lack any understanding of the situation in which the clergy found themselves. The decision in 1838 to remove control of religious orders from the vicars-apostolic was an example of Rome's failure to appreciate the situation in England. The result was a decline in the cooperation between monks and secular clergy, which affected the lives of the laity. In some areas the feuds between monks and secular clergy became a significant problem. The vicars-apostolic felt that the root of most of their problems was principally England's mission status, which denied them a constitutional hierarchy of bishops. Rome, influenced by Cardinal Acton, who was suspicious of English priests, denied repeated requests for a hierarchy. In part Acton was right, the English vicars-apostolic did not cooperate with each other, apart from their meetings held annually after 1825, at which the episcopal differences were frequently evident. Nor were the vicars-apostolic able to assert their control over patronage, which tended to lie with the local laity.

The British government's attitude to Catholicism was driven more by pragmatism than by principles of church government. It suited the Whig government of Russell in 1847 to court the votes of the Irish Catholic MPs on which the government – after the collapse of Peel's ministry – was dependent. It was also important to the Whigs to forge diplomatic links with the apparently liberal Pius IX (whom they saw as a bulwark in Italy against Austrian autocracy). Moreover, with Acton's death in the same year, Rome seemed willing to consider approving a plan for the creation of bishoprics across England. Delayed by the revolutions of 1848 the plan for thirteen dioceses was promulgated in the late summer of 1850. The hierarchy was careful to avoid the names of English see cities, as forbidden by the 1829 Act. Nevertheless, Wiseman's inflammatory pastoral letter, announcing the hierarchy and his own elevation as Cardinal Archbishop of Westminster, drew attacks from *The Times* for the presumptuousness of calling the archiepiscopal see Westminster. *Punch* depicted Pope Pius using a burglar's jemmy to break into a church, and also as Guy Fawkes trying to blow up Parliament;[2] its editorial even proposed the repeal of Catholic emancipation. It was particularly unfortunate that Wiseman talked in a high-flown manner in his letter of 'governing' his diocese. – Queen Victoria asked, when she heard of it, 'Am I Queen of England or am I not?' – though she also confided to her diary that she could not bear the abuse heaped upon the many 'good and innocent' Catholics by Wiseman's foolishness. Some windows were stoned, priests were hooted, and a number of cartoons took a swing at the new bishops, but there was no major disturbance.

The cry of 'papal aggression' emerged some weeks after the announcement of the creation of a Catholic hierarchy, and was in part generated by the prime minister's letter replying to Bishop Maltby. Russell's letter appeared to denounce the creation of the hierarchy as 'insolent and insidious'. He promised to consider whether a law was necessary to restrain the papacy but suggested that the greatest danger was not from Catholicism, but from the Catholic tendency within the Church of England, which he said was leading England to the 'edge of the precipice'. Why Russell should abandon years of commitment to religious toleration in this way is not easily explained: perhaps he was piqued by Pius IX's renunciation of liberalism and his uncooperative attitude to the problem of Ireland, or it may have been a ruse to avoid the admission that the government had been in direct contact with the papacy for some months. Machin sees it as a thoughtless attempt by Russell to gain some easy popularity. Either way, it prompted an outburst of violent opinions from all quarters, including Wiseman who gave up a self-imposed silence to respond. Battle-lines were drawn between Protestants and Catholics, even the Duke of Norfolk ranged himself on the side of the Church of England. Protests against the 'papal aggression' were arranged in most Anglican dioceses. They acted as a rallying call for Protestants so recently stimulated by the Gorham judgment in which Bishop Phillpotts held that George Gorham's strong Protestantism disqualified him from institution to a parish. Much of the protestation emphasised the supremacy of the Crown and the Establishment: Hook saw the hierarchy as a direct challenge to English laws, Church and independence. Only a few dissenters saw the value of the hierarchy in promoting religious pluralism, thereby strengthening their position; for the most part their strong Protestant views led them into the hysterical fray.

The cabinet was bounced into support for anti-papalism by drafting legislation to criminalise the use of territorial titles by Roman Catholic bishops. The government was resigned to the loss of Irish Catholic support, and extended the bill to include

Ireland, which had always had its own hierarchy. The Ecclesiastical Titles Bill was hacked about in the Commons and did not contain any real penalties for the use of titles, but it received the royal assent in July 1851 and re-established a disability for the Catholic Church. Perhaps it was the revenge of a government which expected gratitude for its magnanimity and toleration, but felt it had been roughly treated by Wiseman.[3] Chadwick's view is that the benefits of the episode, the establishment of a hierarchy, outweighed the short-term turbulence of the 1851 Act which few people took seriously.[4] There were occasional disturbances against priests and chapels during the 1850s, but 'papal aggression' was soon forgotten. Ralls holds that the anti-Catholic feeling was a product of four popular attitudes in Britain. These were the huge increase in the Catholic numbers; a sense that Catholicism was 'foreign'; a belief that Catholicism was challenging Protestantism in the creation of monasteries and the use of robes which indicated the intention of the Catholics to convert England, and a sense of insecurity within the Church at the rise of other denominations.[5]

Thus the issue of 'papal aggression' was perhaps as much a statement of the position of Protestantism, and particularly Anglicanism, as it was of Catholicism. Fuelled by Palmerston's xenophobic foreign policy there was a sense of fear and insecurity in the attitudes which emerged in 1850, that was only massaged away by the Great Exhibition of 1851. The 'papal aggression' episode was essentially an anachronism which was a throwback to the days of Anglican monopoly. It suggested that the toleration of 1829 was not unlimited, although the religious census suggested that this view could not last long. As the diversity of religious provision in Britain became apparent it was more difficult to assert the foreign nature of Catholicism, particularly as ritualism grew in scale. This was emphasised by the irony that the Ecclesiastical Titles Act was considered by Parliament at the same time as the Jewish Relief Bill. No bishops were prosecuted under the Act, which was quietly abandoned in 1871. It was a bitter irony for Russell that his government was brought down in 1852 by the votes of Irish Catholic MPs.

The episode also marked an important transition within the Catholic Church to greater control by the clergy and bishops.

Throughout the eighteenth and early years of the nineteenth centuries the Catholic Church had been dominated by the prosperous laity; it was they who had won the gradual removal of disabilities and had earned the acceptance of successive governments. After 1850 the clergy were more prominent: authority and leadership of the hierarchy were emphasised. It was this clerical control which allowed a steady development after 1850 towards ultramontanism.

The New Dissent: the Development of Methodism

The relationship between the Church of England and Methodism after the death of Wesley was a complex one. The decision in 1795 to allow each Methodist church to hold a eucharist service, administered by Methodist rather than Anglican clergy was in effect the final breach which created a new denomination out of the existing Wesleyan Methodist Connexion. Wesley's ordination of Alexander Mather in 1788 had opened a breach between the Church and Methodism, but Wesley had been careful to avoid calling such men priests; they were generally ordained deacons and then referred to as elders or superintendents. By 1791 oversight of the Methodist societies was placed in the hands of the Methodist Conference, establishing a new authority to which the Methodists could look, which fulfilled the role of bishops. The Methodist's Leeds Conference in 1793 resolved to abolish the distinction between preachers, ministers and laity (robes and titles were to be disused). Contemporary opinion was unclear whether this supported the views of those Methodists who favoured the retention of the link with the Church of England, or those who favoured a breach with the Church. The Conference in Manchester, in 1795, was therefore an attempt to clarify the situation for the Methodists with a Plan for Pacification. A committee representing different viewpoints in the Methodist Connexion was formed to address the question of sacraments. The committee's decision was an attempt at compromise. Sacraments could be held in such chapels and at such times as the local leaders, stewards and trustees decided, subject to the conference. However, the rite was to be that of the Church of England. The decision was broad enough to allow the younger preachers to seek Wesleyan ordination and to develop their own chapels, and to allow the preachers of the older tradition to continue their proximity to the Church of England.

This did not allow for the independent minds of Alexander Kilham and his supporters who wanted complete local democratic autonomy, and as a result in 1797 they left the Conference to form the Methodist New Connexion. 'High Wesleyanism', though, was slow to develop a separate identity. This was in part a product of the Wesleyan insistence on respectability and loyalty to the government. Thomas Coke, for example, volunteered intelligence to the Home Office on radical activities in the north-west; Wesleyans opposed the revivalism of the first few years of the nineteenth century as too closely akin to Quakerism; and in his interview with Prime Minister Perceval in 1812 Thomas Allan, a Methodist solicitor, emphasised the absence of any threat to the government from Methodism. This desire for respectability spilled over into worship: as late as 1826 Henry Moore was the first preacher in his chapel to preside at a eucharist service, which had hitherto been administered by Anglican clergy. Only in 1836 did the Methodists officially accept ordination by the laying on of hands. At the same time, cooperation with the Church of England was supported. Many Methodists attended Anglican services, even after the Marriage Act of 1836 allowed civil marriages. Only in the second half of the nineteenth century did the Methodists entirely abandon the abstention from holding services which clashed with those of the parish church. It was only in 1868 that *Punch* portrayed 'Miss Methodist' as refusing to go to church with a Puseyite clergyman. The moderation of the Wesleyans was in part a product of the leadership of Jabez Bunting. Bunting was an itinerant preacher who was drafted in to the secretariat of the conference in 1806, becoming its secretary in 1814. Bunting, like the leaders of the Clapham Sect and the Hackney Phalanx, became a powerhouse of the Wesleyan Conference. By 1820 he was its president and editor of the *Wesleyan Methodists' Magazine*.

Bunting quickly mastered the missionary work of the conference

and attained membership of every committee. A Wesleyan
Blomfield, it was said that the conference could hardly function
without Bunting's attendance. As well as being a manager,
Bunting was a conservative in theology and ritual. He supported
decorous services rather than the ranting of the radical Methodists. He maintained the Methodist model of central government
by clergy and local control by laity. Above all, he was content to
see those more radical Methodists who opposed him expelled from
the conference. While Bunting did protest against Puseyism, he
did not sour relations with the Church of England over it. His
sympathy for the Church of England even led him to say that if he
ever left Methodism he would join the Church of England,
because he could not bear the independent congregationalism of
other nonconformist sects.[6]

The radical Methodists, however, were necessarily unhappy
with this evolutionary denominationalism. From the end of the
eighteenth century there emerged, what Methodist historians
have named, 'the second awakening', a radical popularist
upsurge of evangelical Methodism. John Turner has suggested
its taproots were the radical Methodism of the USA – and
particularly the fiery itinerant preaching of Lorenzo Dow – and
the ranting Methodism of the Potteries and Yorkshire. In the
Potteries the traditions of Quakerism, left wing puritanism and
charismatic Methodism combined with the radicalism created
among unemployed weavers to create a revivalist brand of
Methodism. The revivalist camp meetings held by this Methodist
group, and in particular that held at Mow Cop, were formally
disavowed by the conference in 1807, and Hugh Bourne and
William Clowes – the two principal advocates of camp meetings –
were expelled from the conference. Primitive Methodism was too
vivid and uncontrolled for the Wesleyans: extemporary prayer
and even exorcisms were popular. Above all these Primitive
Methodists were strongly unclerical, placing far greater reliance
on lay control. When they established their own conference it
contained two lay members for every minister. By 1814 it had
spread to the Midlands and the Trent Valley and north to the
East Riding. Steadily increasing numbers of preachers 'toured
these areas, and scandalised the Wesleyan Conference by their

failure to separate men from women. Primitive Methodism seemed to flourish in both industrial and rural areas.

A political dimension to Primitive Methodism was added by the American, Dow, who had been troublesome to the government of Ireland and was the subject of anxiety on Lord Sidmouth's part. Dow promoted republicanism and supported the radical tendencies of the Primitive Methodists. Eventually, Dow's passage back to America was paid by the Wesleyans. Later in the century the Primitive Methodists were particularly strongly represented in Chartism in Lancashire, the West Riding of Yorkshire and the Midlands. As Hempton and Epstein have suggested, Methodism added a crusading zeal and a working-class sense of moral superiority to Chartism. Some historians have been quick to connect the rise of Primitive Methodism with social and economic distress, though the most recent work suggests that the post-war period of economic difficulty was not uniformly one of Primitive Methodist expansion. It may be that Primitive Methodists gained most ground from their Wesleyan brothers, rather than tilling new soil, though in Norfolk they gained from other denominations. Their strength lay in the extraordinary reliance on 'feasts and fasts' and on what has been called the 'three Rs' of ruin, repentance and redemption.[7]

The Primitive Methodists recruited largely from a slice of society below that of Wesleyan Methodism. In many areas the local shopkeeper or craftsman was the leading Primitive Methodist laymen. Gilbert calculated that the farmers, shopkeepers and higher classes made up as little as 12 per cent of the total membership of the Primitive Methodists in the first half of the nineteenth century. Their success led Sydney Smith to refer to the 'nasty numerous vermin of Methodism'. There was, however, a tendency of Primitive Methodists to graduate to respectability, Bourne and Clowes were both men who started as itinerant preachers and ended in established chapels wearing black robes and white bands.[8] This was perhaps unsurprising. The experience of itinerant preachers was generally a dispiriting one, often being attacked with stones by villagers. Once the apocalyptic days of the 1830s were over their ranting sermons carried less weight with the mid-Victorian poor. Nevertheless, they experienced enormous success in recruitment. The increase was extraordinary, Ward estimates the growth as 50,000 in eighteen years, easily out-stripping the Wesleyan rate of recruitment. In 1821 they numbered 16,394, by 1831 they had risen to 37,216 and within a further five years they had reached 62,306. By the religious census of 1851 they had easily exceeded 100,000.

This level of support required an element of organisation, and with this came policies which caused schisms. During the 1840s rules were developed regarding administration of the sacrament using bread and water, preaching on political issues and mixing teetotalism and the gospel. Splits were particularly liable to emerge over rites, music and extemporary prayer. They were perhaps the only denomination which actively saw the poor as their constituency, Wesleyans and the Church of England long having wooed the bourgeois. The Primitive Methodists developed and maintained links with trades unions (particularly agricultural unions) as the century developed. Moreover, the split with the Wesleyans allowed some Methodists to retain independent congregational control rather than a central organisation, and this also allowed radicalism to flourish. Above all revivalism and the emotional aspects of religion maintained a radical spirit within Primitive Methodism long after it had waned in Wesleyan-ism. Nevertheless, as Rosemary O'Day has indicated, even the Primitive Methodists found that in training their clergy it was impossible to maintain a radical flavour among settled commu-nities with their own clergymen.

By the mid-nineteenth century the Methodists had split into Wesleyans and the Primitive Methodists, and there were also the Methodist New Connexion, Calvinist Methodists, Wesleyan Reformers and a host of other minor free Methodist congrega-tions across the country. Gowland's study of Methodist secessions in the north of England suggests that secession was principally a product of congregational desire for independence in style of worship, rather than deep doctrinal divisions. Conflicting social divisions over issues like teetotalism, sabbatarianism and the operation of Sunday schools also promoted secession. But apart from the Wesleyans and Primitive Methodists the other sects were a small element in the two and a half million or so Methodists (of what ever brand) counted by the 1851 religious census. However, the binds that tied Methodists and other nonconformists together were as important as those that divided them. The 'Evangelical consensus', as Gilbert called it, included the importance of personal piety and conversion which was shared by most nonconformist churches. In some areas the nonconformists visited each other's churches and chapels for their respective festivals and anniversaries. And whilst there were doctrinal differences between Methodists and Baptists (on the nature of baptism for example) these rarely spilled over into disputes.

Methodism also shared with other branches of nonconformity the direction of resources into the conversion of neighbouring communities. Itinerancy, where it remained into the nineteenth century, tended to direct itself to neighbouring villages and towns. Sunday schools often spread their work to other neighbourhoods. But as a result of this lateral expansion Methodism and nonconformity shared a model of religion which necessarily involved variety and diversity. It was impossible to maintain homogeneity within a church which relied so heavily upon local circumstances and local effort. Even Wesleyan preaching circuits often faced periods in which the impetus for services had to come from within the community. In part this was the basis of the popularity of Methodism, but it also generated an individualism which legitimised diversity. Even Bunting was unable to eradicate local tastes and preferences in services and attitudes. The ability to standardise religious services and regularise the activities of each church could emerge only once the training and status of the clergy had been established in the second half of the nineteenth century.

As well as promoting social and religious diversity, Methodism, in common with other churches, promoted a particular view of self-improvement. Methodism, and especially Wesleyanism, viewed money as a gift which could be earned through labour and used for self-improvement. Gilbert has claimed that this was one of the immediate benefits some workers perceived in joining Methodism, which otherwise Thompson has branded as a 'Thou Shalt Not' sect.[9] This model should not be limited to financial advantage; it meant also social improvement and respectability through the assumption of responsibility within a community and within a congregation. It meant liberation from the traditional dependency upon a gentry or other elite. Gilbert has suggested that this escape from dependency arose largely from the non-residence of the gentry, the weakness of the parochial system, patterns of landholding and the problems of the urban parishes. All these factors played a part, but there was also the positive effect of nonconformist values permeating society. Methodism taught people of the equality of mankind in piety and faith and it was impossible to prevent this message from affecting a wider social view which eroded deference and traditional roles in society. As laymen, often Primitive Methodists from the lowest strata in society, assumed responsibility for the religious life of their village or community, it was difficult for them to accept that they could not do the same in society at large. It was clearly an incremental, creeping process, and one often unconsciously taught by nonconformity, but it shifted the ground of Victorian society fundamentally.

Old Dissent: Variety and Convergence

Britain had always retained significant numbers of dissenters whose sects pre-dated the eighteenth century: Presbyterians who rejected the Restoration settlement of 1660, the independent Congregational causes which were set up in the wake of the Glorious Revolution – of which the Baptists became the largest group – and the Quakers. They had been legally tolerated during the eighteenth century and afforded annual relief from legal penalties. Some historians, following Isaac Watts's claim that dissenters were in danger of being found only in books, have seen a danger that they were on the verge of collapse by the middle of the eighteenth century; but the evidence of their support suggests that they were moderately healthy. There was certainly a decline in the numbers of licensed places of worship for Congregationalists, Baptists and Quakers but this is not an entirely reliable measure of popular support as these groups often met in a variety of homes and other premises. By the end of the eighteenth century most of these groups experienced a major surge in support, just as the 'new' nonconformist groups did.

The Presbyterian congregations, led by Scottish theologians, during the eighteenth century became strongly rationalist and almost entirely Unitarian. There were problems in this drift to Unitarianism, as judges were prone to rule that endowments of Presbyterian chapels might not be applied to Unitarian purposes. For example, Lady Hewley's fund for Presbyterian clergy and their widows was challenged in 1833 and ruled to be available only for Trinitarians. By 1836 there was something of a split in the London Presbyterian ranks as a result on the issue of Trinitarianism, and only in 1844 did Peel's government legislate to allow endowment of Unitarian chapels. The Dissenters' Chapels Bill was subject to attack from all quarters: Wesleyans combined with High Church Tories to propose that Unitarians, far from being relieved of a disability, should be excluded from the protection of the law. Only the Whig bishops of Norwich and Durham voted for the bill, the remainder abstained or opposed it. The Presbyterians and Unitarians were principally Whigs and Liberals. Like most dissenters they had high expectations of the Whig governments of the 1830s, though few of these were realised. As late as the 1840s *The Times* refused advertisements from Unitarians and they were denied admission to King's College London and the right to present the Queen with addresses.

Chadwick's view is that the Unitarians held the ground that many Christians passed through in a journey to agnosticism or loss of faith, and certainly this is the case with Francis Newman, John Sterling and Arthur Clough. However, the Presbyterians and Unitarians claimed an educated support among the middle classes, and one with considerable commitment. The 1851 religious census suggested that they were more likely than other denominations to experience double attendance on a Sunday. As a result the life of a Unitarian or Presbyterian preacher could be comparatively comfortable: *Punch*, quoting the *Morning Post*, claimed that popular dissenting preachers could expect 'the pick of popular chapels with a crowded audience, a thousand a year, and endless invitations to 5 o'clock dinners'.

The Unitarians produced theologians as well as fashionable preachers. From the 1790s onwards they worked hard to produce their own translations of the Bible and in the nineteenth century there remained a strong tradition of unitarian theology represented principally by James Martineau. Unitarianism also had a dramatic impact on Victorian religion by denying the popular image of hell and by questioning the High Church reliance of the Cross as an image of redemption. To the orthodox Anglicans these views promoted scepticism and doubt. Unitarians also had a propensity to be men of business. E. W. Field, the reforming lawyer who gave significant evidence to the parliamentary select committee on laws of partnership, was a Unitarian. They were active in civic politics: in Leicester, they ranked just behind the Anglicans in supplying twelve councillors, and they had significant support on the councils of Birmingham, Manchester and Liverpool. The Unitarians however, were not an expanding denomination; they established a plateau in the 1820s from which they neither rose nor fell significantly. Attempts to promote activity in 1825 by the creation of the British and Foreign Unitarian Association and later in the establishment of the Unitarian Domestic Mission achieved only minor increases in support.

Those Presbyterians who retained Trinitarian doctrines tended to look to Scotland for support and leadership, and in 1839, after numerous requests, the General Assembly of the Church of Scotland recognised an independent Presbyterian church in England, though their name referred to them as 'in connexion' with the Church of Scotland. Their chapels often became, as a result, the resort of emigrant Scots laymen and ministers living in England, and it was only in the second half of the nineteenth century that they achieved their own identity. This was also an effect of the scattered geographical distribution of Presbyterianism, which precluded any level of organisation or control before the mid-nineteenth century.

They were in strong contrast to the Society of Friends, which during the nineteenth century found itself moving towards a developed form of church government. As the century progressed Quakers dropped their antique forms of address and dress, and overcame their suspicion of central organisation. They began to use their local monthly meetings, regional quarterly meetings and national annual meetings for business which touched on the interests, doctrine and worship of the whole society. They created committees to support the slave abolitionist cause and to promote Quaker education. Younger Quakers were less willing to abide by the tradition of deferring to older senior Friends at the Yearly Meetings. One of the emergent strengths of Quakerism was the diversity of theology it tolerated. There were deist Quakers, Quakers who accepted the authority of the Bible, those who responded to the rationalism of the Society, and those who responded to it emotionally. The doctrine of 'Inward Light' was one which contributed to the Victorian ideal of individual accomplishment and enlightenment.

In spite of these features, the Quakers were wedded to principles which damaged their ability to recruit in large numbers. In particular the society's insistence that Quakers might not marry outside the society lost many members. It was an unattractive tenet for those who might wish to join the society, particularly to a denomination which had a privileged position for its marriage rites under the Toleration and Marriage Acts. The vast majority of expulsions from the society was for breach of the marriage obligation, but the senior Friends saw it as a major pillar of their faith. In north Warwickshire, after 1800, there were more expulsions for marriage outside the society than there were marriages within it. A similar position was adopted by the Quakers on the issue of the permanent ministry. They believed that the ministry should be conditional upon the inspiration of God, open to all members of the society, and not monopolised by a single clerical caste. Whilst this may have promoted the involvement of members of the society in worship, it meant in many places that there was no leadership, and no direction to the work of the society. As a result therefore the collapse of the society seemed likely in the first half of the century. From 1799 to 1861 the membership fell from just under 20,000 to 13,844 and meeting attendance fell in the same period from 8000 to 3000. In Wiltshire, for example, there were eleven meetings in 1785; this fell to seven in 1800 and two by 1828. Only gradually, after 1860, did the younger Quakers, like John Bright, fight for greater liberalism within the society and as a result recruitment increased. In spite of the sympathy for their principles that many churchmen felt, they were regarded as an anachronism. Like the Unitarians the Quakers were dominated by both the middle class and by men of business. Where the poorer classes attended they did so usually as the servants or dependents of other Quakers.

However, unlike other nonconformists the Quaker frowned on activity in civic life, on the magistrates' bench or in Parliament. Thus one of the central paradoxes of the Society of Friends was that whilst they cultivated a separateness from the State which was rare among nineteenth-century Dissent, they were involved in social reform through the work of individuals like Elizabeth Fry, Joseph Sturge and Joseph Rowntree. Thomas Chalmers, who moved in the philanthropic circles of the nation, ranked the Quakers as the most philanthropic people he met. For some Quakers philanthropy arose from their prosperity: Joseph Gurney claimed that the most 'salutary chastisement' he had from God was his money. Men like Gurney and Sturge saw the various fluctuations in the markets and economy as divine purgations.

The independent or Congregational dissenters were, until the foundation of the Congregational Union in 1832, a patchwork of independent chapels. In 1800, they numbered 35,000 but afterwards their growth was dramatic, rising to 165,000 by 1850. Some congregations had been founded in the seventeenth century during the Commonwealth, others were Anglican proprietary chapels which had become independent through the lapse of a patron's interest. They shared with the new Dissent a greater level of working-class support than their old Quaker or Unitarian dissenting cousins, though this changed during the nineteenth century. By 1848 Thomas Binney addressed the union claiming that the Congregationalists' mission was 'neither to the very rich nor to the very poor'. By definition the independents valued the autonomy of their chapels. One of the few factors which drew them together before the establishment of the union was the training of their ministers in the dissenting academies, and the financial support of the Congregational Fund Board which funded poor clergy. Otherwise, the only visible signs of coherence in the Congregationalists were the Congregational Library and the London Missionary Society, which the Congregationalists dominated.

The nature of the union they formed in 1831 was paradoxical; it was to be purely advisory in nature, not a structure of denominational discipline. It lobbied Parliament, collected statistics and held an annual meeting at which it was emphatically stated that no chapel had the right of appeal. It also acted as a focus, attracting other independent chapels to the Congregational banner. Inevitably, whatever the objectives of the founders of the union, it also gradually became the focus of a denomination. In 1833, it adopted a declaration of faith and church order, albeit a loose one. Like so many religious endeavours the union's success was built on the work of a single man, Algernon Wells, who was secretary to the union from 1837 to 1850. Under his leadership a new edition of Isaac Watts's hymnal was developed and its huge sales managed to bring the union out of the jaws of bankruptcy. Wells also managed to draw those independent congregations, which had refused to join in 1831, into the union. Committees were set up for tracts, education, missions and even pensions. Wells's strength was his ability to manage all these ventures without giving the congregations a fear of encroachment of their independence. There was, however, some greater homogeneity, principally encouraged by the union's annual meeting. There was pressure to avoid use of the *Book of Common Prayer*, there was an avoidance of revivalism and 'ranting' in their worship, and the use of extemporary sermons was considered important. As Machin has noted, in politics there seems to have been a remarkably strong trend to Whig-Liberalism in the Congregational Union. They were swift to take advantage of the 1834 Municipal Corporations Act and enter the corporations of the large cities, and by the 1850s they were actively seeking election to parliament, and were successful in Hull and Cambridgeshire. They were also active in the free trade debate, denouncing protection on religious and humanitarian grounds.

The Baptists were often formerly independent congregations which rejected Congregational views on infant baptism. Well into the nineteenth century many Baptists were happy to attend Congregational services and shared their forms of worship, other than for baptism, and on occasion the two groups shared chapel accommodation. However, the Baptists, who might be expected to have a homogeneity of theology, were as diverse and varied as the Congregationalists. They were particularly divided over the nature of salvation, splitting between Arminianism and Calvinism. In 1770, the Arminians had split away to form the Baptist New Connexion, but Arminianism remained strong in many Baptist congregations. There were also disputes over the admission of the unbaptised to the sacraments. Even the establishment of the Baptist Union in 1831 did not eradicate these disputes. Like other groups they were led by a strong secretary, J. H.Hinton, founded a denominational newspaper, the *Baptist Magazine*, and produced a hymnal, but they were often debt-ridden and unable therefore to undertake greater activity. In the religious census of 1851 the Baptists, who had numbered 27,403 in 1800, numbered 930,000, a large increase in support. But their obscurity, relative to their numbers, stemmed in part from a conservative outlook. Few Baptist ministers liked the new gothic style of chapel and church; Charles Spurgeon even avoided it in his London Metropolitan Tabernacle. But this symbolised a tendency to reject the new: garb, preaching and conversion were all essential to the Baptist tradition. Paradoxically, as with so many dissenters, the Baptists valued the progressive commercial spirit: in their Bloomsbury Mission they emphasised the benefits of 'the moral influence' of commercial endeavour. They, like the Congregationalists, were in the forefront of the campaign for free trade.

The development from sect to denomination by the old and new dissenting groups in the nineteenth century was largely achieved in the years between 1800 and 1851, the same years in which the Church of England moved towards the status of a pluralist–voluntary denomination. Many of the factors which effected this shift were held in common by the dissenting groups. The increase in their support was crucial, as was the creation of some level of central organisation or coordination. Most denominations had leading figures, Bunting, Wells, Hinton and their colleagues, who drove the work of the unions or annual meetings, and promoted the creation of a central form of church government. These were the dissenting equivalents of Blomfield, younger men of business who were able to shake off the old 'connexional' traditions and had a vision of the future of their organisations which led them towards denomination. The paraphernalia of periodicals, hymnals, foreign missions and assemblies confirmed in the eyes of the clergy and laity that they were part of a larger whole that accorded a legitimacy and status to them.

It was this self-confidence that encouraged the dissenters to engage in the evangelical revival in which most groups were involved after 1820. For Parsons the evangelism of the dissenters was one of the focuses of convergence between them at the dawn of the Victorian era.[10] It also drew the various groups together in their demand for removal of disabilities, for without religious liberty there was no foundation for home or foreign missions, seeking the recruitment of the unenlightened. Other writers, like Richard Helmstadter, have argued that it was the old and new dissenters' ability to synthesise religious, political and social views that built their success in the nineteenth century.[11] Central to this synthesis was the dissenters' commitment to individualism, which played a crucial role in conversion and salvation, in conscience, in political commitment, in efforts to avoid poverty and to achieve prosperity.

Perhaps the level of unity has been overstated, but the importance of individualism has been emphasised in Boyd Hilton's work on the impact of evangelicalism on social and political thought. Evangelical opinion, both Anglican and dissenting, promoted a view of the morality of trade and the validity of economic endeavour. The old traditions of the providence of God, so strong in the seventeenth and eighteenth century, fell away; it was too random and arbitrary, no longer a sufficient view of the world for an industrial era. In its place was raised up the importance of the external features of religion. Equally important was salvation over which man exercised control, which superseded the nature of creation over which man had no control. The emphasis on the contractual nature of salvation and the 'share' in redemption that religion offered were in close harmony with, and perhaps promoted, the economic ideas of the age. Equally, argues Boyd Hilton, ideas of social reform were affected by the shift in religious views of heaven and hell. The mid-Victorian era saw the decline in the belief in a literal hell, which in turn allowed the softening of social attitudes and a greater willingness to allow government intervention to solve social problems. This generated ideas of 'the limited liability of sin', though of course where the liability was that of mankind it could produce a sharp response, particularly the sin of poverty. Sin was in part a product of the world and thus prevention was a religious duty as well as a social obligation.[12] The Board of Health, the investigations into social conditions and the plethora of interventions which eroded the Benthamite ideal, all traced their origin to ideas which encouraged men to achieve the justice in this world. Many of these ideas are ephemeral, and difficult to tie to the ideas which religion promoted. But the abiding belief in individual conscience lay behind many of the social and political reforms of the nineteenth century.

The transition of Dissent, old and new, into self-confident denominations was also in part effected through the training of ministers and clergy which became a significant feature of most denominations. When, in 1816, the Revd William Griffiths of Burry Green was appointed to the Welsh Calvinist congregation in Gower, it was an informal affair, dominated by the Gower trustees. But he was one of the last nonconformist clergy to be appointed after only self-directed study and part-time preaching experience. From the 1820s onwards most denominations developed their own systems for training their clergy and most created theological colleges and institutes for this purpose. In doing so the various denominations had to focus on the sort of pastoral care and liturgy they wished to promote. Such colleges tended to develop their own brands of theology and spirituality, and this tended to generate a greater sense of identity within each church. Inevitably, they tended to emphasise the role of the clergy and promoted a clerical caste, comparable to that which had developed within the Church of England.

Religion without Christianity: the Jews

Numbering 6030 attendances in the 1851 census, and with a total Jewish population exceeding 35,000, the Jews were larger than both the orthodox churches and the foreign Protestant churches in England (though in Scotland the latter easily outnumbered them). Their comparatively low attendance rate indicates the way in which the synagogues were dominated by the prosperous Jews, who tended to establish fashionable synagogues rather like clubs. Even the more modest synagogues were expensive to join and tended to celebrate the wealth of their members. However, their significance in the early nineteenth century lies in the developing attitudes towards toleration of non-Christians that they highlight.

The murder in 1771 of a man by a Jew in Chelsea produced an upsurge of anti-semitism. Francis Place recorded in his *Improvement of the Working Classes* that 'every Jew was in public opinion implicated, and the prejudice, ill will and brutal conduct this brought upon the Jews . . . did not cease for many years . . . Dogs could not be used in the streets in the manner many Jews were treated.' It was 1787 before a Jewish figure emerged who could claim to be truly popular among the urban poor of London. This was Daniel Mendoza, a boxer and the founder of a boxing school. Mendoza was the champion of the London poor and his victories were celebrated in spite of his religion.

In the early nineteenth century the Jewish community made great efforts to integrate into British culture. In 1809, *The Times* recorded that the jubilee of George III was celebrated in cathedral, abbey, church, meeting house, chapel and synagogue. George III's sons were visitors to the affluent and fashionable London synagogues. Of course such compliments reflected, in part, the gratitude of the State for the Jewish financial commitment to Britain during the Napoleonic Wars.[13] The principal disability for Jews was the Christian oath required on taking a seat in Parliament. The nature of the discrimination was not simply anti-semitic; it excluded any who were not were not prepared to swear an oath on their 'true faith as a Christian'. Quakers were able to assent to it but a conscientious Jew, like a conscientious atheist or Hindu, took the rubric to imply Anglicanism and was excluded. Men like Disraeli, Anglicans who came from Jewish families, were thus not excluded by the restriction. Attempts were made unsuccessfully in 1833, 1834 and 1836 to allow Jews to take an alternative oath, and in 1835 Peel passed an Act allowing them to hold civic offices. In 1846 an ancient and unused statute was repealed which disbarred Jews from owning land. But Parliament was reluctant to allow the admission of Jews to their ranks. The issue came to a head in 1847 when the Jewish merchant David Salomons was elected MP for the City of London. Russell and the Whigs favoured admitting him to the Commons, in part because of the heavy reliance of the financial and banking system on men like Lionel Rothschild. With the support of Peel and Gladstone (who ignored Tractarian appeals to oppose it) the government tried twice to allow Jews to swear an alternative oath; both failed, spurred on by the occasional petition from London churches against the admission of Jews to the Commons as against the Established Church. During the debate on the second bill, Blackwood wrote that the admission of Jews to parliament would be 'an injury to the Constitution, a peril to the public principle and an insult to humanity'. Salomons's attempt to swear on the Old Testament, and omitting the offending words, was rejected and his subsequent election for Greenwich in 1851 led him to be expelled from the House. It was only in 1858 that the Lords relented and allowed Jews to swear an oath, on condition that any Jewish government minister, like a Roman Catholic, should surrender control of any ecclesiastical patronage.

Elsewhere in society the Jews played an extraordinarily full role. Salomons was elected Lord Mayor of London in 1855, and he with other City Jews, was particularly active in making charitable gifts – even to Christian charities and to church building. In part this was because the status of Jews in England was not controlled by law as it was in some other European countries. There was no confinement to ghettos, no exclusion from occupations. Jews were admitted to King's College London and University College London to read for degrees. As a result the Anglo-Jewish population in England was comparatively stable, with few demographic movements other than a dribble of continental Jews into London. Equally the focus of Jews on the trade in luxury goods brought them into contact with the highest social classes. In the lower reaches of society Jews were strongly represented in the ranks of street traders and itinerants, although there was an increase in the numbers of Jewish wage labourers. Rural Jewry was rare; Jewish populations were centred on London, Leeds, Liverpool, Manchester, Birmingham and South Wales. Whilst many Jews conformed to the lives of the artisan or middle classes, East End Jewry was as notoriously violent as that of other local groups. The position of this class of Jews was seen not as a threat to property, but rather to the position of more prosperous Jews. Prosperous Jews were determined that there should be no cause of grievance against them, and spent freely in establishing Jewish institutes for the poor. There was an attempt to establish a Jewish system for poor relief, which would allow the deportation of 'undesirable' Jews, but parliament refused to hand such powers to the Jewish community. However, *Chevra*, open houses for Jews, were set up across the East End where poorer Jews could pray and even sleep overnight.

The consciousness of Jewishness was, like that of the dissenting denominations, aided by the growth of a structure of religious government. There had been no tradition of a centralised rabbinate before the election of Nathan Adler to the office of Chief Rabbi of the United Hebrew Congregations in 1844. Adler, in 1847, published a set of laws which gave the Chief Rabbi control over all religious matters. No synagogue could be built, rabbis appointed or changes made without his permission. A year later the creation of the Jewish Board of Guardians established similar control over the social life of Jews, over charity and other aspects of communal life. Both 'wings' of the Jewish establishment were attempts to conform to the Anglican model of religion. Worship was shifted away from the moaning and swaying of traditional Jewry to a more 'Anglican' sermon and ordered prayers. Rabbis increasingly took up the model of English clergy, by visiting the sick, helping the poor and undertaking numerous pastoral duties. Some even wore clerical collars and referred to each other as 'the reverend'. The strongest contrast with the dissenting churches was the absence of any missionary or evangelical fervour. Preaching in English and other English affectations were more to achieve integration than to attract converts to the faith. The traditional references to the Election of Israel and the return to Israel were not calculated to attract English converts. However, they shared a commitment to biblical study which the Victorian Christians undertook. Whilst biblical scholars differed over the emphasis that should be placed on the Talmud, they shared a scholastic interest. The existence of the Readership in Talmudic Studies at Cambridge, albeit held by a Christian, provided a focus for Jewish studies.

The position of Jews in mid-nineteenth century England is perhaps best illustrated in *Punch*. Mark Lemon, the first editor of *Punch* was himself of Jewish extraction, but this did not prevent him from depicting Jews as slippery in trade, wearing bright flashy clothes and surviving on usury. *Punch* declared that attempts to convert Jews to Christianity were useless and that only money would tempt them to apostasy. All this anti-semitic material was set in a context that was remarkably hypocritical. *Punch* remarked that wealthy Jews were reluctant to help their poorer brethren, an unjust charge that many gentiles might more reasonably have faced. The 1850s, however, saw a remarkable turn-about in the depiction of Jews in *Punch*. There was a willingness to depict them as Englishmen, rather than foreigners; Tzar Alexander of Russia was portrayed as a brute for his attacks on Russian Jewry and celebrated English Jews like Disraeli (though an Anglican) and the millionaire philanthropist Sir Moses Montefiore were drawn with greater affection and sympathy. The change also expressed itself in the written contributions: Jews were increasingly praised for their abilities, their economic contribution to the life of the country, their faith in efficiency, and above all, their role as model citizens.

6

RELIGION IN MID-VICTORIAN ENGLAND

The Religious Census of 1851

The Religious Census of 1851 was the child of Sir George Lewis, the under-secretary at the Home Office in 1850, who felt that discovery of information regarding religion would be useful. The questions were included in the census under the power of the secretary of state, Russell, to ask such questions as he saw fit. But the law officers doubted whether refusal to answer could be punished by the law, and as a result the questions on religious behaviour were voluntary. There were opponents of the scheme, notably Bishop Wilberforce of Oxford who felt that the danger of eliciting inaccurate information invalidated the census. The work of preparing and analysing the returns was entrusted to Horace Mann, whose inexhaustible patience served the census well. Failure to respond to the initial enquiry led to a second questionnaire, after which Mann estimated the likely reply. In total nearly a 1000 of the 14,000 Anglican parishes refused to make a return. Years later, when the figures had been disputed by all sides, Mann admitted that there had been errors and that the figures gave only a general picture of the religious life of the country.

The raw figures on which Mann worked were those of attendance at church on 30 March 1851 (though clergy were asked about church accommodation and other matters). The figures revealed that, of a total population of nearly 18 million, 5,292,551 people attended the services of the Church of England, 4,536,264 attended the main Protestant dissenting churches (Methodist, Presbyterian, Congregational and Baptist) and 383,630 people attended the Roman Catholic services.[1] In general, the public seem to have felt that the figures for Catholic attendance was very low (considering the furore aroused by the 'papal aggression' episode). The fact that nearly half the attendances were at the dissenting Protestant churches was a revelation. Few people had realised how strong Protestant Nonconformity was, least of all the Whigs who had courted their votes. When localities were examined it came as a shock to those in the south that in some northern cities like Bradford attendance at the Nonconformist churches exceeded that at Anglican churches by over two to one. It was no surprise to men like Hook of Leeds, who in 1837 conceded that the religion of Leeds was Methodism. But it was a greater shock that rural Nonconformity was so strong; after 1851 no one could dismiss Nonconformity as the religion of the industrial classes only. In Wales, the massive preponderance of Nonconformity in rural and urban areas fuelled the demands for disestablishment of the Anglican Church which attracted only 9 per cent of the population. Many, with some justification, argued that the Nonconformist figures were most prone to inflation by double attendance by members and that the real figures were lower for Protestant Nonconformity, although conversely the Nonconformist Liberation Society claimed that the figures did not give a true reflection of the strength of support.

Making detailed calculations, usually based on guesses, Mann estimated that excluding the children, elderly and infirm, those who worked on Sundays and other groups, about 70 per cent of the population (or 12.5 million people) was free to attend church on Sunday. Making allowances for those who had probably been counted twice, Mann concluded that about five and a quarter million people, who were free to do so, did not attend church. He was aware that there was probably a 'turnover' in attendance, and that the real figure for habitual non-attenders was much lower. Mann's own diagnosis of the situation was that many people felt that the churches did not respond to the needs of the poor and perpetuated social distinctions. There was also the problem of accommodation which his census revealed: in cities there was a shortage of a million and a half seats, and across the country as a whole there was a need for 2000 new churches. Shoreditch could accommodate only 18 per cent of the population, and even the wealthy clergy of Durham had a problem accommodating all members of their congregations. In using these explanations, Mann assumed that the census revealed religious indifference rather than complete loss of faith.

There are other explanations for the presumed decline in church attendance which consider the wider social context of the era. First, and most important, was the decline in the social cohesion which effected communal attendance at church. The processes of urbanisation and industrialisation broke down smaller communities which could promote widespread attendance. Peer pressure was less effective in maintaining church attendance in the mass slums of the large cities. Equally, the wider range of leisure opportunities offered by an industrial society, particularly to those who lived in towns, has been advanced as a cause of declining religious observance by some social historians. Most practical was the desire by some to avoid the discipline on Sundays that they experienced during the week: Ann Eggly gave evidence to a parliamentary commission in 1842 that she 'went a little to Sunday-school, but . . . soon gave it over [sic]. I thought it too bad to be confined both Sundays and weekdays. I walk about and get fresh air on Sundays.' Her sister admitted she stayed in bed on Sundays to rest.

The most significant achievement of the census was the shattering of the remaining illusion that the Established Church was the Church of the whole nation. Establishment had either to be abandoned or reasserted on other grounds. Churchmen were quick to claim that Establishment could be defended on the grounds of history and of being the majority church in England, if not in Ireland and Wales.[2] But they were hard pressed to defend church rates, the exclusion of dissenters from the universities and from burial by their own ministers, and the host of other disabilities which remained for nonconformists. Some evangelicals threw themselves into redeeming the situation, like Bickersteth, who targeted the towns and cities of his diocese for Anglican renewal. Others like Palmerston and his mentor Shaftesbury sought to relieve the dissenters from their disabilities.

Parsons has indicated that the census was significant in the indication it gave of the diversity of nonconformity in England and Wales. There were over thirty nonconformist churches and sects; a few were genuinely national churches, others were isolated congregations. Nevertheless, the greatest impact the census had on the nonconformists was the self-confidence it inspired. *The Patriot* and the Anti-State Church Association both propagated the figures that the census revealed. By 1855 the Anti-State Church Association renamed itself the Liberation Society and founded a new monthly newspaper called *The Liberator*. By the end of the decade the society had divided the country into districts for the collection of funds and a parliamentary committee drafted bills for supportive MPs to introduce, removing remaining disabilities and promoting disestablishment. After 1851 the training of clergy and the creation of institutions multiplied within nonconformity largely because it saw itself as a legitimate alternative to the Church of England.

Religion and Cultural Change

By the middle of the nineteenth century religion had made significant moves away from the religious culture of the previous century, although perhaps these changes were not dependent on the reforms of the 1830s. There were the visible changes of church building, new denominations, greater efficiency in pastoral care, less pluralism and less non-residence. But these external and visible changes were perhaps the least significant evidence of the changes which influenced religion. Of far greater import was the way in which the Church of England's monopoly had been eroded into the status of one denomination among many. By 1850 even the most conservative churchmen acknowledged that the Church operated in a pluralistic society and religious behaviour was becoming, by definition, voluntary behaviour. All denominations had to grapple with surrender of some secular responsibilities and the assumption of others. These had important implications for the role of the clergy, not least in the mid-Victorian drift downwards in the social status of the clergy. The steady erosion of the role that clergy played in local society, on the bench of magistrates and in the various functions of charity and local government, made Orders less attractive for the sons of the gentry and landed classes. Perhaps also the expansion of the numbers of clergy through the growth in the variety of religious denominations effected a decline in the status of the clergy. Few sons of the gentry would relish comparison with the local Wesleyan or Baptist minister, who might be the son of a shopkeeper. Numbers of Oxford or Cambridge educated clergy declined as the numbers of men coming forward increased.[3]

The increasing spiritual functions of the clergy attracted the pious and those who had a vocation, but their status relied increasingly upon their efforts and achievements. This trend was affected by two emergent factors in the nineteenth century. The first of these was the growing meritocratic ideals generated by the public schools for the middle classes and effected by mechanistic changes, like the competitive examination for entry to the civil service. The second was the growth in religious apathy and scepticism. Whereas in 1760 faith could be taken for granted, no such assumption could be made in 1850. Thus the clergy took to the citadel of professionalisation. Training and esoteric knowledge, the two touchstones of a profession, steadily developed during this period. Parish clergy were no longer talented amateurs, with a dilettante approach to their various duties. They were specialist preachers, ritualists, theologians and missionaries. Lesser functions could be delegated to lay men and women. For the Church of England, as much as for the nonconformist churches, influence and control increasingly arose from the commitment of the clergy, rather from their inherent status as clergy. This was not always a benefit to the churches. As Josef Altholtz has indicated the Victorian 'crisis of faith' was perhaps less an attack from outside by scientific ideas than a conflict within religion between narrow dogma and the calls upon the layman's pluralistic conscience.[4] Thus as clergy specialised their role, they were less able to respond to the challenges of science.

Challenges abounded from theology as well as science. German theologians like David Strauss advocated a theology which seemed to reject the revelatory element in the New Testament. Miracles, the historical nature of the Gospels and the dogmas of the church were rejected. Strauss's views, like those of traditional Deists were deeply rationalistic. He also shared a humanitarianism which the Utilitarians recognised; God's role in the world was to develop the divine aspects of mankind. English theologians stood shoulder to shoulder to reject Strauss's blasphemy, but the trickle of ideas soon became a flood. Anthony Froude's *Nemesis of Faith* which recounted the agonised decline of faith in the mind of a clergyman suggested that even the strongest minds were prey to doubts and questions. John Sterling also abandoned the Church, leaving after his death a collection of essays which traced the path of his apostasy. But these were pin-pricks compared with the onslaught from geology, which by 1840 had seriously eroded the literal interpretation of *Genesis* by Anglicans. For a time, some clergy claimed that geologists like Buckland and Lyell were continuing in the tradition of Newton, proving the harmony of nature and religion. But it soon became clear that it was more than the date of creation and of Noah's flood that was at stake. Geologists were joined by anatomists and astronomers in questioning the divine order of the world. Before Darwin ideas of some mutation of species gained currency in Scottish scientific circles.

All these ideas unsettled the mid-Victorian middle class educated conscience. Their impact on the non-specialist theologian was not great, but they opened the door for other agnostic disciplines such as the infant studies of psychology and sociology to question the divine order. As the physical sciences diverged from the moral sciences they exerted a gravitational pull on economic and social ideas. These changes coincided with the gradual professionalisation of the scientific world. Lyell's appointment to the chair in Geology at King's College London, established the first lay geologist. By 1847 the reform of the rules of the Royal Society made nomination far more dependent on the candidate's scientific knowledge; clerical fellowship of the Royal

Society collapsed as a result from 10 per cent of its membership in 1849 to just 3 per cent in 1899. As the clergy withdrew from scientific endeavour, science asserted itself as a secular study prepared to challenge orthodox religion.

Religion, the Family and Women

A major feature of the social impact of religion in the nineteenth century was the influence it sought over the family. The decline of family prayers during the seventeenth and eighteenth century was reversed during the nineteenth century. The churches targeted the family as a major institution which could effect both commitment and recruitment to Christianity. In a world in which, demonstrably after 1851, there was no guarantee or assumption of faith, the family was a principal mechanism that allowed entry into the hearts of the people. The churches placed much emphasis upon it since other conduits were gradually being secularised, namely schools, universities, literature and work. The increasing emphasis on the family as a Christian institution led to the elevation of the rites of passage, always a significant element in church life, to a higher status in society. Many of the ceremonies and traditions of the baptism, confirmation, marriage and funeral services were invented and developed in the Victorian era. In some families, particularly those of the middle classes, catechising was as much a feature of the home as of the church. They were the grappling hooks which bound the churches to the family. Most denominations produced their own hymnals, books of devotions and prayers for use in homes, as well as children's devotional literature. Evangelical groups often used the family home as the centre for weekday meetings, with men, women and children involved in the worship. It was a symbiotic relationship. The family also gained greater status from the religious emphasis placed upon it. In the middle classes the head of the family was endowed with a quasi-religious duty in monitoring moral discipline, religious observance, and in reading prayers and leading the worship. Roberts regards the principal role of the Victorian *paterfamilias* as one of admonishment, and this was derived from religious ideas. Children and other family members were inculcated with religious ideals such as thrift, piety, modesty and other Victorian values by the male head of the household.

The role of women in religious life was often marginalised in the eighteenth century into one of superstition. According to François de la Rochefoucauld, in 1784, women were superstitious about the sacraments, on occasion being confirmed every time that a bishop undertook a confirmation tour. He also concluded that women were more prone to unitarianism.[5] Certainly, women were in the forefront of opposition to Catholic emancipation in 1828. Colley ascribes this to a greater assiduousness on the part of women in church attendance, and they were therefore subject to organised church opposition to emancipation.[6] It is also the case that women were perhaps more dependent on oral tradition than men, and thus drew upon the long memory of anti-Catholic behaviour among working men and women. Outside the Established Church women were incorporated into the work of the church: visiting the sick and poor and arranging the plethora of mothers', clothing and friendly clubs. For women, frequently excluded from society and the educational system, religion was a legitimate area of both study and other activity. Carpenter claimed that 'apart from "parish work" . . . there was not much scope for the activity of Christian women'. During the nineteenth century, as Linda Colley has noted, increasing numbers of women enjoyed freedom from their domestic role, many devoting this time to religion. As the century progressed women increasingly wrote works of religious devotion. Hannah More wrote religious tracts and novels, and the daughters and wives of clergy edited letters and wrote biographies. The wives and daughters of Bishops Hampden, Ridding, Thompson, Owen and Creighton immortalised them in print.

Quakers were particularly willing to abandon social prejudices against active involvement by women in worship and ministry. At a local level they arranged separate weekly and monthly meetings of men and women and chose women as elders of societies. Local meetings allowed women to investigate and report on the morals of other female members of the society, and embraced ideas of marriage as a partnership between man and woman. At Witney, in 1851, Hannah Smith responded to the religious census as overseer of the Friends Meeting House. At the national level there was greater patriarchy, but women were still involved. Women were particularly targeted by evangelical groups, especially during revivalist campaigns. In studies of both the Cotswolds and East Cheshire women in particular were successfully recruited by evangelical groups, often making up the majority of a congregation. Urdank's research suggests that women were more likely than men to seek out religious support after a family had migrated from one area to another in seek of work, and as a result often acted as the anchor which attached a family to a particular denomination or connection.[7] Women also played a significant role in the religious campaign for the abolition of the slave trade. The sugar strike of the 1820s, against slavery in the West Indies, was able to express the opposition of ordinary women to the religious and moral offence.[8]

The role of women in the nineteenth-century household was also prey to religious dogma. Evangelicals in particular were liable to emphasise obedience in marriage, and the domestic arena was elevated in status and acted as a transparent instrument of social control. Hannah More in 1783 wrote of the 'almost sacred joys of home' and Coventry Patmore's poem *The Angel in the House* elevated the domestic role of women into a quasi-religious duty. Froude even claimed that 'home is the one pure earthly instinct which we have'. Trudgill indicates that even childbearing and motherhood were endowed with an angelic status during the Victorian era.[9] There were few areas of women's lives unaffected by religious ideas. Dr William Acton's treatise on sex in 1857 suggested that High Church ladies should sleep separately from their husbands during Lent. Moreover, the churching of women became an established Anglican ritual: Caroline Clive, wife of the rector of Solihull, was churched after the birth of her son in 1842 and the historian Edward Vaux found evidence of it thriving in 1870.[10] The ceremony of churching placed emphasis on the principle of the purity of women, and this became one of the important ideas inculcated into Victorian women by the churches. On the stage, in literature, and in wider society prudish emphasis on purity restrained women. Those who were not restrained by ideas of prudence and decency were, of course, in religious and social terms 'fallen', attracting the opprobrium and also the charity of society.

The religious image of women was confined principally to the Virgin Mary and Mary Magdalen. Within Roman Catholicism the cult of Mary, often adopted by the Tractarians and ritualists, provided a representation of women. But for the Protestants there were few opportunities. Colley argues that as a result nineteenth-century women turned to Princess Charlotte and then Queen Victoria to fill this gap. As the century progressed the position of Queen Victoria as the supreme governor of the Church of England, and a monarch who played a major part in the appointment of bishops, may have strengthened the hand of those women who sought a role in the Church.[11] However, women who sought a formal role in the Church were often dissuaded by the number of obstacles placed in their way. One woman who approached Samuel Wilberforce in 1844 in the hope of establishing a link with the Sisters of Charity found a plethora of problems. What would such women do? Would they mix with society? Would they visit schools? Would they own land and religious houses? Wilberforce concluded that the matter needed 'much thought and many prayers'. Nevertheless, during his episcopate he received letters from women asking about a number of theological issues, including the validity of confession and of a range of ritualist practises, suggesting a growing involvement of women in theological controversies.[12]

The lives of children were similarly open to the strong influences of religion. The State maintained a formal attitude to children that required them to be maintained in a Christian environment. Shelley, for example, was denied access to his children since the courts held that as an atheist he would not bring his children up in a religious tradition, and well into the second half of the nineteenth century courts used atheism as a cause of denial of a parent's custody. Sunday schools also drew the children into the orbit of the Church. Laqueur has estimated that 75 per cent of working class children were in Sunday schools by 1851, though this may overstate the position in some industrial cities.[13] Hempton claims that the attraction of Sunday schools to the working classes was that they were cheap and did not inhibit the earnings of children during the week.[14] This underestimates the cultural impact and attraction of Sunday schools which developed a paraphernalia and culture of their own. Parades, festivals, readings, prizes, visits and local celebrations were incorporated into the cycle of the Sunday school year. They offered the opportunity for the young to spend time together, without their parents, and as has been noted already were the forerunner of a youth culture.

Religious schools for the poor were not without their abusers, however. In some cases, religious schools reinforced and disguised the appalling nature of industrial conditions that many children had to endure. In the report of the 1843 Children's Employment Commission it was revealed that some 'Bible schools' were in reality opportunities for child exploitation, providing a few verses from the Bible, followed by hours of rote learning whilst lace-making or other drudgery was undertaken. Elsewhere in manu-facturing, children grew up in isolation from either Sunday schools or religion. The degradation and brutality in which they were raised immured them against religion and its teaching. Child prostitution, begging and appalling forms of abuse were common-place in many cities. At the turn of the eighteenth century the founders of the Philanthropic Society were horrified to learn of the godlessness of the children of convicts and set up schools to catechise and educate them. Such reformatory experiments as were undertaken tended to place great store by religion. The government's experiment in 1825 using HMS *Euraylus*, a prison hulk, as an experiment to imprison convicts under 16 years of age, insisted on prayers and hymns morning and evening, and leisure time was spent in reciting hymns and scripture. Children in workhouses were treated to a similarly stern religious regime in the hope that the spiritual nourishment would encourage them to be productive citizens. This was not always effective in promoting religion; the thousand-strong school run by Mr Aubin at Nor-wood for London workhouse children was judged 'extremely defective' in religious and moral training. The Poor Law rule that children should be trained in the religious persuasion of their parents was often ignored and in 1861 Roman Catholics gave evidence to the commission that they were ridiculed in strongly Protestant workhouses. Nevertheless, for the majority of the children of the urban poor the churches may have been even more remote. In 1851, the Birmingham Conference of the Reformatory and Refuge Union emphasised the need to 're-claim' the children of the 'neglected classes' for religion. By 1851 two or three generations of urban poor had endured a childhood either devoid of religion or in which the Sunday school was the chief means of inculcating religious ideas.

Religion and the Working Classes by 1851

While religious attitudes to the role of women and the family predominantly reflected the values of the middle and upper classes, among the working classes immorality and vice were as prevalent as they had been. Religious ideas filtered down to the worker in the mine or the pauper in the street only very slowly. Some clergy were shocked by the position of the poor they were expected to administer to. In the 1840s, for example, Sidney Godolphin Osborne, rector of Durweston, commented that Yetminster was 'the cesspool of everything in which anything human can be recognised'. For much of the period under review the impact of the churches on the working class who lived in such squalor was of a far less even quality than on the middle or upper classes. The evidence in Chapter 4 regarding the level of church accommodation and other provision suggests that it was a minority of the working class who had a developed religious life in the period between 1780 and 1840. Osborne wrote in the Christian Socialist journal, *Politics for the People*, in 1848 that only 'fair wages . . . and decent dwellings' would release the poor from the bonds that prevented them from worshipping God. A similar view was expressed by Augustus Hare when he commented that the souls of his parishioners at Alton Barnes must be 'got at through their bodies'. But Osborne and Hare were comparatively rare; few clergy or denominations accepted that it was the physical conditions of the poor that affected their spiritual lives. The position of those clergy who did subscribe to such a view was often difficult. Canon Edward Girdlestone, who supported the militancy of agricultural labourers, found that the farmers and landowners deserted his church for the Wesleyans and refused to pay their church rates.

Where the working classes were committed to religion they often developed a distinctive religious flavour. The working class, for example, was far more prey to the distractions of superstition and eccentric religious beliefs. Joanna Southcott's extraordinary role as a prophetess and apocalyptic visionary found followers principally, though not exclusively, among the working class. Her progress from the West Country to London stirred up local superstition. It was the working men of Sheffield who were convinced by the prophesies in her *Book of Wonders* that the world would end in 1817, and the working class of Taunton whose belief in the 'Samford Ghost' was stirred up by Southcottian fever. Joanna herself regarded her mission as being principally to the poor, 'the true heirs' as she called them. In areas like the West Riding even Joanna's death in 1814 did not undermine the conviction that she was right, and her male followers continued to wear beards, as she had ordered. While Joanna Southcotts were rare, the working class was always prey to extravagance in religion. Preachers and visionaries attracted support often by appealing to sensationalism, which became the lowest common denominator of working-class religious experience. Revivalism could obtain a grip on a community, as Thomas Cooper a teacher, recognised in the 1820s, when Gainsborough was affected by a spate of religious conversions. Cooper suggested that the whole town was affected for weeks, until in time the religious fervour passed.

Rural society was perhaps even more prone to superstition and paganism than urban. The 'Mad Thoms' revival of 1838 in Kent was turned into a revolt by peasant farmers who believed Thoms to be Christ, and took up arms to support him. Pamela Horn's examination of rural life suggests that witchcraft and paganism remained a strong feature of rural life in the nineteenth century. Women were attacked for witchcraft well into the nineteenth century, and smaller superstitions about livestock and everyday life were endemic.[15] Obelkevitch goes as far in his study of Lindsey to claim that paganism was a stronger influence than Christianity on the lives of the rural poor, who nevertheless considered themselves Christian. Thus, for example, confirmation was believed to cure rheumatism and Christmas and harvest festivals were thinly disguised pagan feasts.[16] There must have been few clergy who were not dismayed by the ignorance of religion of the poor. The plethora of superstitions Vaux recounted in 1894 were for the most part contributed by clergymen from their own experiences.

One of the principal problems for the poor was that religion, of whatever form, tended also to demand too much of the working man and woman. It wanted all their leisure time, perhaps to deny opportunities for sin. Few denominations approved of ordinary working class leisure activities. Horse races, wakes, dances, fairs, playhouses, pubs and the more vicious pastimes of dog and cock fighting and bear-baiting were frequently denounced by the churches. Thompson claims that even the least participation in local festivals was, to Sheffield Methodists, 'fellowship with the unfruitful works of darkness'. Entertainment was associated with the waste of money and with worldliness; the only entertainment necessary was Bible reading and hymn singing. Some denominations believed that the paucity of references to dancing in the Bible meant that it was not permissible. And the Society for the Suppression of Vice prosecuted over 600 people for breaking Sabbath laws in 1801 and 1802 alone. In Lancashire in the 1820s the athletic festivals of wrestling, quoits and archery were declared unacceptable.

In part such teaching by the churches aimed to debrutalise the working people and restore self-respect. Certainly, the Bartholomew Fair in London, which attracted an enormous onslaught from the pulpits in the 1820s, was notorious for its drunkenness and violation of women. But too often the churches raised up a counsel of perfection, unattainable by the majority, and thus turned the poor away from religion. All too easily the church-goers obtained the reputation among the poor as kill-joys and prudes. Rural and urban traditional customs were subsumed within a bland and sombre attitude to enjoyment and entertainment, local folk customs were replaced by Whit walks and harvest festivals. Those folk customs that survived were driven into subcultures and stripped of their respectability. In this way religion divided society between the idle and industrious, the religious and the profane. There was no *via media* between the pious mentality of men like Gladstone, who began his rescue work among prostitutes during the 1850s, and the degradation of the women he sought to save.

NOTES

Introduction

1. R. Newton, *Eighteenth Century Exeter* (Exeter, 1984), p. 74.
2. A. Smith, *The Established Church and Popular Religion, 1750–1850* (London, 1971), p. 6.

1 The Established Church in 1760

1. D. R. Hirschberg, 'The Government and Church Patronage, 1660–1760', *Journal of British Studies*, 20 (1980) p. 139.
2. M. W. McCahill, *Order and Equipoise: The Peerage and the House of Lords, 1783–1806* (London, 1978), pp. 28, 162. W. C. Lowe 'Bishops and Scottish Representative Peers in the House of Lords, 1760–1775', *Journal of British Studies*, 18 (1978), pp. 86–93.
3. J. Cannon, *Aristocratic Century* (Cambridge, 1987), 64–65.
4. N. Sykes *Church and State in England in the Eighteenth Century* (Cambridge, 1934), p. 186.
5. G. F. A. Best, *Temporal Pillars* (Cambridge, 1964), p. 204.
6. W. B. Maynard, 'Pluralism and Non-residence in the Archdeaconry of Durham, 1774–1856: The Bishop and Chapter as Patrons', *Northern History*, 26 (1990), p. 112.
7. F. C. Mather, *High Church Prophet: Bishop Samuel Horsley...* (Oxford, 1992), pp. 272–3.
8. P. Virgin, *The Church in an Age of Negligence* (Cambridge, 1989), p. 153.
9. O. F. Christie (ed.) *The Diary of The Revd William Jones 1777–1821* (London, 1929), p. 111.
10. Mather, *High Church Prophet*, p. 282.
11. J. Barber '"A Fair and Just Demand?": Tithe Unrest in Cardiganshire, 1796–1832', *Welsh History Review*, 16, 2 (1992).

12. A. Smith, *The Established Church and Popular Religion, 1750–1850* (London, 1971), p. 27.
13. Virgin, *The Church in an Age of Negligence*, p. 153.
14. Best, *Temporal Pillars*, pp. 185 *et seq.*
15. Best, 'The Road to Hiram's Hospital', *Victorian Studies* (1961), p. 136.
16. O. W. Jones, 'The Welsh Church in the Eighteenth Century', in D. Walker (ed.), *A History of the Church in Wales* (Penarth, 1977), p. 104.

2 Church and State, 1760–1830

1. C. Bridenbaugh, *Mitre and Sceptre* (New York, 1962), pp. 261, 293.
2. R. W. Greaves, 'The Working of the Alliance' in G. V. Bennett and J. Walsh (eds), *Essays in Modern English Church History* (London, 1966), pp. 173 *et seq.*
3. C. J. Abbey, *The English Church and its Bishops, 1700–1800* (London, 1887), pp. ii, 165.
4. Quoted in E. Norman, *Church and Society in England, 1770–1970* (Oxford, 1976), p. 17.
5. Abbey, *The English Church and its Bishops*, pp. ii, 157–8.
6. National Library of Ireland, Richmond Ms 66., ff 888–9.
7. British Library, Add. Ms. 41,856, ff 220–8.
8. Public Record Office, Chatham Papers, p. 189.
9. G. F. A. Best, *Temporal Pillars* (Cambridge, 1964), p. 261.
10. W. Gibson, 'Tory Governments and Church Patronage, 1812–1830' *Journal of Ecclesiastical History*, 41, 2 (1990) *passim*.
11. A. Webster, *Joshua Watson* (London, 1954), p. 25.
12. C. Dewey, *The Passing of Barchester* (London, 1991), pp. 5–6.
13. K. Hyslon-Smith, *Evangelicals in the Church of England, 1734–1984* (Edinburgh, 1989), p. 86.
14. J. H. Overton and F. Relton, *The English Church from the Accession of George I to the End of the Eighteenth Century* (London, 1924), p. 235.
15. F. K. Brown, *The Fathers of the Victorians* (Cambridge, 1961), pp. 354 *et seq.*
16. J. A. Patten, *These Remarkable Men: The Beginning of a World Enterprise* (London, 1945), p. 107.
17. B. Hilton, *The Age of Atonement* (Oxford, 1988), pp. 15, 28.
18. E. Norman, *The English Catholic Church in the Nineteenth Century* (Oxford, 1985), p. 44.
19. J. Clark, *English Society, 1688–1832* (Cambridge, 1985), *passim*.

Notes

3 Religion and Social Change

1. E. Halevy, *History of the English People in the Nineteenth Century*, 3, (London, 1949–51), p. 53.
2. E. P. Thompson, *The Making of the English Working Class* (London, 1979), pp. 390–8.
3. A. Urdank, *Religion and Society in Cotswold Vale: Nailsworth, 1780–1865* (Los Angeles, 1990).
4. D. Hempton *Methodism and Politics in British Society 1750–1850* (London, 1987), chapter 2.
5. Ibid, 231.
6. M. Watts, *The Dissenters*, 1 (Oxford, 1978) J. E. Bradley, *Religion, Revolution and English Radicalism* (Cambridge, 1990), p. 423.
7. H. B. J. Armstrong, *A Norfolk Diary* (London, 1949), pp. 79–80.
8. All statistical information in this chapter is drawn from R. Currie, A. Gilbert and L. Horsley, *Churchmen and Churchgoers* (Oxford, 1977), *passim*.
9. O. F. Christie (ed.), *The Diary of the Revd William Jones, 1771–1821* (London, 1929), p. 81.
10. R. A. Soloway, *Prelates and People, 1783–1852* (London, 1969), pp. 259 *et seq.*
11. A. Rowden, *The Primates of the Four Georges* (London, 1916), p. 336.
12. L. Colley, *Britons* (New Haven, 1992), p. 227.
13. E. R. Wickham, *Church and People in an Industrial City* (London, 1957), pp. 58 *et seq.*
14. Ibid., p. 90.
15. A. Trollope, *Clergymen of the Church of England* (Leicester, 1974), p. 68. *Guardian*, 10 December 1856, p. 937.
16. Trollope, *Clergymen of the Church of England* p. 96.
17. Quoted in G. Kitson Clark, *Churchman and the Condition of England, 1832–1885* (London, 1973), p. 187.

4 The Church and the Reforms of the 1830s

1. M. Brock, *The Great Reform Act* (London, 1973).
2. O. Chadwick, 'The Ecclesiastical Commission', in *The Spirit of the Oxford Movement* (Cambridge, 1990).
3. W. Gibson, 'Continuity and Change: The Cathedral Chapter at Winchester in the Nineteenth Century', *Proceedings of the Hampshire Field Club and Archaeological Society*, 45, (1989).
4. O. Brose, *Church and Parliament* (London, 1959).

5. Trinity College, Cambridge, Houghton Ms, Thirlwall to Houghton 5 July 1851; C. Thirlwall, *Charge to the Clergy of the Diocese of St David's* (np, 1851).

6. W. Gibson, 'The Professionalisation of an Elite', *Albion*, 23, 3 (1991).

7. G. F. A. Best, *Temporal Pillars* (Cambridge, 1964), p. 329.

8. P. J. Welch, 'Blomfield and Peel: A Study in Cooperation between Church and State 1841–1846', *Journal of Ecclesiastical History*, 12, (1961) *passim*.

9. O. Chadwick, *The Victorian Church*, 1 (London, 1971), pp. 108 *et seq.*

10. A. Russell, *The Clerical Profession* (London, 1980), pp. 110–12.

11. E. J. Evans, *The Contentious Tithe* (London, 1976), p. 170.

12. G. F. A. Best, 'The Constitutional Revolution 1828–32, and its Consequences for the Established Church', *Theology*, 62 (1959), pp. 226–34.

13. B. Palmer, *High and Mitred* (London, 1992).

14. W. Palmer, *A Narrative of Events Connected With the . . . Tracts for the Times* (London, 1843), pp. 4–5.

15. O. Chadwick, 'The Oxford Movement and its Reminiscencers', in *The Spirit of the Oxford Movement* (Cambridge, 1990).

16. For the extraordinary appointment of Hamilton see W. Gibson 'Disraeli's Church Patronage', *Anglican and Episcopal History* (1992).

5 Religion and Society Outside the Establishment

1. W. R. Ward, *Religion and Society in England, 1790–1850* (London, 1979).

2. D. W. Duthie, *The Church in the Pages of Punch* (London, 1912), p. 35.

3. G. I. T. Machin, *Politics and the Churches in Great Britain, 1832–1868* (Oxford, 1977), p. 58.

4. O. Chadwick, *The Victorian Church*, 1 (London, 1971), pp. 287 *et seq.*

5. W. Ralls, 'The Papal Aggression of 1850: A Study of Victorian Anti-Catholicism', *Church History*, 43 (1974).

6. W. R. Ward, (ed.) *The Early Correspondence of Jabez Bunting, 1820–1829* (London, 1972), *passim*.

7. J. M. Turner, *Conflict and Reconciliation: Studies in Methodism and Ecumenism in England, 1740–1982* (London, 1985), p. 79.

8. O. Chadwick, *The Victorian Church*, pp. 388–91.

9. E. P. Thompson, *The Making of the English Working Class* (London, 1979), pp. 396 *et seq.*

10. G. Parsons (ed.), *Religion in Victorian Britain* (Manchester, 1988), *passim*.

11. R. Helmstadter, 'The Nonconformist Conscience', in P. Marsh (ed.), *The Conscience of the Victorian State* (Brighton, 1979).
12. B. Hilton, *The Age of Atonement* (Oxford, 1988), p. 102.
13. L. Colley, *Britons* (New Haven, 1992), p. 231.

6 Religion in Mid-Victorian England

1. All data in this chapter derived from: R. Currie, A. Gilbert and L. Horsley *Churches and Churchgoers* (Oxford, 1977), and A. D. Gilbert, *Religion and Society in Industrial England, Church, Chapel and Social Change, 1740–1914* (London, 1976).
2. G. Parsons, 'Reform, Revival and Realignment: The Experience of Victorian Anglicanism', in G. Parsons (ed.), *Religion in Victorian Britain* (Manchester, 1988).
3. A. Haig, *The Victorian Clergy* (London, 1984), pp. 194–7.
4. J. L. Altholz, 'The Warfare of Conscience with Theology' in G.Parsons (ed.) *Religion in Victorian Britain*, 1, (Manchester, 1988).
5. J. Marchand, (ed.) *A Frenchman in England in 1784* (Cambridge, 1933), 86.
6. L. Colley, *Britons* (New Haven, 1992), Chapter 6.
7. A. Urdank, *Religion and Society in a Cotswold Vale: Nailsworth, 1780–1865* (Los Angeles, 1990), pp. 281–4; G. Malmgreen, 'Domestic Discords: Women and the Family in East Cheshire Methodism, 1750–1865', in J. Obelkevitch, L. Roper and R. Samuels (eds), *Disciplines of Faith: Studies in Religion, Politics and Patriarchy* (London, 1987).
8. *Urdank Religion and Society in a Cotswold Vale*, pp. 241, 276.
9. E. Trudgill, *Madonnas and Magdalenes* (New York, 1976).
10. J. E. Vaux *Church Folklore...* (London, 1894), p. 213.
11. Colley, *Britons*, p. 272.
12. R. K. Pugh, *The Letterbooks of Samuel Wilberforce, 1843–68*, Oxford Record Society, 47 (1969), pp. 29 *et seq.*
13. T. W. Laquer, *Religion and Respectability: Sunday Schools and Working Class Culture, 1780–1850* (London, 1976).
14. D. Hempton, *Methodism and Politics in British Society, 1750–1850* (London, 1987), 85–92.
15. P. Horn, *The Rural World, 1780–1850* (London, 1980), p. 246.
16. J. Obelkevitch, *Religion and Rural Society: South Lindsey, 1825–1875* (Oxford, 1976).

A NOTE ON SOURCES

A number of books have been published in the last few years which have considerably enhanced the study of religion and society in this period. Foremost amongst these has been Jonathan Clark's *English Society, 1688–1832*. Clark refuses to accept the traditional view of the Church of England in the eighteenth century as moribund, arguing that it was vibrant and far more effective than historians have traditionally allowed. Moreover, Clark suggests that English politics and society were the products of a nexus of political and religious attitudes. He also recognises the close relationship between Church and State in the period. This view has been supported by Linda Colley's *Britons*, which argues that Britain's economic, military and political success in the eighteenth century were a product of, among other things, her strong Protestantism. Like Clark, Colley sees the development of Catholic emancipation as an achievement of proportions equal to, if not exceeding, that of the Reform Act 1832. There are other important works which have moved forward our understanding of religion in this period. Clive Dewey's *The Passing of Barchester* has refreshed the view of the High Church 'wing' of the Church of England and of nepotism in the Church. Another work which advances our knowledge of the High Church element is Frederick Mather's posthumous *High Church Prophet . . .*, a biography of Bishop Samuel Horsley.

The broader picture of Methodism, Nonconformity and politics have been enhanced by David Hempton's excellent *Methodism and Politics in British Society, 1750–1850* and James Bradley's *Religion, Revolution and English Radicalism*. Boyd Hilton's *The Age of Atonement*, in indicating the influence that evangelicals had on the development of social and economic thinking, advances our understanding of the link between ideas and the material world. Robert Hole's *Pulpits, Politics and Public Order in England, 1760–1832* also adds valuable insights to the subject by focusing on the social impact of some of the religious developments of the era. The four volume *Religion in Victorian Britain* presents some excellent essays on specific themes like Judaism, Nonconformity and the development of a denominational feeling in the churches. A synthesis of economic, social and religious ideas can be found in Albion Urdank's outstanding *Religion and Society in a Cotswold Vale: Nailsworth, 1780–1865*. Books which set the religious issues of the nineteenth century into a political context include G.I.T. Machin's *Politics and the Churches in Britain, 1832–1868* and P. Mandler's *Aristocratic Government in and Age of Reform*.

It would be careless, however, to suggest that only the most recent books can shed light on the themes of this period. There are also a number of books which are becoming classic works and which no student can ignore. These include E. P. Thompson's *The Making of the English Working Class* which has a great deal to say on the issue of the moderating influence of Methodism. R. A. Soloway's *Prelates and People* presents the episcopal reaction to the emergent social and political ideas in the years after 1780. James Obelkevitch's study of *Religion and Rural Society: South Lindsey, 1825–1875* and Diana McClatchey's *Oxfordshire Clergy, 1777–1869* both advance a rounded view of religion in rural society which are still very valuable. Eric Evans's *The Contentious Tithe* is also an invaluable guide to a feature of rural religion, which has yet to be surpassed. Owen Chadwick's two-volume history of *The Victorian Church* and Geoffrey Best's remarkable *Temporal Pillars* are also worth examining. The former for its breadth and the scale of the narrative it incorporates, and the latter for its focus on the major changes in the funding of the Church in this period.

In order to gain a feeling for religion at this time it is worth reading some of the primary source material. Of these diaries and letters are perhaps the most interesting. *A Parson in the Vale of the White Horse . . . 1753–1761*, *The Diary of the Revd William Jones, 1777–1821* and *The Journal of a Somerset Rector* are perhaps the best. It is also worth looking at the evidence of visitations in the period. John Guy's analysis in *The Diocese of Llandaff in 1763* is an excellent example. Later visitations by archdeacons are also worth examination: *The Church in Derbyshire in 1823–4* and *Visitations of the Archdeaconry of Stafford, 1829–1841*.

BIBLIOGRAPHY

C. J. Abbey, *The English Church and its Bishops, 1700–1800* (London, 1887).

C. J. Abbey and J. H. Overton, *The English Church in the Eighteenth Century* (London, 1887).

J. L. Altholz, 'The Warfare of Conscience with Theology' in G. Parsons (ed.), *Religion in Victorian Britain* (Manchester, 1988), vol. 1.

C. B. Andrews (ed.), *The Torrington Diaries* (London, 1954).

S. Andrews *Methodism and Society* (London, 1970).

H. B. J. Armstrong (ed.), *A Norfolk Diary* (London, 1949).

F. Arnold, *Our Bishops and Deans* (London, 1875).

A. Aspinall (ed.), *The Later Correspondence of George III* (Cambridge, 1970).

M. R. Austin, 'The Church of England in the County of Derbyshire 1772–1832', London, University Ph.D. thesis, 1969.

M. R. Austin, *The Church in Derbyshire in 1823–4: The Visitation of the Archdeacon of Derby. . .*, Derbyshire Archaeological Society Record Series, 1972.

W. J. Baker, *Beyond Port and Prejudice* (Toronto, 1981).

J. A. Banks *Victorian Values* (London, 1981).

J. Barber ' "A Fair and Just Demand?": Tithe Unrest in Cardiganshire, 1796–1832', *Welsh History Review*, 16, 2 (1992).

L. W. Barnard, *An Eighteenth Century Archbishop: John Potter* (London, 1989).

A. Barrow, *The Flesh is Weak* (London, 1980).

G. V. Bennett and J. Walsh (eds), *Essays in Modern English Church History in Memory of Norman Sykes* (London, 1966).

E. Berens, *Church Reform. . .* (London, 1828).

G. F. A. Best, *Temporal Pillars* (Cambridge, 1964).

G. F. A. Best, 'The Constitutional Revolution 1828–32, and its Consequences for the Established Church', in *Theology* (1958).

G. F. A. Best, 'The Whigs and the Church Establishment in the Age of Grey and Holland', *History*, 45, (1960).

G. F. A. Best,'The Road to Hiram's Hospital', *Victorian Studies* (1961).

D. Bowen, *The Idea of the Victorian Church . . . 1833–1889* (London, 1968).

J. E. Bradley, *Religion, Revolution and English Radicalism* (Cambridge, 1990).

R. Brent, *Liberal Anglican Politics* (Oxford, 1987).

C. Bridenbaugh, *Mitre and Sceptre* (New York, 1962).

M. Brock, *The Great Reform Act* (London, 1973).

O. Brose, *Church and Parliament* (London, 1959).

F. K. Brown, *The Fathers of the Victorians* (Cambridge, 1961).

R. L. Brown, *Lord Powis and the Extension of the Episcopate* (Cardiff, 1989).

R. V. H. Burne, *Chester Cathedral* (London, 1958).

J. R. M. Butler, *The Passing of the Great Reform Bill* (London, 1963).

P. Butler, *Gladstone: Church State and Tractarianism, 1809–1859* (Oxford, 1982).

J. Cannon, *Aristocratic Century* (Cambridge, 1987).

E. Carpenter, *Thomas Sherlock* (London, 1936).

J. Carswell and L. A. Dralle, *The Political Diaries of George Bubb Doddington* (Oxford, 1965).

O. Chadwick, *The Victorian Church* (London, 1966).

O. Chadwick, *The Spirit of the Oxford Movement* (Cambridge, 1990).

I. R. Christie, *Stress and Stability in Late Eighteenth Century Britain* (Oxford, 1984).

O. F. Christie (ed.), *The Diary of the Revd William Cole 1771–1821* (London, 1929).

J. C. D. Clark, *English Society, 1688–1832* (Cambridge, 1987).

W. K. Lowther Clarke, *Eighteenth Century Piety* (London, 1945).

L. Colley, *Britons* (New Haven, 1992).

H. Combs and H. Box (eds), *The Journal of a Somerset Rector, 1772–1839* (London, 1930).

R. Currie, A. Gilbert and L. Horsley, *Churches and Churchgoers* (Oxford, 1977).

L. P. Curtis, *Chichester Towers* (New Haven, 1966).

E. T. Davies, *The Story of the Church in Glamorgan, 560–1960* (London, 1962).

C. Dewey, *The Passing of Barchester* (London, 1991).

S. Drescher, *Capitalism and Slavery* (London, 1986).

D. Englander, 'Anglicised not Anglican: Jews and Judaism in Victorian Britain', in G. Parsons (ed.), *Religion in Victorian Britain*, 4 vols (Manchester, 1988).

E. J. Evans, 'English Rural Anti-Clericalism c. 1750–1830', *Past and Present*, 66 (1975).

E. J. Evans, *The Contentious Tithe* (London, 1976).

Bibliography

G. N. Evans, *Religion and Politics in Mid-Eighteenth Century Anglesey* (Cardiff, 1953).

C. F. Fedorak, 'Catholic Emancipation and the Resignation of Williams Pitt in 1801', *Albion*, 24, 1 (1992).

E. G. Forrester, *Northamptonshire County Elections and Electioneering, 1695–1832* (Oxford, 1941).

W. Gibson, 'Bishop Charles Moss and the Finances of the Diocese of St David's', *Journal of Welsh Ecclesiastical History*, 3 (1986).

W. Gibson, 'A Hanoverian Reform of the Chapter of St David's', *The Journal of the National Library of Wales*, 25 (1988).

W. Gibson, 'Continuity and Change: The Cathedral Chapter of Winchester in the Nineteenth Century', *Hampshire Field Club and Archaeological Society Proceedings*, 45 (1989).

W. Gibson, 'Tory Governments and Church Patronage, 1812–1830', *Journal of Ecclesiastical History*, 41, 2 (1990).

W. Gibson, 'The Professionalisation of the Nineteenth Century Episcopate', *Albion*, 23 (1991).

A. D. Gilbert, *Religion and Society in Industrial England: Church, Chapel and Social Change 1740–1914* (London, 1976).

D. Gowland, *Methodist Secessions* (Manchester: Chetham Society, 1979).

R. W. Greaves and M. Macauley (eds), *The Autobiography of Thomas Secker, Archbishop of Canterbury* (Kansas 1988).

J. R. Guy, *The Diocese of Llandaff in 1763* (Cardiff, 1991).

A. Haig, *The Victorian Clergy* (London, 1984).

E. Halevy, *A History of the English Speaking People in the Nineteenth Century* (London, 1949–51).

E. Halevy, *The Birth of Methodism* (Chicago, 1971).

A. T. Hart, *The Eighteenth Century Country Parson* (London, 1955).

A. Hartshorne (ed.), *The Memoirs of a Royal Chaplain, 1729–1763* (London, 1905).

B. Heeney, *A Different Kind of Gentleman* (Hampden, Conn., 1976).

R. Helmstadter, 'The Nonconformist Conscience', in P. Marsh (ed.), *The Conscience of the Victorian State* (Brighton, 1979).

D. Hempton, *Methodism and Politics in British Society, 1750–1850* (London, 1987).

D. Hempton, 'Bickersteth, Bishop of Ripon: The Episcopate of a Mid-Victorian Evangelical', in G. Parsons, *Religion in Victorian Britain* (Manchester, 1988).

B. Hilton, *The Age of Atonement* (Oxford, 1988).

D. R. Hirschberg, 'A Social History of the Anglican Episcopate, 1660–1760', Michigan University Ph.D. thesis, 1976.

D. R. Hirschberg, 'The Government and Church Patronage, 1660–1760', *Journal of British Studies*, 20 (1980).

D. R. Hirschberg, 'Episcopal Income and Expenditure' in R. O'Day and F. Heal (eds), *Princes and Paupers in the English Church, 1500–1800* (Leicester, 1981).

E. Hobsbawm, 'Methodism and the Threat of Revolution in Britain', *History Today*, VII, (1957).

R. Hole, *Pulpits, Politics and Public Order in England, 1760–1832* (Cambridge, 1989).

G. Holmes, *Augustan England* (London, 1982).

P. Horn, *The Rural World, 1780–1850* (London, 1980).

E. M. Howe, *Saints in Politics: The Clapham Sect and the Growth of Freedom* (London, 1953).

E. Hughes, 'The Bishops and Reform, 1831–2: Some Fresh Correspondence', *English Historical Review*, 61 (1941).

E. Hughes (ed.), *The Letters of Spencer Cowper, Dean of Durham, 1746–1774*, Surtees Society, vol. CLXV, 1956.

K. Hylson-Smith, *Evangelicals in the Church of England, 1734–1984* (Edinburgh, 1989).

O. W. Jones and D. Walker (eds), *Links wth the Past* (Llandybie, 1974).

J. H. S. Kent, 'Methodism and Revolution', *Methodist History*, 12, 4 (1973).

G. Kitson Clark, *Churchmen and the Condition of England, 1832–1885* (London, 1973).

T. W. Laquer *Religion and Respectability: Sunday Schools and Working Class Culture, 1780–1850* (London, 1976).

J. Wickham Legg, *English Church Life from the Restoration to the Tractarian Movement* (London, 1914).

C. L. S. Linnell, *Some East Anglian Clergy* (London, 1961).

W. C. Lowe, 'Bishops and Scottish Representative Peers in the House of Lords, 1760–1775', *Journal of British Studies*, 18 (1978).

M. McCahill, *Order and Equipoise: The Peerage and the House of Lords, 1783–1806* (London, 1978).

D. McClatchey, *Oxfordshire Clergy, 1777–1869* (Oxford, 1960).

G. I. T. Machin, *Politics and the Churches in Great Britain, 1832–1868* (Oxford, 1977).

G. Malmgreen, 'Domestic Discords: Women and the Family in East Cheshire Methodism, 1750–1865', in J. Obelkevitch, L. Roper and R. Samuels (eds), *Disciplines of Faith: Studies in Religion, Politics and Patriarchy* (London, 1987).

P. Mandler, *Aristocratic Government in the Age of Reform* (Oxford, 1990).

F. C. Mather, 'Georgian Churchmanship Reconsidered', *Journal of Ecclesiastical History*, 36 (1985).

F. C. Mather, *High Church Prophet: Bishop Samuel Horsley. . .* (Oxford, 1992).

W. B. Maynard, 'Pluralism and Non-residence in the Archdeaconry of Durham, 1774–1856: The Bishop and Chapter as Patrons', *Northern History*, 26 (1990).

F. V. Mills, *Bishops by Ballot* (New York, 1978).

W. T. Morgan, 'The Diocese of St David's in the Nineteenth Century', *Journal of the Historical Society of the Church in Wales*, 20–3 (1970–1973).

E. Norman, *Church and Society in England, 1770–1970* (Oxford, 1976).

E. Norman, *The English Catholic Church in the Nineteenth Century* (Oxford, 1985).

R. O'Day, 'The Clerical Renaissance in Victorian England and Wales' in G. Parsons (ed.), *Religion in Victorian Britain* (Manchester, 1988).

J. Obelkevitch, *Religion and Rural Society: South Lindsey, 1825–1875* (Oxford, 1976).

J. H. Overton and F. Relton, *The English Church from the Accession of George I to the End of the Eighteenth Century* (London, 1924).

R. Pares, *George III and the Politicians* (Oxford, 1953).

J. P. Parry, *Democracy and Religion* (Cambridge, 1986).

G. Parsons (ed.), *Religion in Victorian Britain* (Manchester, 1988).

G. Parsons, 'Reform, Revival and Realignment: The Experience of Victorian Anglicanism', in G. Parsons, *Religion in Victorian Britain.*

G. Parsons, 'From Dissenter to Free Churchmen: The Transitions of Victorian Nonconformity' in G. Parsons, *Religion in Victorian Britain.*

The Lives of E. Pocock, Z. Pearce and T. Newton. . . (London, 1816).

D. T. W. Price, *Bishop Burgess and Lampeter College* (Cardiff, 1987).

A. I. Pryce, *The Diocese of Bangor Through Three Centuries* (Cardiff, 1929).

R. K. Pugh, 'Bishop Hoadly: A Plea in Mitigation', *Proceedings of the Hampshire Field Club and Archaeological Society*, 41 (1985).

E. Ralph (ed.), '. . .Bishop Secker's Diocese Book', in *A Bristol Miscellany*, Bristol Record Society, 37 (1985).

W. Ralls, 'The Papal Aggression of 1850: A Study of Victorian Anti-Catholicism', *Church History*, 43 (1974).

M. Ransome (ed.), *The Visitation Returns of 1783*, Wiltshire Record Society, 1971.

N. Ravitch, 'The Social Origins of French and English Bishops in the Eighteenth Century', *Historical Journal*, 8 (1965).

N. Ravitch, *Sword and Mitre* (The Hague, 1966).

K. Robbins (ed.), *Protestant Evangelicalism* (Oxford, 1990).

D. Roberts, 'The Paterfamilias of the Victorian Governing Classes' in A. S. Wohl (ed.), *The Victorian Family* (London, 1978).

D. Robinson (ed.), *Visitations of the Archdeaconry of Stafford, 1829–1841*, Staffs. Record Society (and RCHM), 1980.

R. J. Robson, *The Oxfordshire Election of 1754* (Oxford, 1949).

A. W. Rowden, *The Primates of the Four Georges* (London, 1916).

A. Russell, *The Clerical Profession* (London, 1980).

B. Semmell, *The Methodist Revolution* (London, 1974).

R. Sharp, 'New Perspectives on the High Church Tradition: Historical Background 1730–1780' in G. Rowell (ed.), *Tradition Renewed* (London, 1986).

J.J. Slack, *The Grenvillites 1801–1829* (Illinois, 1979).

A. Smith, *The Established Church and Popular Religion 1750–1850* (London, 1971).

R.A. Soloway, *Prelates and People* (London, 1969).

F.G. Stokes (ed.), *The Bletchley Diary of the Revd William Cole, 1765–7* (London, 1931).

N. Sykes, 'Episcopal Administration in England in the Eighteenth Century', *English Historical Review*, 47 (1932).

N. Sykes, *Church and State in England in the Eighteenth Century* (Cambridge, 1934).

N. Sykes, 'The Duke of Newcastle as Ecclesiastical Minister', *English Historical Review*, 57 (1942).

N. Sykes, *William Wake* (Cambridge, 1957).

S.J. Taylor, 'Church and State in Mid-Eighteenth Century England: The Newcastle Years 1742–1762' (Cambridge, University Ph.D. thesis, 1987.

S.J. Taylor, 'The Bishops at Westminster in the Mid Eighteenth Century', in C. Jones (ed.), *A Pillar of the Constitution: The House of Lords in British Politics, 1640–1784* (London, 1989).

E.P. Thompson, *The Making of the English Working Class* (London, 1979).

K.A. Thompson, *Bureaucracy and Church Reform* (Oxford, 1970).

E. Trudgill, *Madonnas and Magdalenes* New York, 1976).

F.M. Turner, 'The Victorian Conflict between Science and Religion: The Professional Dimension' in G. Parsons (ed.), *Religion in Victorian Britain* (Manchester, 1988).

J.M. Turner, *Conflict and Reconciliation: Studies in Methodism and Ecumenism in England, 1740–1982* (London, 1985).

A. Urdank, *Religion and Society in a Cotswold Vale: Nailsworth, 1780–1865* (Los Angeles, 1990).

J.E. Vaux, *Church Folklore. . .* (London, 1894).

D. Verney (ed.), *The Diary of a Cotswold Parson* (Gloucester, 1979).

P. Virgin, *The Church in an Age of Negligence* (Cambridge, 1989).

J. Walsh, 'Methodism and the Common People' in R. Samuel (ed.), *People's History and Socialist Theory* (London, 1981).

W.R. Ward, *Victorian Oxford* (London, 1965).

W.R. Ward, (ed.), *The Early Correspondence of Jabez Bunting, 1820–1829* (London, 1972).

W.R. Ward, *Religion and Society in England, 1790–1850* (London, 1972).

A. Warne, *Church and Society in Eighteenth Century Devon* (Newton Abbot, 1969).

M. Watts, *The Dissenters* (Oxford, 1978).

R. F. Wearmouth, *Methodism and the Common People of the Eighteenth Century* (London, 1949).

A. Webster, *Joshua Watson* (London, 1954).

P. J. Welch, 'Blomfield and Peel: A Study in Cooperation between Church and State 1841–1846', *Journal of Ecclesiastical History*, 12, (1961).

E. R. Wickham, *Church and People in an Industrial City* (London, 1957).

The Life and Letters of Rowland Williams edited by his wife (London, 1874).

INDEX

Dates represent tenure of office.

American Revolution, 41–6
Anderson, Parson, 7
Armstrong, the Revd Benjamin of
    E. Dereham, 83–4, 86, 141
Arnold, Thomas, 66, 109, 134
Ashburnham, Sir William, Bishop
    of Chichester (1754–98), 12
Association for Preserving Liberty,
    50
Astrop (Northants), 7
Athol, 4th Duke of, 54
Atkinson, the Revd Miles of
    Kippax, 27
Aubin, Mr, 178
Auckland, 1st Earl of, 71
Axbridge (Som.), 20

Babbington, Thomas, 64
Bagot, Lewis, Bishop of Bristol
    (1782–3), of Norwich (1783–
    90), of St Asaph (1790–1802),
    97, 102
Bagot, Richard, Bishop of Oxford
    (1829–45), of Bath and Wells
    (1845–54), 22
Balguy, Thomas, Archdeacon of
    Winchester (1759–95), 68
Ballard, the Revd **John of**
    Cropredy, 103
Banbury (Oxon.), 103
Baptist Union, 161
Baptists, 82, 85, 88, 100, 154, 155,
    161, 169, 172
Barrington, Joseph, 71
Barrington, 2nd Viscount, 12
Barrington, Shute, Bishop of
    Llandaff (1769–82), of
    Salisbury (1782–91), of
    Durham (1791–1826), 12, 19,
    89, 92, 97
Bath and Wells diocese, 31, 108
Bathurst, Henry, Bishop of
    Norwich (1805–37), 55, 107,
    129, 130
Bathurst, 3rd Earl, 54

Beadon, Richard, Bishop of
    Gloucester (1789–1802), of
    Bath and Wells (1802–24), 54
Beauclerk, Lord James, Bishop of
    Hereford (1746–81), 11
Bedford, 6th Duke of, 57
Bedminster, Bristol, 20
Benson, Edward, Bishop of Truro
    (1877–82), Archbishop of
    Canterbury (1882–96), 99
Benthamism, 130, 163
Berens, Edward Archdeacon, 23,
    113
Bethell, Christopher, Bishop of
    Gloucester (1824–30), of
    Exeter (1830), of Bangor
    (1830–59), 57
Bickersteth, Robert, Bishop of
    Ripon (1857–84), 94, 170–1
Binney, Thomas, 159
Birmingham Constitutional
    Society, 51
Birmingham, 144, 157, 166
bishops in the House of Lords, 6, 7,
    68–71, 89, 97, 103, 106–12,
    117, 129, 132, 134
bishops, character of, 16–19,
    128–37
bishops, social status, 11–12
Blackstone, Sir William, 130.
Blomfield, Charles J. Bishop of
    Chester (1824–8), of London
    (1828–57), 57, 61, 89, 95, 96,
    98, 100–1, 102, 103, 108, 110,
    111, 112, 113, 114, 115, 117,
    119, 120, 122, 128, 135, 140,
    162
Blunt, the Revd J. H., 124
bonds of resignation, 15
Bonney, the Revd Mr, 5
Bourne, Hugh, 151, 152
Bowdler, John, 60
Bowstead, James, Bishop of Sodor
    and Man (1838–40), of
    Lichfield and Coventry
    (1840–3), 132, 134

Durham, 24, 39, 44, 60, 80, 82, 85, 92, 108, 110, 116, 125, 136, 170
Durham, 1st Earl of, 108, 109
Durnford, Richard, Bishop of Chichester (1870–95), 101

Ecclesiastical Commission, 35, 36, 90, 108, 112–22, 135
Eden, Robert, 3rd Earl of Auckland, Bishop of Sodor and Man (1847–54), of Bath and Wells (1854–70), 133, 134
education grants, 123–5
Egerton, Henry, Bishop of Hereford (1724–46), 11
Eggly, Ann, 170
Eldon, 1st Earl of, 56, 108
Elton, the Revd Edward of Wheatley, 101
Ely, 11, 113
Ely, 2nd Marquess of, 54
enclosure, 2, 29
Euraylus, HMS, 178
evangelicalism, 23, 63–7, 94, 95, 97, 98, 102, 106, 107, 152–4, 160–2, 170, 174
Ewer, John, Bishop of Llandaff (1761–8), of Bangor (1768–74), 42
Exeter, 1, 5, 20, 22, 25, 57, 107, 109
Eyre, the Revd Charles, 93

factory reform, 66, 89, 90, 100
Feathers Tavern petition, 67–8
Field, E. W., 157
Fisher, John, Bishop of Salisbury (1807–25), 54
France, 11
Fraser, James, Bishop of Manchester (1870–85), 93
French Revolution, 1, 46, 48, 51, 53, 55, 57, 68, 71, 76, 82, 97
Froude, the Revd Hurrell, 110, 137–43, 176
Fry, Elizabeth, 159

Gainsborough (Lincs), 180
Galley the Revd H., 9
George III, King (1760–1820) 33, 41, 53, 54, 55, 56, 68, 70, 164
George IV, King (1820–30) and Prince Regent, 55, 56, 59, 90, 130
Gibson, Edmund, Bishop of London (1720–48), 6, 27, 42, 117
Gilbert, Ashurst, Bishop of Chichester (1842–70), 143
Girdlestone, Canon Edward, 180
Gisborne, Thomas, 63
Gladstone, William Ewart, 53, 117, 134, 137, 139, 165, 182
Glandford (Norfolk), 29
Gloucester, 13, 115, 117, 118
Goderich, 1st Viscount, later Earl of Ripon, 57, 58
Goodenough, Samuel, Bishop of Carlisle (1808–27), 53
Gordon riots, 70
Gorham, the Revd George, 147
Goulburn, Henry, MP, 113
Grafton, 3rd Duke of, 17, 43
Graham, John, Bishop of Chester (1848–65), 143
Grant, Charles, 63, 65
Green, John, Dean (1756–61) and Bishop of Lincoln (1761–79), 5, 19, 38, 41
Gregory, the Revd Robert, 94
Grenville, George, 11, 48, 53, 54–5
Grenville, 1st Baron, 35
Grey, 2nd Earl, 61, 107, 108, 109, 110, 112, 125, 129–31, 135, 136
Grey, Edward, Bishop of Hereford (1832–7), 57, 131
Griffiths, the Revd William of Bury Green, 163
Gurney, Joseph, 159

Hackney Phalanx, 34, 58–63, 97, 150
Hagley (Birmingham), 98

Halevy thesis, 76–9
Hall, Sir Benjamin, MP, 1st Baron
    Llanover, 118
Hamilton, Walter Kerr, Bishop of
    Salisbury (1854–69), 143
Hampden, Renn Dickson, Bishop
    of Hereford (1848–68), 140,
    175
Hanoverian Succession, 4
Harcourt, 3rd Earl, 8
Harcourt, Edward Vernon, Bishop
    of Carlisle (1791–1807) and
    Archbishop of York (1807–
    47), 54, 108, 109
Hardwicke, 1st Earl, 5, 38
Hare, the Revd Augustus, 179
Harrison, Benjamin, 61
Harrison, the Revd H. B., 7
Harrowby, 1st Earl of, 57, 113
Headington (Oxon.), 29
Henley, 3rd Baron, 1st Baron
    Northington, 43, 111, 113
Herbert, Sidney, MP, 92
Herring, Thomas, Bishop of
    Bangor (1737–43), Archbishop
    of York (1743–7), and of
    Canterbury (1747–57), 8
Hewley, Lady, 156
Hinchcliffe, John, Bishop of
    Peterborough (1769–94), 43
Hinds, Parson, 7
Hinton, J. H., 161, 162
High Churchmanship, 3, 6, 27, 34,
    42, 58–63, 86, 92, 98, 106, 111,
    116, 137–43, 144, 156, 157, 176
Hoadly, Benjamin, Bishop of
    Bangor, Hereford, Salisbury
    and Winchester (1734–61), 16,
    17, 27
Hobhouse, John, 1st Baron
    Broughton de Gyfford, 113
Holland, 3rd Baron, 69, 107, 129
Hook, the Revd Walter, 92, 93, 99,
    103, 104, 110, 139, 147, 169
Hooper, George, Bishop of Bath
    and Wells (1703–27), 15

Horne George, Dean of
    Canterbury (1781–90), Bishop
    of Norwich (1790–2), 51, 97
Horne, Parson, 5
Horsley, Samuel, Bishop of
    St David's (1788–93), of
    Rochester (1793–1802), of
    St Asaph (1802–6), 6, 7, 31,
    38, 39, 42, 46, 47, 49, 51, 71,
    97, 102
Horsman, Edward, MP, 114, 121
Howley, William, Bishop of
    London (1813–28),
    Archbishop of Canterbury
    (1828–48), 23, 56, 57, 62, 95,
    108, 109, 110, 112, 113, 114,
    117, 119, 120. 124, 128, 135
Huddersfield, 14
Hughes, the Revd E.J.R., 98
Hull, 63, 64, 160
Hume, Joseph, MP, 98, 107
Huntingdon, Countess of, 88
Huntingford, George, Bishop of
    Gloucester (1802–15), of
    Hereford (1815–32), 53
Hurd, Richard, Bishop of Lichfield
    and Coventry (1774–81), of
    Worcester (1781–1808), 97

Ilfracombe (Devon), 20
Inglis, Sir Robert, MP, 61, 112,
    117, 137
Ireland, 17, 70–5, 80, 85, 108, 110,
    113, 127, 132, 144–6, 147, 152,
    170
Islington, 14, 63

Jackson, William, Bishop of
    Oxford (1812–15), 55
Jackson, John, Bishop of Lincoln
    (1853–69), of London (1869–
    85), 96
Jacobite risings, 4, 8, 69
Jenkins, the Revd John, 7
Jenner, Sir Herbert, 113
Jews, 123, 125, 148, 164–7

Lushington, Dr Stephen, 131
Lyall, William, Dean of
    Canterbury (1845–57), 61–3
Lyell, Sir Charles, 173
Lyndhurst, 1st Baron, 113
Lyttelton, the Revd W. H., 98

Macauley, Thomas, 48, 129
Macauley, Zachary, 63, 65
Macclesfield, 2nd Earl, 8
Mackenzie, the Revd Henry, 93,
    94
Mackonochie, the Revd Alexander,
    94
Majendie, Henry, Bishop of
    Chester (1800–9), of Bangor
    (1809–30), 52, 54, 100
Maltby, Edward, Bishop of
    Chichester (1831–6), Durham
    (1836–56), 96, 107, 118, 130,
    147
Manchester, 74, 90, 95, 100, 113,
    115, 117, 118, 127, 128, 149,
    157, 166
Mann, Horace, 168–73
Manners-Sutton, Charles, Bishop
    of Norwich (1792–1805),
    Archbishop of Canterbury
    (1805–28), 49, 55, 59, 97
Manning, Cardinal Henry, 116
Mansel, William, Bishop of Bristol
    (1808–20), 53
Mansfield, 1st Earl of, 67, 70
Marlborough, 3rd Duke of, 8
Markham, William, Bishop of
    Chester (1771–7), Archbishop
    of York (1777–1807), 43
Marsh, Herbert, Bishop of
    Llandaff (1816–19), of
    Peterborough (1819–39) 39, 56
Martineau, James, 157
Massingberd, the Revd F. C. of
    S. Ormsby, 84
Mather, Alexander, 149
Melbourne, 3rd Viscount, 61, 114,
    117, 127–8, 129–37, 141, 142

Mendoza, Daniel, 164
Merthyr Tydfil, 39
Methodism, 26, 27, 48, 51, 76–89,
    90, 91, 149–55, 169, 181
Middleton, Sir Charles, 46
Middleton, Thomas, Bishop of
    Calcutta (1814–22), 59
Mill, J. S., 111
Milner, John, Roman Catholic
    Bishop (1803–26), 72
Minstead (Hants), 15
modus decimandi, 28
Monk, James, Bishop of Gloucester
    (1830–56), 57, 95, 108, 110,
    117, 128
Montefiore, Sir Moses, 167
Moore, Henry, 150
Moore, John, Bishop of Bangor
    (1775–83), Archbishop of
    Canterbury (1783–1805), 27,
    38, 44, 46, 50, 65, 68, 71
More, Hannah, 20, 79, 97, 175, 176
Moss, Charles, Bishop of St Davids
    (1766–73), Bath and Wells
    (1773–1802), 15, 18, 20, 21, 30,
    38
Moss, Charles, Jr, Bishop of
    Oxford (1807–11), 54
Mothers' Union, 87
Moule, the Revd Henry of
    Fordington, 104
Mow Cop, 151
Munro, the Revd Edward, 98
Munslow (Salop), 15
Murray, George, Bishop of Sodor
    and Man (1814–27), of
    Rochester (1827–54), 57
Musgrave, Thomas, Bishop of
    Hereford (1837–47),
    Archbishop of York (1847–
    60), 132, 133, 134, 136

Nailsworth (Glos), 78, 176
Napoleonic Wars, 29, 30, 52, 72,
    85, 92, 102, 164

Index